"ESCORT PASSING OVERHEAD!"

The periscope streaks down. For the first time the crew is conscious of a new noise, a drumming noise—propeller beats—coming closer. With a roar like that of an express train, the high-speed destroyer screws sweep overhead.

"This is a shooting observation! Are the torpedoes ready?" Unconsciously, the captain's voice has become clipped and sharp. This is the moment they have worked for all night. He must not fail!

"Shooting observation. All tubes are ready, sir. Range one five double oh, angle on bow starboard eight five. We are all ready to shoot, sir!"

There is no wavering, no lack of confidence.

"Up periscope! Looks perfect! Bearing—mark!"

"Zero zero one!"

"Set!"—from the TDC officer.

And then that final word, the word they have been leading up to, the word they have all studiously avoided pronouncing until now.

"FIRE!"

"A story of high adventure, endurance and suspense . . . so graphically written that it gives the armchair sailor a firsthand idea of what it was like to dive on a sub, stalking the enemy for a kill or diving desperately to evade the avenging destroy~~~."

—*Saturday Review Syndicate*

SUBMARINE!

EDWARD L. BEACH,
Captain, USN (Ret.)

POCKET STAR BOOKS
New York   London   Toronto   Sydney

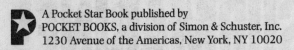 A Pocket Star Book published by
POCKET BOOKS, a division of Simon & Schuster, Inc.
1230 Avenue of the Americas, New York, NY 10020

First Pocket Books printing September 2004

10 9 8 7 6 5 4 3 2 1

POCKET STAR BOOKS and colophon are registered
trademarks of Simon & Schuster, Inc.

Cover photograph © Philip Gendreau/Corbis
Cover design by Patrick Kang
Interior design by Melissa Isriprashad

Manufactured in the United States of America

For information regarding special discounts for bulk purchases,
please contact Simon & Schuster Special Sales at 1-800-456-6798
or business@simonandschuster.com.

To the two *Triggers*—the old and the new

ACKNOWLEDGMENTS

Aside from the thousands of officers and enlisted men of the United States Navy and the United States Submarine Forces, I am indebted to:

Captain Edward L. Beach, USN, my father, who many years ago also wrote about the Navy;

Donald Kennicott, forty years with *Blue Book*, who first put me in print and kept me there—as he has so many others;

Helen Grey, editor and adviser, who helped make this book a reality;

Henry Sell, of *Town & Country*, who provided the spark;

Jonathan Leff, editor at Henry Holt & Company; and

Ingrid, my wife, who would still like a ride in a submarine.

FOREWORD

Commander Edward L. Beach, in *SUBMARINE!*, tells a story which not many men survived to tell. All too often the careers of our most daring submarines and submariners were terminated, after weeks of prayerful watching and waiting back at ComSubPac's operating base, by the issuance of that fateful message, "Overdue, presumed lost." Thus were written the epitaphs of *Trigger, Wahoo, Seawolf, Harder, Albacore, Tang,* and some twoscore more of those silent gray ships which carried the war to the enemy and held the line while the Fleet licked its wounds, and shipyards beat pruning hooks and plowshares into replacements for Pearl Harbor losses. Three hundred seventy-four officers and three thousand one hundred thirty-one enlisted men gave their lives in a submarine offensive that finally swept enemy shipping from the Pacific, yet Ned Beach, veteran of twelve war patrols, providentially was spared to recapture for us the moments of triumph, desperation, quiet humor, and numbing fear which were the daily portion of those devoted warriors.

Serving the apprenticeship of his deadly trade in *Trigger* and *Tirante* under such daredevils as Roy Benson, Dusty Dornin, Fritz Harlfinger, and George Street, he early experienced the wild elation of hearing torpedoes explode against enemy hulls, the stomach-fluttering thrills of night surface battles, the spine-chilling sound of enemy depth charges, and the frustrated fury caused by "dud" and "premature" torpedoes. He felt the sorrow which every true seaman feels in his heart as he watches fine, sturdy ships—even though enemy ships—take the last, despairing plunge to their graves.

Finally, in recognition of excellent service and outstanding ability, Ned was given command of the brand-new *Piper*. He had achieved the ambition of every submariner—command of his own boat in a hot war area. Deep below the surface, guided by equipment as fabulous as any ever dreamed by Jules Verne, Ned snaked his way through row upon row of mines into that last enemy stronghold, the Sea of Japan.

There the war ended and mothballs took over.

Now Ned has a new command, the brand-new *Trigger*, named for that gallant ship whose story he has so ably told. It is most fitting that this honor should be accorded him. I know that I speak for his shipmates, living and dead, when I wish Ned Beach and *Trigger* "Good luck and good hunting."

Charles A. Lockwood
VICE-ADMIRAL, USN (RET.)

CONTENTS

I'M THE GALLOPING GHOST OF
THE JAPANESE COAST

by Constantine Guiness, MoMM1/c, United States Navy, 1943

I'm the Galloping Ghost of the Japanese coast,
    You don't hear of me or my crew—
But just ask any man off the coast of Japan
    If he knows of the *Trigger Maru.*

I look sleek and slender alongside my tender,
    With others like me at my side,
But we'll tell you a story of battle and glory,
    As enemy waters we ride.

I've been stuck on a rock, felt the depth charges' shock,
    Been north to a place called Attu,
And I've sunk me two freighters atop the equator—
    Hot work, but the sea was cold blue.

I've cruised close inshore and carried the war
    To the Empire island Honshu;
While they wired Yokohama I could see Fujiyama,
    So I stayed—to admire the view.

When we rigged to run silently, deeply I dived,
    And within me the heat was terrific—
My men pouring with sweat, silent and yet
    Cursed me and the whole damned Pacific.

Then destroyers came sounding and depth charges
  pounding;
    My submarine crew took the test.
For in that far-off land there are no friends on hand
    To answer a call of distress.

I was blasted and shaken—some damage I've taken;
    My hull bleeds and pipe lines do, too;
I've come in from out there for machinery repair,
    And a rest for me and my crew.

I got by on cool nerve and in silence I served,
    Though I took some hard knocks in return—
One propeller shaft sprung and my battery's done—
    But the enemy ships I saw burn!

I'm the Galloping Ghost of the Japanese coast,
    You don't hear of me or my crew—
But just ask any man off the coast of Japan
    If he knows of the *Trigger Maru.*

1
TRIGGER

MY STORY BEGINS on January 1, 1942. Two and a half years out of the Naval Academy, and fresh out of Submarine School, I reported to Mare Island Navy Yard for "duty in connection with fitting out USS *Trigger* (SS237), and on board when commissioned." Before presenting myself at the office of the commandant I drove down to the submarine outfitting docks looking for my future home. There she was, a great black conning tower sticking up over the edge of the dock, with a huge white 237 painted on her side. A swarm of dusty nondescript men were buzzing around her, and wood scaffolding, welding lines, hoses, temporary ventilation lines, and other miscellaneous gear hung haphazardly about.

"There's my new home," I thought, "wonder if I'm looking at my coffin." To me, she certainly wasn't impressive, beautiful, or anything at all but an ugly chunk of steel. "No life, no spirit, no character," I thought.

I remembered my old "four piper" destroyer, which I had left three months before after two years of steaming up and down and across the Atlantic on Neutrality Patrol. She was old—launched within a week of the day I was born—and ungainly, but she was a lovely thing to me. I knew and loved every part of her. I'd cussed at, slaved over, and stolen for her, and when orders arrived for me to report to Submarine School I'd sent back a dispatch saying I wished to remain where I was. But the Bureau of Navigation had insufficient applications for Submarine School and had decided to draft a few. One of the draftees was Ensign Beach, and here I was.

As I turned my back on number 237, I did not know that two and a half of the most crowded and thrilling years of my life were to be spent with her. She was to become the ruler of my life, and the most beautiful and responsive creature I had ever known; a hard, exacting mistress, but loyal, generous, and courageous. All ships have souls, and all sailors know it, but it takes a while to learn to commune with one. It took me a long time, for *Trigger* had to find her own soul, too, but in the end she was my ship, and nobody else's. I never became her skipper, but I spent nearly a year as her exec, and when finally I left her I was the last "plank owner" left—except for Wilson, the colored mess attendant. Having three times failed to cajole Wilson into taking a transfer and a rest, I finally booted him off ahead of me, with the remark that nobody was going to be able to say he'd been aboard longer than I. Five hours after I left, good old competent Wilson was back aboard. He is the only man alive who can say he served with *Trigger* from her birth to just before her death.

On January 30, 1942, Lieutenant Commander J. H. Lewis read his orders, and put submarine number 237 in commission. From that moment *Trigger* was a member of the United States Fleet. In no other type of ship is it so vital that all hands know their jobs and be constantly alert. A submarine operates in three dimensions, and her very ability to float, submerge, or surface is an expression of the will and effort of her personnel. Neptune is her medium, her friend, her protector, and she embraces the sea eagerly at every opportunity—carefully, with wholesome respect. You never hear a submariner speak of the sea as his enemy, for subconsciously he recognizes this peculiar relationship. He uses the sea and knows its properties. The effect of bright warm sunlight on it, for example, interests him greatly. The type of bottom, far down though it may be, affects him and what he does. The temperature of the water, the depth, and the amount of marine life—all are of consuming importance. All sailors—submarine or surface—know one great experience in common. They have a certain feeling of identity with their ships, and in extreme cases may even be said to be possessed by them. In analyzing the submariner you are invariably struck by these two traits: the sense of loyalty to his ship, and an indefinable oneness with, and deep understanding of, the sea.

Naturally, this temperament is rare. The men who have it are hard-working, thorough, and idealistic. The submariner is always aware that an error during underwater operations jeopardizes everyone's life. Always present, too, is the realization that any slip, any mistake, is unworthy.

Because a ship, no matter how modern and fine, is only as good as her crew, the United States Navy concentrates on its *men* as the most important factor affecting over all efficiency. If they lack judgment and initiative, so does the ship. If they lack the indomitable spirit, the absolute determination to succeed, so will the inanimate steel. But if they possess these attributes, they and their ship are unbeatable.

The embodiment and personification of this perspective is the captain. His men and his ship reflect his will, and a properly organized crew operates with the unity of purpose of an ant colony. Whatever the state of the individual and of internal affairs, the composite exterior is smooth, unruffled; it acts under a single directive force—a single brain—the captain's. It is in tacit recognition of this basic understanding that a sailor, in speaking of a ship other than his own, frequently will use the pronoun "he" instead of "she."

Weeks and months of strenuous training and organization go into a new submarine before she is considered ready to venture against the enemy. All our crews are organized into three sections, each able to dive and surface the ship, fire torpedoes, and run all machinery—in fact, operate the entire mechanism of the vessel. On patrol each section customarily stands watch for a period of four hours in rotation. While off watch the members of a section eat, sleep, make necessary repairs, and, if there is nothing else to do, read magazines, play cards, or write letters.

The progress of *Trigger* from building yard to Pearl Harbor is slow. First come the builders' trials, including the testing of all machinery to be sure that it operates as designed; then the first few dives, slowly and carefully; then more dives, gradually increasing the tempo of the operations. Finally, when the crew becomes quite expert in diving against time, try to catch them by surprise! Eleven seconds for all bridge personnel to get below and shut the hatch! By this time the vents are opened, and water is pouring into the tanks. Also by this time the engines are shut off; inboard and outboard exhaust valves are closed; motors are disconnected from the engines and connected to the batteries; the bow planes are rigged out; and the ship is half under water. In twenty seconds water pours around the bridge plating and covers the hatch, now tightly shut, through which, just a moment before, eight men had scrambled. Fifty seconds, and all that may be seen of the submarine is the top of the tall towerlike periscope support structure. Sixty seconds, and the ship is completely out of sight, cruising under water with possibly a little foam to mark the place where she disappeared. If you look hard enough you might notice a thin rod the size of a broom handle project vertically out of a wave for a moment and then disappear. Sixty seconds, and a ship displacing 1,800 tons, more than 300 feet long, rushing across the waves at a speed of 20 knots, has completely submerged. No time for error, no time to wait for the flash of genius to tell you what to do. Only by constant repetition of each tiny operation leading to accomplishment of the great operation is it possible to perform this tremendous feat.

Trigger's first test dive was in San Francisco Bay. After the first few weeks of tests in the shallow waters of the Bay, she left for San Diego, where she remained for a month completing her training. Then back to Mare Island for final loading for war.

Fill her up with torpedoes, diesel oil, food, and spare parts. Make any necessary repairs and take care of the many last-minute items which always come up. Then, one May afternoon about two o'clock, good-bye—this is it! The admiral comes down to the dock, shakes hands with the skipper, wishes him good luck and good hunting. The ship backs into the Mare Island Slough, twists gracefully, and is gone, through Carquinez Straits, past Alcatraz, and under the Golden Gate Bridge. *Trigger* probably had a soul already, but we were too new to each other, too much taken up with the details of operating her complicated mechanism, to appreciate it.

No one who saw it will ever forget the awful vista of Pearl Harbor. Although we had been prepared for it, the sight of four of our great battleships lying crushed into the mud staggered us. That day I first sensed a more purposeful note in the gentle throb of the *Trigger*'s diesels, but she was only a neophyte, just joining up, and almost apologetically nosed her way into her berth at the Submarine Base.

We expected to get additional training and indoctrination at Pearl Harbor—such, we understood, was the normal routine for a new arrival. But all we received was an additional officer—another ensign, Dick Garvey—and next day *Trigger* was at sea again, bound for Midway to join a group of boats on station off that island. Things were tense in Pearl Harbor, and "strategic planning" was in an uproar—although it seemed to know fairly well what it was doing. The Jap fleet was coming, that we knew, and maybe—*maybe*—we'd get a shot at it!

Our chance came suddenly. A dispatch addressed for action *Trigger* said: MAIN JAP LANDING EFFORT EXPECTED JUNE SIXTH X CLOSE MIDWAY AND PATROL SUBMERGED TWO MILES OFF SHORE BEARING ZERO SIX ZERO. All night long we raced through the darkness, and shortly before dawn sighted the lights of Midway, dead ahead. With just an hour to go before daylight would force us to submerge, we had to cut the eastern reef much too close for comfort, and suddenly, catastrophically, with a horrible, shattering smash, *Trigger* ran head-on into a submerged coral wall! Her bow shot skyward. Her sturdy hull screamed with pain as she crashed and pounded to a stop.

When all forward movement had ceased we hurriedly took soundings. Plenty of water aft, but only six feet or so under our bow, with zero feet a few yards ahead, where the malevolent coral mass alternately glistened in the starlit blackness and gurgled as a wave washed over it. Apparently this reef had very steep sides; that was a break—maybe we could get her off. We backed emergency—no luck. We were much too firmly aground. Only one thing to do: lighten ship, and this task we feverishly began. We also sent a message to ComSubPac telling him of our trouble, and one to Midway, asking for help.

And then came dawn—the day the Japs were to land—and here poor *Trigger* lay, bruised, battered, and *hors de combat*. At any moment we expected to see the enemy fleet, and high and dry as we were, our complete destruction was inevitable.

As it grew light a pint-sized tug steamed out of the channel from Midway lagoon, put a hawser on our stern, and nonchalantly began to pull. We backed with everything we had—no luck. We didn't budge. Then, to our dismay, the hawser broke. Surely this was the end!

But as the tug maneuvers to get the remains of the hawser to us again, Gunner's Mate Third Class Howard Spence, one of the lookouts, suddenly shouts, "She's moving!" Incredulously we look over the bow at the reef, and if you look hard enough, the slightest movement is discernible. No time to figure it out. *All back emergency! Maneuvering, make maximum power!* The four faithful diesels roar. Clouds of smoke pour out of the exhaust trunks. The reduction gears whine in a rising crescendo, and the propellers throw a boiling flood of white foam over our nearly submerged stern. Line up your eye with the bow and the reef. She trembles. The water foams along her sides and up past her bow. Her stern is now completely submerged. She feels alive! Is that a slight change? Yes—yes—she moves! She bounces once and is off the reef. She is free! Thank God!

For the second time I sensed a quick, live spirit in the *Trigger.* It seemed as though she responded just a little more when the chips were down.

It wasn't until several days later that we learned the Japs had been thoroughly beaten the day before, and what was left of their fleet had been in headlong flight.

Although we knew *Trigger* had a gaping hole in number one ballast tank, we remained on patrol for a few days, in case some Jap ships might still be around. Finally we returned to Pearl for repairs, and after dry-docking we started the training period we should have had when we first arrived.

The *Grunion* had just arrived from New London, and she and *Trigger* went through their training together. My classmate and close friend, Willy Kornahrens, whose wedding I had attended in New London a few months before, was aboard *Grunion.* And when *Trigger* set forth on her first patrol, bound for Attu, *Grunion* followed a few days later. When she reached Attu, we were shifted to Kiska, and then after about a week *Grunion* and *Trigger* exchanged areas.

As we were heading back to Attu, we sighted a submarine and instantly submerged. The other submarine must have dived also; Captain Lewis couldn't see her through our periscope.

We could not be sure whether it was a Jap submarine or *Grunion,* and I made a mental note to ask Willy next time I saw him. It's one of the things I shall never find out. A week later we intercepted a message from *Grunion,* which I decoded out of curiosity:

FROM GRUNION X ATTACKED TWO DESTROYERS OFF KISKA HAR-
BOR X NIGHT PERISCOPE SUBMERGED X RESULTS INDEFINITE BELIEVE
ONE SANK ONE DAMAGED X MINOR DAMAGE FROM COUNTERATTACK
TWO HOURS LATER X ALL TORPEDOES EXPENDED AFT . . . and then
the message, which until that moment had decoded per-
fectly, turned into an unintelligible jumble.

GRUNION was never heard from again. For several days
we intercepted messages addressed to her, but she never
acknowledged any of them.

Years later I read an account of an interview with a
Japanese submarine skipper, now master of an American-
owned merchant ship operating out of Yokohama. As
skipper of the *I-25* he had made three patrols from Japan
to California. On one return trip, when passing the
Aleutians, he had torpedoed a surfaced submarine. The
date he gave was July 30, 1942, which tallied exactly with
our interception of *Grunion*'s last transmission.

We sank no ships on this first patrol, and returned to
Pearl Harbor for reassignment. Upon our arrival Captain
Lewis was hospitalized with pneumonia, and Lieutenant
Commander Roy Benson, irreverently known as "Pigboat
Benny" during his days on the Naval Academy faculty,
took command of *Trigger.*

It took *Trigger* a long time to develop her personality. I
felt the impact of her rowdy, brawling, fierce spirit a third
and fourth time, and after that it was as if we had always
been together. In a way, I suppose, I became a sort of slave
to her rather terrifying presence, but she gave me far
more than she received.

That third time was when I watched her first ship sink,
and heard her snarl. It was on her second patrol.

A day or so after arriving off the eastern coast of
Kyushu, the southernmost island of Japan, shortly after

0100, we sighted a large black shadow, blacker than the night. A few true bearings indicated that the shadow moved, and we knew it for what it was—a cloud of smoke from the funnel of a ship. So we commenced to close this unwary fellow, went to battle stations, and soon made out the silhouette of a moderate-sized freighter. Although he was darkened, Captain Benson and I could see him plainly from the bridge at about four thousand yards' range. He was steaming along steadily, puffing out a fair-sized cloud of dense black smoke, with not so much as a hint of a zigzag, or of having sighted us.

Here was one of the reasons for American supremacy over the Jap whenever they met. Undeniably, our low black hull was harder to see than the lofty-sided merchantman, but nevertheless he was so plainly visible that his inability to see us was then, and continued to be, astounding. We turned *Trigger*'s bow toward him, and ghosted in, presenting at all times the minimum possible silhouette.

He sees nothing, steams blindly and confidently along. Closer and closer we draw. *Make ready the bow tubes!* Estimated range, 1,500 yards. Track, ninety starboard. Gyro angle, five left. Stand by! He's coming on—coming on—*Fire One!* One, two, three, four, five, six, seven, eight, nine, ten. *Fire Two!*

Two white streaks leave the bow and, diverging slightly, arrow for the point ahead of the freighter where our calculations say he will be at the instant the torpedoes get there. This is the longest minute in the world. Depending on the range, of course, the torpedoes must travel about a minute before they reach a target, and during that minute a target making 15 knots goes 500 yards, or a quarter of a nautical mile. Few ships are as long as 150 yards.

So we watched our two white streaks of bubbles. "Torpedoes running all right, looks good!" Suddenly we are galvanized into action. If those torpedoes stop the target, on our present course we will run right into him! If they miss, he'll be sure to see us passing so close under his stern and make a follow-up shot immeasurably more difficult by radical maneuvers, to say the least. Besides, he might happen to have a well-trained armed guard aboard.

Left full rudder! All ahead full! Trigger's bow commences to swing left as she gathers speed. The ship is just crossing in front of the torpedo wakes now. Will they get there or will he skin by? All hands on the *Trigger's* bridge watch tensely. Let's go—what's wrong with those torpedoes?

Wham! . . . Wham! Two perfect geysers of water rise alongside the freighter's bow. Almost immediately he slows down, his bow sinks deep, his stern rises. Lights flash on and off about the decks. A cloud of smoke and escaping steam envelops his bridge and center section. Some hardy soul finally unlimbers a gun on the stern and shoots about wildly.

Trigger slid past the now-stopped and crazily canted stern, at a distance of about two hundred yards, and that's when I heard her snarl. All right, it was just the rumble of the hydraulic plant, or the echo of the diesel exhaust returning from the hull alongside—so say you land lovers. I know better. She snarled a message of hatred for all things Japanese, and a warning that this was but the beginning.

We circled slowly about half a mile away, waiting for our victim to sink, debating the advisability of hitting him again. Morning twilight began to seep in from the east, softening the darkness into a musty, unhealthy greenishness, tinged with the dampness of the unhappy sea. Two lifeboats were in the water, long oars sticking out in every direction, the round black heads of their crews bobbing jerkily back and forth as they frantically plied their oars—and caught innumerable crabs.

They were ludicrous and pathetic, but we felt no pity. Only twenty miles from land, these fellows would probably cause trouble for us when they got ashore. Besides, well we knew what had happened to certain of our people who had fallen into the clutches of the Jap. Why shouldn't we sink the two boats and make sure there was no one to tell the tale? But of course, we couldn't.

So we circled, and our target, still barely under way, also circled, bow now at the water's edge. Suddenly a cry, "He's going!" Slowly at first, irresistibly, then more quickly, his bow plunged down and his stern swooped into the air, until he was straight up and down in the water, his long, dusty stack flat on the greedy, splashing sea. The old-fashioned counter stern, crude square rudder, and massive propeller, still slowly revolving, hung high above us, dripping and gleaming. Loud rumblings and crashing noises—his cargo tearing loose from its stowage and falling through the forward bulkheads—came loudly to us as we stared from the bridge of the *Trigger.* He dipped a little lower, the stack disappeared, and the great steel fabric began to swing back and forth, about ten degrees from the vertical. Then, as though in the grip of some playful Gargantuan monster, the hull commenced to lurch, and twice spun completely around, accompanied by squeaks and groans of tortured steel and a bewildered cacophony of internal crashings and bangings. Still lower he sank, till only his propeller and after deckhouse were out of water. At this juncture some shred of lost dignity returned, the lurches ceased, the stern remained momentarily poised about fifty feet in the air, and then quietly, without fuss, slipped swiftly beneath the sea.

Just as the stern disappeared we heard a loud explosion and felt a heavy shock through the water. Evidently his boilers had finally exploded. The water boiled a bit as the tip of the wreck went down, and then, as if to eradicate all signs of the tragedy, hurled itself from all directions upon the cavity suddenly formed in its midst. It met itself in the middle of the whirlpool and, having overdone its enthusiasm, unavoidably bunched up, forming an idiotic topknot surmounted by a little plume of smoke, to mark the grave.

Dawn was approaching, so we dived.

The next night we surfaced even closer to the shore near the Bungo Suido, the southern entrance to the Inland Sea, hoping for another contact. We got one almost immediately.

"Object bearing zero eight zero!" from a lookout. We look, and there against the gloomy hills flanking the Bungo Suido we see a peculiar white V. No radar in these early days.

"What is it? Can you make it out?"

"No, sir. It looks mighty funny, though!" The V gets bigger.

"What in the Sam Hill——?"

The explanation, when it hits, is blinding. "My God! A destroyer—coming right at us!"

"Clear the bridge!" *"Dive! Dive!"* The diving alarm sounds. "All ahead emergency! Two hundred feet! Rig for depth charge! Rig for silent running!" Down we go, but with maddening slowness. *Trigger,* in common with her sisters, always "hangs" on a dive at about thirty-five feet.

Full dive on everything, making emergency speed, we can do no more.

We can hear it now. A throb, throb, throbbing noise coming from outside the hull, steadily and rapidly increasing in volume—thum, thum, thum, THUM, THUM, THUM, THUM, THUM! Only one thing it can be! Pray we can get under! Shut all watertight doors and bulkhead flappers, secure all unessential machinery. "What's the depth now?" "Thirty-six feet." Will she ever break through? All hands are out of their bunks, all officers in the control room, startled by this unexpected dive.

"What is it? What is it?" Then they hear this horrible drumming noise, THUM, THUM, THUM, THUM, look at the depth gauges, and fall silent.

Forty feet. She's going through at last. Fifty feet. We're under! And not a split second too soon, for the drumming at that moment increases to an unbearable pitch, resounding through *Trigger*'s thick hull until all other noise is drowned out, and thinking is frozen in the hypnotic rhythm which rises to an incredible, screaming, maddening horror of sound that stops the heartbeat, then abruptly drops in tone, continues loud, but evidently dimishing now.

We look at each other and smile weakly. Click . . . WHAM! swish! click, WHAM! swish! click—WHAM—WHAM—WHAM! swish swish swish. We knew that was coming. This little evening is just starting. These are the first Japanese depth charges we've heard, but we knew what they'd sound like. First the click, as the first concussion wave hits you. Then the noise of the explosion, and afterward a prolonged swishing of water through your superstructure. The length of time between the "click" and the "wham" is a rough measure of the distance of the depth charge. If the click and explosion come close together, he's getting warm. If they come almost simultaneously, he's hot.

Trigger was strong and ruggedly built, but the shock of the exploding depth charges shook her sturdy hull as though it were made of light sheet metal. The noise was as if a giant were swinging a thousand-pound sledge hammer time after time against her side. We inside were flung about by each succeeding shock, until we hit upon the idea of not leaning heavily upon any piece of gear secured to the ship. With each charge the whole hull whipped, the great steel frames bent, and piping, ventilation lines, and other internal gear set up a strong sympathetic vibration, until we thought they would fall off the bulkheads and overhead. We had something new—light bulbs separated from the overhead light fixtures by two-inch pieces of insulated wire—hence few bulbs were broken although they danced around crazily. Broken bits of cork and dust flew through the air and carpeted the deck. With ventilation and air conditioning secured, the temperature shot up to 120 degrees, and all hands began to shed clothes; our uniform became sandals and skivvy-shorts with towels or rags flung around our necks.

Leveling off at sixty feet, finding we had successfully withstood the initial salvo of depth charges, "He can't get away with this!" Benson said. "We have tubes full of fish. We can play rough too!" So began one of the war's strange battles. Since he had only moonlight, the enemy destroyer could probably not see our periscope, but it was light enough to see him through it.

Battle stations! We'll fix this bastard! He has contact on us by sound. We'll have to wait him out, wait till he lines himself up for a shot. Up periscope. Bearing 045. Angle on the bow five starboard. Oh, oh! He's starting a run. Pass astern this time, but close. No chance to shoot. Here he comes! Hang on! click—WHAM swish-swish-swish, click—WHAM swish, WHAM, WHAM, WHAM, WHAM! swish, swish, swish, swish, swish! *Trigger* shivers and reels from the pounding, but all still seems well. Check through the boat. Report all damage. Now is the time to find out if, indeed, she is "well and truly built." One area in the after end of the forward engine room seems to be the center of shock effect. When you stand there on the deck plates each explosion throws you a foot into the air. A weak spot? Hope not, but we'll soon find out.

Back in the conning tower. Bearing 285, range 1,500, angle on the bow zero. Here he comes! Still no shot. Down periscope! Coming right overhead this time. The fast Thum—Thum thum of his screws is the same as before. Here it is! WHAM—WHAM—WHAM—WHAM—WHAM! Really close that time! Locker doors burst open to strew their contents on the decks running with human perspiration. One man gets sick and vomits into a slop bucket, but the bucket overturns and the slop gets all over its sides and on the deck. Someone throws a rag on the mess on deck, leaves it. A valve wheel flies off a gauge in the conning tower, bounces twice on the deck plates, ringing fantastically loud in the silence between charges, then drops into the periscope well, ringing as it caroms off the steel sides of the well until it splashes into the bilge water at the bottom. A hoarse whisper more like a cry from below, "Pump room's flooding!" We stare at one another, aghast. "How bad?" Penrod Schneider, our executive officer, dives down the pump room hatch. It must not be too bad—water hasn't welled out of that hatch yet. It never does. "Grease fitting in negative tank flood valve operating gear carried away, sir. We put a plug in it. Not much water come in." The speaker is covered with grease, sweat, and salt water. He glares indignantly. Somebody got excited down below, panicked. Evidently not this guy. "Very well," says the skipper.

"Screws slowing down bearing zero seven zero," says the sound man.

"Up periscope! Yes, he's turning. Bearing—mark!—zero six five. Angle on the bow ninety port. Range, two oh double oh. As soon as he swings toward us, we'll swing toward him, let him have a whole salvo, set shallow, down the throat! Bearing—mark!—zero two five. Angle on the bow thirty port. He's swinging toward. Right full rudder, port ahead full. Steady on one six five. . . . All ahead one third. Where is he, Sound? Keep the sound bearing coming!"

"Zero one zero, screws speeding up. Shifting to short scale!"

"Stand by forward! I see him! Bearing, zero zero seven-a-half, range, one two double oh, angle on the bow five port. Here he comes again. Bearing, zero zero seven. Bearing, zero zero six-a-half. Gyro angles, one right. Stand by—zero zero six—five-a-half—Fire ONE! Fire TWO! Fire THREE! Fire FOUR!"

"Forward room reports all torpedoes fired electrically, sir."

"Torpedoes running on zero zero zero, sir. Merging with target's screws."

WHAM! WHAM! We look around unbelievingly. Can those have been hits? Impossible. Prematures!

What about the other two? Thirty seconds. Any time now. Thirty-five seconds. Forty seconds. Forty-five seconds. Oh, God! We've missed!

"He's seen the fish! He's turning away! That explosion dead ahead must have worried him, anyway. We've spoiled this run for him. Here's a sixty-starboard angle on the bow. Chance for another shot! Bearing zero zero five. Stand by forward! Bearing zero one zero. Gyro forty right. Stand by . . . fire FIVE! Fire SIX!"

But we hear no explosions even though we see one torpedo pass directly beneath him.

"Take her deep, boys. We're dry forward now, and there's nothing else to do."

Down we go and prepare for a beating.

We got it, too, but after a while the Jap went away, and a little later so did we. No doubt he enthusiastically reported destruction of one United States submarine—for a night or two later Tokyo Rose said she regretted to inform all American submarines that off the Bungo Suido one of their number had recently fallen victim to a destroyer of the Imperial Japanese Navy. And then she played a recording of "Rocked in the Cradle of the Deep!"

Plagued with more bad fish, we sank one other ship, a large tanker, and damaged still another before running out of torpedoes and having to return to Pearl Harbor. There we found to our dismay that since we had not seen our tanker sink, we could not get credit for him. We vowed that we would not make this mistake again!

2

SEAWOLF

FROM DECEMBER 7, 1941, until the end of the war, our undersea fleet operated in strictest secrecy, which resulted in the well-deserved sobriquet—the "Silent Service." Concealment of results of submarine operations was intended to keep from the enemy knowledge of what we were doing, how it was accomplished, and who was responsible. Consequently, it was not until the end of the war that the full extent of our submarine campaign became known to the people of the United States. Only recently has it been appreciated that although we never had as many submarines as the Germans, ship for ship and man for man the United States Submarine Force was the more effective.

There were two additional reasons why secrecy was deemed desirable. Unrestricted warfare had been outlawed by international convention. Although that rule already had been thrown out on two counts—prior violation by Axis belligerents and indiscriminate arming of enemy merchant ships—there was still a feeling that it might be desirable to protect the identity of individuals engaged in such warfare. Second, at the same time that the first successes were reported, reports of strange and inexplicable failures also were received. Without exaggeration, the effectiveness of our submarine force was approximately 15 percent of what it should have been in the early days of the war. In the Asiatic Fleet, until its final dissolution, the percentage of failure was nearly 100 percent. There is no question in the mind of any submariner today that if the submarines of that ill-fated fleet had had the percentage of successes that was achieved later, the outcome of the battles of Corregidor and the Java Sea, and possibly the whole Asiatic Pacific campaign, might have been much different.

It was not long before submariners knew the answer. Faulty torpedoes! Our submarines were being sent to war with defective weapons. They had not one but two enemies, and the whisper of suspected sabotage or irresponsible stupidity began to take its toll of morale. No one, even now, dares hazard a guess as to how many submarines sleep the everlasting sleep because of this insidious foe.

Time after time, in the early days of the war, our submarine skippers reported that their torpedoes were not running where they were aimed; were not exploding when they got there; were going off impotently before they arrived; or were running in circles, with consequent danger to the firing ship. Written deep into many patrol reports, pathetic now in their vehemence, can be found the bitter words:

"Torpedoes ran true, merged with target screws, didn't explode."

"Fired three torpedoes, bubble track of two could plainly be seen through the periscope, tracked by sound and by sight right through target. They looked like sure hits from here. No explosions. Cannot understand it."

"Fired full salvo of stern tubes at ideal setup. Through

periscope observed personnel on deck of target watching torpedo track which apparently passed under the ship. No hits. Commenced receiving depth charge counterattack."

"Fired two torpedoes down the throat of attacking destroyer. Both prematured, enemy was not damaged. Went deep, prepared for depth charge attack."

Letter after letter was sent to the Navy's Bureau of Ordnance and to the Naval Torpedo Station at Newport, Rhode Island, pleading that something be done.

But the desk-bound moguls in Washington and Newport, from their deep knowledge and great experience, were sure they knew the answer. Fire-control errors in the excitement of combat, or sheer lack of competent technique could only be responsible for the misses. The torpedo, a mechanical marvel of perfection, obviously could go only where it was aimed. Q.E.D., it must have been improperly aimed, "and don't complain about faulty torpedoes until you can prove the rightful blame does not lie with your own personnel!"

So, in exacerbation, wrote the men responsible for development of our torpedoes.

Submariners are a sincere and hard-working lot of men. That is one of their innate characteristics, fostered by careful selection and training. Blandly accused of inefficiency and carelessness, they redoubled their efforts to make successful attacks. Torpedo after torpedo was fired under ideal circumstances. More often than not the only reward was the blank futility of "no explosions."

The story of defective torpedoes is a sordid one, and it is part of the tale of the *Seawolf.*

Among the submarines based in Manila, during the long summer and fall of 1941, was USS *Seawolf* (SS197).

Commissioned on December 1, 1939, she had spent formative months at New London and Pearl Harbor, and finally was assigned to the Asiatic Fleet, along with her squadron mates of Submarine Squadron Two. On December 8, 1941, east longitude date, she lay anchored in Manila Bay, scheduled to enter Cavite Navy Yard to join her sisters, *Sealion* and *Seadragon*, in their first overhaul.

That burning evening, which saw *Sealion* sunk by Japanese bombs as she lay helpless, unable to submerge or get under way, and *Seadragon* severely wounded, was *Seawolf*'s introduction to total warfare. From then until October 3, 1944, when the veteran warrior fell victim to a friendly destroyer which she could not counterattack and which would not listen to her frantic signals, her story is the epitome of our undersea campaign as it developed. Under four commanders, *Seawolf* built for herself a reputation for straight shooting and original thinking which carried through her career and won her two prized Navy Unit Commendations—the only submarine to be so honored up to this time.

Her battle with defective torpedoes began on March 31 and April 1, 1942, when she engaged three Japanese cruisers off Christmas Island. For two days her skipper, Lieutenant Commander Frederick B. Warder, remained in the area, almost the entire time under search and attack, and delivered three deliberate, well-planned torpedo attacks upon three different Japanese cruisers. Already furious, as were all his fellows, with unexplainable torpedo "misses," Skipper Freddie made all his attacks from such short range that failure to hit was nearly as impossible as it was inexcusable. In two cases the target screws were definitely heard to stop after the torpedo explosions, and all indications were that at the very least all three must have been damaged.

Certainly the working over *Seawolf* received from the numerous escorts present also appeared to be real enough, as any of the men on board will testify. Either of the first two depth charge attacks which lasted more than six hours should have been enough to convince anyone of the serious intentions of the droppers.

Following *Seawolf*'s third attack, the Japanese delivered the most impressive, sustained, uncompromising beating of the whole period, as the Seawolves well knew they could expect. It is conceivable that had the Nips stuck to it a bit longer they might have finished the submarine, for her battery was depleted, the temperature in the boat had reached extraordinary heights, and the crew—after two days and nights of virtually continuous attack and counterattack—was exhausted. Shortly before midnight of the third day, however, *Seawolf* managed to break away and come to the surface.

So Warder reported sinking or damaging three cruisers. But since they had been fairly well identified, it soon became known that all three ships were still very much in action.

A high-ranking Japanese naval officer was asked about this engagement after the war. His reply, as translated, was a classic understatement: "We realized that you were experiencing a little difficulty with your torpedoes."

But the failure wasn't from lack of trying and taking fantastic risks, and it wasn't from lack of expert technique on the part of her crew, or of daring and skill on the part of her skipper. If Warder had been as intrepid with a pen as he was with torpedoes, his report of the two days' action would read like the wildest fiction. And when the brethren of the undersea service heard of *Seawolf*'s exploit, the nickname of "Fearless Freddie" was immediately bestowed upon the skipper, much to his disgust, and USS *Seawolf* became renowned across the broad Pacific. And Warder redoubled his efforts to make his torpedoes pay off.

One thought was that they might be running too deep. Instructions were to set them to run beneath the hull of an enemy vessel so that the magnetic feature of the warhead exploder would function under the keel and thus blow the bottom out. If the torpedoes ran deeper than set, they might easily pass harmlessly beneath the target. Conversely, if the patent magnetic exploder were too sensitive, the torpedo might "premature"—that is, go off before reaching the target. The best guess anyone could make at this juncture was that either of these suppositions might be right.

Driven by bitter experience, the old-time skippers gradually had been learning to cope with their ineffective armament and devising means and stratagems to deal with it. Most of them simply set the torpedo running depth to zero, although this was directly contrary to instructions from the Bureau of Ordnance. Since it was generally accepted that submarine torpedoes ran from ten to twenty feet deeper than Washington said they did, a zero depth setting gave the best chance of hitting deep-riding ships. Hardly the optimum situation, since it was still largely a matter of luck if one could hit a shallow draft vessel such as a destroyer.

It was soon realized that with the most meticulous and constant care, the torpedoes sometimes increased their percentage of hits—somewhat. Although German, British, and Dutch submariners were able to take their torpedoes to sea, expose them to the most rigorous service conditions, and still expect efficient performance, our submariners were forced to baby their "fish" to a ridiculous degree. It was found necessary to give them routine overhauls every few weeks when on patrol. Any time salt water touched them for any reason, certainly if it got into any of the working parts, they had to be thoroughly overhauled. At sea and ashore our submarine torpedomen became the most efficient torpedo overhaul personnel ever known.

Although a full report of the circumstances of *Seawolf*'s action was rushed to the Naval Bureau of Ordnance, submariners by this time were learning the hardest of all lessons: when there is a job to be done, do it yourself. At Brisbane, Pearl Harbor, Fremantle, Surabaya, Mare Island, and New London, the work went forward. By word of mouth the warning also went the rounds: "Don't take anything on trust. Check every torpedo you receive from warhead to afterbody!" This philosophy went so far that submarines going on patrol would overhaul every one of their torpedoes before firing them. And the base overhaul crews passed no torpedoes to a submarine about to leave on patrol without the most careful and thorough preparation.

Of its own accord a sort of competition sprang up. Every submarine, upon return from patrol, reported the number of actual or suspected torpedo failures and the actions in which they had been involved. The base, or tender, with an abnormally high percentage of torpedo failures usually had some explaining to do, but this was nothing compared to the unofficial disapproval of the Submarine Force as a whole. Service reputation means much to any man, or any organization, and violent battles sometimes raged over the responsibility for a particularly bad bunch of torpedoes.

In the meantime a quieter campaign was also going on. Besides the possibility of minor errors in functioning of the fish there was undeniable evidence of something inherently wrong with their design. The submarine high command ordered a searching investigation into the minutest details of torpedo design, construction, and performance.

But it all took time. As might have been expected, the most immediate progress was made by the men of the force themselves. They became perfectionists—especially the skippers—and gradually the causes of our early troubles came to light.

On November 3, 1942, *Seawolf* has penetrated far into Davao Gulf, in Mindanao, in her search for enemy shipping. Warder and company have reasoned that their torpedoes are passing under the targets without exploding, and have resolved to prove it. Their first requirement is to find a ship which will present no fire control problem whatsoever, thus disposing of that possible cause of failure. Their second requirement is for the torpedo—if it misses—to explode after passing beyond the target. The location of the explosion should furnish conclusive proof of its path. Taken together, these requirements spell out an anchored or moored ship in a harbor, where torpedoes fired from seaward will go off upon hitting the shore after passing the target. For a clincher, Warder has taken two types of torpedoes on this patrol—the Mark XIV, recently put in service, and the obsolete Mark X. Maybe, he thinks, a little comparative performance data might be useful.

The blame for failure in this attack, if failure there is to be, will rest squarely where it belongs—where Warder has for months known it belongs—on the torpedo itself. *Seawolf* will fire each fish carefully and deliberately, and will record the performance of each. Rather a heroic test, this, and one which should have been performed by the Naval Torpedo Station in the calm and peaceful waters of Narragansett Bay years ago!

At last Warder and his Seawolves sight what they seek: *Sagami Maru*, an 8,000-ton transport lying at anchor in Talomo Bay, a small harbor. Warder surveys the harbor, the anchorage, indication of current; he pores over the chart of the area and carefully selects and memorizes the "getaway" course. He has the torpedoes given one final check, then he quietly calls his crew to battle stations.

With Fred Warder at the periscope and Bill Deragon, Executive Officer, backing him up, *Seawolf* creeps into position, running silent. Every bit of machinery not essential to firing torpedoes is secured.

Closer and closer creeps the submarine, her periscope popping out of the water at irregular intervals, never for very long. Finally, *Seawolf* is in position. Range, 1,400 yards. Target speed, of course, is zero. Target course, not applicable. Current, zero, indicated by *Sagami Maru*'s anchor chain, which is hanging straight up and down.

Ever an enthusiastic and ingenious fellow, young Reserve Lieutenant Jim Mercer has rigged up a new gimmick to try out: a system of taking pictures through the periscope. If *Seawolf* can get a series of half-decent photographs there will be indisputable evidence to back up the arguments about torpedoes!

"Up periscope!" Fred Warder snaps. "Bearing—mark! Range—mark! Down periscope!" The data are fed into the old-fashioned Torpedo Data Computer, located in the control room.

"Angle on the bow, one one oh starboard!—Control, what is the generated gyro angle?"

Don Syverson, torpedo officer, checks his TDC carefully before replying. "Gyro angle one degree left, Captain!"

"What do you head, helmsman?" Warder's next question is directed to the man at the wheel.

"Mark! Three oh six, sir!"

"Come left one degree to three oh five, and steady!" Skipper Warder is determined to eliminate all possible points of error or argument. He will fire his torpedoes with zero gyro angles, at the optimum range. The "straight bow shot"—the simplest one in the book.

"Steady on three oh five, sir!" The helmsman's report coincides with one from Don Syverson that the gyros now indicate zero.

Sweat standing out beneath his short stubble of beard, Warder turns to Bill Deragon. "Take a look—fast!"

As Deragon squats before the rising periscope, Warder busies himself with last-minute preparations for firing. "Make ready bow tubes!" he orders. Theoretically the torpedo tube outer doors should have been opened and the tubes flooded long ago, but experience has shown that the longer a torpedo is in a flooded tube the less chance it will run properly.

"Set depth eighteen feet!" With the target's estimated draft of about twenty feet, and with allowance for the torpedo to run only slightly deeper than set, this fish should pass right beneath the dazzle-painted *Sagami Maru* and explode magnetically under her keel.

"Bow tubes ready, depth set eighteen feet!" A young sailor standing in the forward part of the conning tower swiftly relays the telephoned report from the forward torpedo room.

Fred Warder takes over the periscope. "Stand by forward! . . . Stand by ONE! . . . Up periscope. . . . Final observation and shoot!"

The periscope comes up. "Bearing—MARK! Range—MARK! Stand by!"

"FIRE ONE!"

With a hiss of air and the sudden whine of rapidly starting gears, the torpedo in number one tube is on its way. The whole ship recoils as the ton and a half is suddenly expelled. Immediately comes a confused burble of water back-flooding the tube and rushing in through the poppet valve, as the air bubble which would otherwise come to the surface is swallowed within the ship.

Grimly determined, despite previous training and doctrine, to see the whole show, Warder now keeps the periscope up. An ever-lengthening path of fine bubbles streaks unerringly for the dappled side of the target. A mist of oil smoke rises from the water where the torpedo has passed, indicative of excessive oil—a minor matter, but annoying, for it will certainly attract the enemy's attention.

Straight as a die speeds the torpedo. The corners of Fred Warder's mouth curl almost imperceptibly. "If that fish works the way it's supposed to," growls the skipper, "this ship is a goner. It should break him right in half!"

All eyes are on Bill Deragon, who holds the stop watch. The seconds tick away with excruciating slowness. . . .

Suddenly the captain lets out a yelp. "Camera! I nearly forgot! Stand by for a picture!"

Bill snatches the camera off a locker top and hands it to his skipper.

Warder keeps his eyes at the 'scope eyepiece. "How much time, Bill?"

"Forty-seven seconds, Captain!"

"Damn! Should be hitting right now!" The fervent comment echoes the thoughts of everyone in the conning tower.

Suddenly Warder whips the camera toward the periscope eyepiece, feverishly fits it into place. Almost simultaneously the roar of a torpedo explosion fills the conning tower, and a moment later the sound of hoarse cheering wells up from the control room. "We've hit him! A hit with the first shot!"

The skipper furiously quells the incipient jubilation. "Pipe down! That was *not* a hit! Fish passed under point of aim and exploded on the beach!"

Dead silence.

The skipper's voice cuts through the gloom. "That torpedo was a Mark XIV. Deragon, see that the depth we set on that fish is logged and witnessed, and that the serial number and type are noted. This time we've got proof of what happened. This picture will show the torpedo track to the target and the explosion beyond it."

A smile plays around the corners of Warder's mouth. "For the next torpedo, set depth eight feet and have that witnessed and logged also!" If he's going to break specific instructions, Fred Warder is going to do it properly, with malice aforethought.

"Stand by TWO. . . . Range—*mark!* . . . Bearing— mark!

"Standing by TWO, sir! Depth set, eight feet!"

"FIRE TWO!" The crosshair of the periscope exactly bisects the single vertical stack of the target.

Again the wait for the explosion, but this time it is not so long. As the impact of the explosion reaches the submarine, the skipper grins and motions to Deragon to take the 'scope for a look. "I think we really did hit him that time, Bill."

Through the tiny periscope eye can be seen a cloud of spray and mud thrown into the air, accompanied by what looks like pieces of debris. The ship rolls far over toward them, approximately thirty degrees, and immediately returns to an even keel.

Stare as they may, *Seawolf*'s skipper and exec must admit that there is no conclusive evidence of damage. Despite an obvious hit and the subsequent wild rolling, the target has suffered no appreciable increase in draft.

"How long did that torpedo run?" Warder suddenly asks.

Bill Deragon looks at his stop watch. "Forty-four and a half seconds, Captain." The two men look at each other thoughtfully.

Warder speaks first. "Let's see, now. Torpedo run . . . torpedo speed . . . Why, the earliest that fish could have got there is forty-five seconds, probably a little longer! It must have gone off just before hitting the target!"

The exec nods in agreement. "That's why he rolled over so far. What'll we do now?"

"Do? We'll let him have another one, that's what! Set depth FOUR feet!"

And so a few moments later fish number three goes on its way, set even closer to the surface. Again the torpedo track is observed to run straight to the target, but this time there is no explosion whatsoever. Sound hears the torpedo running perfectly normally long after the time it should have hit the target. Suddenly it stops.

"Stand by FOUR! . . . FIRE FOUR!"

Again nothing. *Seawolf* has expended all her bow

tubes, and *Sagami Maru* still rides at anchor in Talomo Bay—unharmed. And now the submarine has drawn upon herself the quite understandable wrath of *Sagami.* Two large guns on the Jap's bow and stern have been manned and are lobbing shells at *Seawolf*'s periscope. The explosions of gunfire on the surface of the water are remarkably loud, and possess a characteristic entirely their own. If *Seawolf* ever had any idea of trying her luck with the deck gun, this battery effectively changes it. But Warder has no thought of quitting with his target still afloat. The Mark XIV torpedoes have failed. Now he will try the old Mark X fish.

Working against time, "topping off," checking and reloading torpedoes in the four bow tubes, the men of the *Seawolf* silently perform a miracle of effort, in spite of a room temperature hovering around the 120-degree mark. And half an hour after the fourth torpedo was fired the submarine stealthily creeps back into Talomo Bay for another try.

Having lost sight of the periscope when it was lowered, the gun crews of *Sagami Maru* are firing blindly and rapidly in all directions. Again Warder approaches as close as possible before shooting—if anything a little closer this time—again gyro angle is zero, and the camera ready, and so are the obsolete torpedoes.

"FIRE ONE! . . ." This one does it. The torpedo explodes in the stern of the ship. When the smoke clears away the after gun crew has disappeared and *Sagami* is sinking at last, with bow up and stern down. Time for the *coup de grâce.*

Seawolf has approached so close to her enemy by this time that it is necessary to turn around before shooting again. Besides, this will enable her to fire a stern tube, and will tend to equalize expenditure of torpedoes, always a concern of the provident skipper.

Sagami's forward gun crew have deserted their posts, and *Seawolf* is allowed to complete her reversal of course within the harbor unmolested. Twelve minutes later she is ready with the stern tubes, and fires one torpedo.

"WHANG!" A solid hit, in the bow. A fire sends billows of smoke into the air, and the target now sags down by the bow, with the more slowly sinking stern up. Several backward looks from *Seawolf*—snaking her tortuous way seaward—confirm that *Sagami Maru* is on the way to Davy Jones's locker with a whole cargo of essential supplies for the Japanese occupiers of Mindanao, and in plain sight of hundreds of native and Japanese watchers from the shore.

And then come the countermeasures. Three aircraft direct two anti-submarine vessels to the vicinity of the submarine. *Seawolf* is forced deep and into evasive maneuvers, but receives only a portion of the licking which by this time she so richly deserves.

A few hours later Fred Warder composes the concluding words to an official report. He has expended six torpedoes, of which the four new Mark XIV were defective. The ship was sunk by the old torpedoes. He has photographic proof of the whole thing. And so he contents himself with a simple statement of fact, leaving much more between the lines than in them: "The failures of the first attack are typical, and merely add weight to the previous complaints of other C.O.s and myself as to the erratic performance of the Mark XIV torpedo and its warhead attachments."

On December 1, 1942, *Seawolf* observed her third birthday as she entered Pearl Harbor after seven consecutive war patrols under the command of Freddie

Warder. Less than a month before, thousands of miles away, she had fought her battle with *Sagami Maru*—or perhaps it should have been said that she had fought her battle against ineffective American torpedoes, with *Sagami* as the prize. The contribution she thereby made to the war effort was far greater than merely the sinking of one vessel.

The torpedo problem was not solved yet, for it takes more than one documented report to change the mind of a whole naval bureau. But the weight of evidence continued to mount.

3

TRIGGER

THERE WAS A NEW IDEA for *Trigger*'s third war patrol: we were to plant a mine field in the shallow coastal waters of Japan before starting a normal patrol. So early in December of 1942 *Trigger* appeared off Inubo Saki, a few miles north of Tokyo. Penrod and the skipper had spent many long hours planning just how we would lay our mines, and where, so as to do the greatest damage to the enemy. We picked a bright moonlit night, so we could see well through the periscope, and selected a spot a few miles to seaward from the Inubo Saki lighthouse, where traffic was sure to pass.

One of the problems in laying a mine field has to do with the excessive air pressure built up inside the submarine. Our poppet mechanism was designed to swallow the impulse bubble made when firing a torpedo tube, and since we were to eject a large number of mines from the tubes, we would swallow lots of air. The problem came because as the air pressure built up within the submarine, the depth gauges, which measured the difference between water pressure outside and air pressure inside, would show a progressively shallower depth.

My job on the mine plant was one worthy of the assistant engineer that I was: I constantly measured the barometric pressure and calculated the change in the depth gauges so that our planesmen could maintain the prescribed depth.

It was a nervy business laying a field of mines in shallow water right under the noses of the enemy, and I know that Penrod and Captain Benson were much concerned over what we should do to defend ourselves in case we were detected in the process. With our torpedo tubes full of mines, there was not much we could do until we had unloaded them and put torpedoes in their places.

Up in the conning tower, Roy Benson kept watch through the periscope. Beside him Penrod checked our course, while standing alongside me in the control room my boss, Steve Gimber, the engineer, coached the planesmen. We laid our first line of mines; all went well. Then we turned around to lay the second line. Halfway through—Benson's voice from the conning tower:

"Bear a hand down there."

We laid a few more mines. Benson's voice again: "How much longer?"

Another mine went out. "About ten minutes," Steve Mann, the torpedo officer, reported from the forward torpedo room.

"Make it as fast as you can," from the skipper.

"What is it? Why the sudden hurry? What's happened up there?"

I ran up the ladder to the conning tower to find out. A large ship and a destroyer escorting it had come into view and were heading directly for us. I whispered the word to Gimber, then ran forward and told Steve Mann. As rapidly as possible we pumped out our remaining mines.

Relieved of our mission, we slunk away, in the meantime hurriedly shoving torpedoes into the now-empty tubes. When that had been completed, we felt better.

Benson had been keeping a watch on the two ships. Suddenly word came down from the conning tower: "Looks like he's going right into our mine field."

We wondered whether he would go over one of our mines, whether any of them had had time to arm, whether they were any good anyway.

"Kerblam!" Three of our questions were answered at once. Through the periscope Benson could see the ship hoisted irresistibly upward on a sudden blossoming of white water beneath him. When it subsided, the ship lay wallowing, broken in half, bow and stern high, center section under water.

Fascinated, our periscope stared at the destruction. Then, recollecting itself, it turned to look for the destroyer, and found him racing rapidly around his broken charge like a hound looking for a scent. Over the sonar gear we could hear him echo ranging, not routinely as he had been, but purposefully, alertly. The same thought struck several of us: "Say—he probably thinks that ship was torpedoed! What if he finds us here?"

The incongruity of our being attacked for torpedoing the ship didn't seem particularly amusing, and we had to admit that it would make little difference anyway if he found us. We could hear the destroyer's propellers flailing the water as he sped around.

Steve Gimber leaned over to me and said quite seriously, "You know, Ned, things could be worse. That little s.o.b. is still in the mine field. If he looks hard enough, he might find another one!"

Hardly had Steve finished speaking when another

huge kerblam was heard and the propellers and echo ranging frighteningly stopped.

Having gone as deep as we could in the shallow water in our attempt to evade the destroyer, we didn't have the pleasure of actually seeing him sink; and, sure enough, when we later reported the incident, *Trigger* received credit for sinking one large freighter only. When we surfaced about an hour later, we could see dead astern of us a tall column of black smoke where the two ships had been.

Three more ships we sank on this patrol. One, a freighter just at the entrance to Tokyo Bay; the destroyer *Okikase* evidently returning from an anti-submarine sweep outside the harbor; and a large freighter loaded with seaplanes on deck farther offshore. This last ship went down on the 31st of December 1942—with our very best wishes for the New Year.

All ammunition expended for the second time in succession, *Trigger* returned to Midway for refit. When we arrived, Penrod Schneider and Steve Gimber were detached—Steve to report to Manitowoc, Wisconsin, to put the new submarine *Rasher* into commission as executive officer—a nice promotion. Penrod got an even better one, for he was ordered to the Electric Boat Company, at Groton, Connecticut, as prospective commanding officer of the submarine *Dorado*, under construction there.

This also was good news to Steve Mann and to me, for though we were sorry to see Penrod and Gimber leave, Mann moved up to executive officer and I became engineer. A large party was thrown for our two departing shipmates, and a couple of days after our arrival in Midway we saw them off in the motor launch which was to take them to the airfield.

A few days later one of their replacements arrived, an ensign fresh from the Naval Academy, John W. Sincavich by name, who unsuccessfully tried to conceal the fact that his nickname had been "Stinky." In particular I appreciated his arrival. I had been assistant engineer for almost a full year, but now I was engineering officer, and, as such, rated an assistant. Stinky was it.

4
WAHOO

TO TELL THE STORY of USS *Wahoo*, it is necessary also to tell the story of Mush Morton. More than any other man, Morton—and his *Wahoo*—showed the way to the brethren of the Silent Service. He was positive, intolerant, quick to denounce inefficiency if he thought it existed; but he was precise by nature, absolutely fearless, and possessed of a burning desire to inflict damage upon the Japanese enemy.

Just why Morton felt that destruction of the Japanese merchant marine was his own private job will probably never be explained, for he and *Wahoo* sleep forever somewhere in the Sea of Japan. But all that is immortal of both of them is indissolubly paired in the archives of a grateful (but forgetful) nation and in the minds and hearts of a few men who knew them.

Morton died, perhaps believing that his message had not been received by those for whom it had been intended, perhaps with a bit of bitterness that he could convince no one to follow where he led. But he need not have worried, for after him came a host of names which, by their very fame, proved that his ideas had fallen upon fertile soil. *Trigger, Tang, Barb, Tirante, Harder*—these were some of his disciples: the school of "outthinking the enemy"; the believers in the coldly logical evaluation of chances, followed by the furious, slashing attack; the devotees of the competition to bring back the most ships.

Morton believed that there was a certain way in which the job should be done. He would have nothing to do with any other way. There is no question but that his search for perfection in his science brought about his own undoing.

On the last day of 1942 Lieutenant Commander Dudley W. Morton took command of USS *Wahoo* at Brisbane, Australia. There was nothing particularly outstanding about the new skipper during the first few weeks of his command, except perhaps an almost fanatical determination to get the items of the refit completed and checked on time, so that there would be no unnecessary delay in starting upon patrol.

Finally, on January 16, 1943, all repairs had been completed, and *Wahoo* was ready for sea for her third war patrol—Mush Morton's first in command. In company with her escorting destroyer—necessary in view of the "shoot on sight" order directed against any submarine in those "friendly" waters—the submarine got under way and headed for the open sea. At nightfall the escort turned back, a dimmed signal light blinking the customary farewell: "Good luck . . . good hunting!" Perhaps the captain of the destroyer wished that he, too, could go forth on his own, like some ancient sea rover, to seek out the enemy. Undeniably there was always a strong element of romance at the sight of a small ship setting out alone for enemy waters, bravely inviting the worst the enemy could offer, confident in her ability to best him in all encounters. Perhaps the destroyer skipper sensed this as he watched his signalman flash out his valedictory; perhaps Morton knew a momentary sense of understanding, also, but his answer was an equally simple: "Thank you!"

Wahoo was on her own.

It wasn't long before the first plan churning around in the restless brain of *Wahoo*'s new captain became evident to the crew, now that the need for secrecy had passed. Only recently had it become known that the Japanese for some time had been using a harbor known as Wewak as a major staging area. The location of this harbor was loosely determined to be somewhere on the northeast coast of New Guinea, but its position was known to our forces only by whole numbers of latitude and longitude. Morton planned to find Wewak, enter the harbor unsuspected, and raise as much fuss as possible.

The preparations he and his officers made for this little expedition were thoroughly characteristic of the man. The only available chart showing even in vague degree the location of Wewak was contained in a school atlas. Using a camera lens and the ship's signal light, a homemade projector was rigged up for the construction of a large tracing, designed to exactly the same scale as the ship's charts of that section of New Guinea. Much study of the *Notices to Mariners* and of other publications resulted in the accumulation of a considerable body of information which aided in the location of the correct spot. After several roundtable discussions, the most likely area—between and behind several small islands off the coast of New Guinea—was selected. A large-scale chart was then made showing all pertinent information, and this chart was the one Mush Morton proposed to use for his entry and egress.

All this time *Wahoo* was proceeding at the best practicable speed toward the general area where Wewak was known to be. Obviously this new skipper was a bearcat, at least insofar as getting into action with the enemy was concerned.

Eight days out of Brisbane, *Wahoo* silently dived, at 0330 just a couple of miles north of the suspected anchorage. As dawn broke, her periscope made continuous and wary observations while her plotting party carefully noted down all landmarks and other data which might aid the attack or the subsequent exit.

If there were any lingering doubts that the new skipper meant to follow through with his daring plan, they must have been dispelled by this time, for he calmly ventured right into the anchorage area, deftly avoiding a patrol of two anti-submarine torpedo boats which had just got under way for their daily sweep. Nothing was seen here, however, except a tiny tug and barge which Mush did not consider worth bothering with.

Some tripod masts on the far end of one of the islands excited his interest, for they might belong to a ship, and a warship at that. An attempt to circumnavigate this island was frustrated by a low-lying reef connecting the island to the next in the chain and thus effectively keeping *Wahoo* from getting around to where the masts had been spotted.

It is difficult to describe the situation in which Morton had deliberately placed himself. He had entered, submerged, but in broad daylight, a suspected enemy harbor. He was in shallow water—a very bad place to be if your presence is detected. Moreover, there were enemy craft about, and in a position to do something about the submarine once its presence became known.

But far from worrying Morton, the fact that there were

two Japanese patrol vessels active on anti-submarine sweeps in the area actually encouraged his belief that he had indeed found Wewak. So he spent the whole morning quietly cruising about the harbor area, nosing (submerged, of course) into all the suspected and possible anchorages, one after the other. By one o'clock he was quite disgusted, for he had seen nothing to show for his pains except a tug, two *Chidori*-class patrol boats, and those unidentified tripod masts which he was unable to approach, and which, later observations showed, had disappeared.

But a few minutes after one, the situation changed. A ship was sighted, about five miles farther into the harbor, apparently at anchor. She was too far away to be clearly made out, because of the mirage-like effect of the glassy bay waters, which also forced *Wahoo* to expose only an inch or two of her periscope per observation for fear of being sighted.

Wahoo alters course, heads for the unknown ship. Two or three quick observations are taken, and the target is identified as a destroyer at anchor, with some smaller vessels alongside—apparently the tug and barge first sighted at dawn.

One of Mush Morton's unorthodox ideas, later adopted to some degree in the submarine force, was to have his executive officer make the periscope observations, while he, the skipper, ran the approach and coordinated the information from sound, periscope, plotting parties, and torpedo director. Thus, so ran his argument, the skipper is not apt to be distracted by watching the target's maneuvers, and can make better decisions. But you really have to have the courage of your convictions to carry out this stunt! And you also have to have an exec in whom you have complete confidence, and who can so work with his skipper that the two think and act together as one. Fortunately Morton has such a man in Dick O'Kane. They have thoroughly discussed and planned how everything should be done in case a chance comes their way—and here it is!

Battle stations submerged! The word is quietly passed through the ship. O'Kane and Morton have both been up in the conning tower of *Wahoo* for hours, looking over their quarry. Now O'Kane keeps the periscope, while Mush handles the rest of the attack details. The plan is to sneak up on the destroyer while he is still swinging around his hook, and to blast him right then and there. *Wahoo* will start shooting from about three thousand yards' range. All is in readiness as the submarine creeps into position. Fully aware of the unprecedented risks they are taking, *Wahoo*'s crew tensely stand to their stations. The temperature inside the ship wavers around 100 degrees, for the air-conditioning plants have been shut down for some time to avoid unneccessary noise. As a concession to morale, however, and in the interests of having at least a bearable atmosphere inside the boat, the ventilation blowers and fans have been kept running—but now even these are stopped. A ship with all auxiliaries stopped can be eerily quiet indeed, and it is with this unnatural, deadly silence that *Wahoo* works into position for her attack.

"Up periscope! One more observation before we let him have it!" The voice is the skipper's.

Rising slowly from his haunches as he follows the 'scope up, his face pressed against the rubber eyepiece, O'Kane sees only greenish-yellow muddy water for a moment until the tip of the instrument breaks clear of the surface. Then bright sunlight strikes the objective lens of the periscope and reflects in multicolored hues as the tiny rivulets of water drain swiftly off the glass. O'Kane's voice rasps out:

"He's under way! Coming this way! Angle on the bow, ten port!"

"Right full rudder! Port ahead full!" The skipper is almost instantaneous in the command. "Stand by aft!" You have to be quick in this business, if you expect to be good, or if you simply hope to survive. Morton's intentions are immediately obvious to everyone: swing around to the right, and let him have a salvo from the stern tubes as he goes by. Still no thought of avoiding action.

"Dick! What speed do you give him?" Mush has to have this information. "Sound! Get a turn count on the target's screws as soon as you can!"

The sound man, intently watching his bearing dials as though by divination they could give him the information sought, shakes his head even while, with one hand gently pounding his knee, he is attempting to count. O'Kane runs the 'scope down without comment, then speaks over his shoulder.

"He's just got his anchor up, and he's speeding up. Not a chance in hell of getting his speed!"

"Well, try again! We've *got* to have some idea of it!"

The 'scope starts up again. O'Kane's voice: "He's zigged! To his left! Crossing our bow! Bearing—mark!"

"Three oh three!"—this from the sailor intently watching the scribe marks on the periphery of the azimuth ring overhead, as the etched hairline on the periscope barrel matches that relative bearing.

"Down 'scope! Give him fifteen knots, Captain. That's just a guess, though!"

Mush Morton has not been idle during this periscope observation period. He has shifted preparations for firing torpedoes from the after room to the forward torpedo room. He has also made a swift approximation of enemy speed, from the meager information available. Quickly he supervises the insertion of the new situation into the TDC. In a matter of seconds *Wahoo* is ready to fire with a third completely new setup.

"Sound bearings!" The command starts the chant of numbers from the sweating sound man.

"Three two oh!—Three two five!—Three three oh!—Three four oh!—Three five three!—" It's difficult to stay on a target going by at such close range and such relatively high speed, and the sound man has his troubles, but he does the best he can.

"Stand by forward. Stand by one!"

All is in readiness. All is quiet. The skipper nods to his exec. "Give us the bearings, Dick!"

Up goes the periscope again. Firing torpedoes on sound bearings is not for *Wahoo*. To make your shots good, you must get the target's exact bearing as shortly before shooting as possible. You take a chance on his sighting your periscope! If you really make them good, you won't have to worry whether he sees it or not!

"Bearing—mark!"

"Three five eight!"

"Set!" The TDC operator reports that he is, at that precise instant, on the target.

The clipped commands, the staccato syllables, are a natural result of the tension generated in the confines of the conning tower. About twelve feet long by eight in diameter, the conning tower is like a cylinder lying on its side, where, during general quarters, ten men must work.

Fire!

"Fire one!" repeats the firing key operator into his sound power telephones, as he presses the firing key.

In the forward torpedo room, the torpedomen are standing anxiously by the tubes. The tube captain wears the telephones and stands between the two banks of torpedo tubes, his eyes glued to his gauge board, his hand poised to fire the torpedo by hand if the solenoid firing mechanism fails to function electrically. But everything operates as it should. The click of the solenoid and the rush of air into the firing valve sound unnaturally loud in the stillness. The whine of the torpedo engine starting is heard momentarily as it leaves the tube, and the ship lurches. The pressure gauge for number one tube impulse air flask dies rapidly down to zero, and just before it reaches the peg at the end of the dial there is a sudden rush of air into the bilges under the tube nest, followed immediately by a heavy stream of water.

The chief torpedoman waits an agonizingly long time, then reaches up to a manifold of valves and levers and pulls one toward him. The roar of the water stops with a tremendous shuddering water hammer, and immediately a sailor, stripped to the waist, vigorously turns a large chromium-plated crank attached to number one tube, thus closing the outer torpedo tube door.

Up in the conning tower, the firing key operator has been counting to himself as he holds down the firing key, but suddenly he is interrupted by a report in his earphones and sings out, "Number one tube fired electrically!" He then releases his firing key—actually a large brass knob fixed to the bulkhead beneath the ready-light and selector switch panel—reaches to the selector switch for number one tube, turns it to "Off," and then, very precisely, turns the selector switch under the number "2" to "On."

Meanwhile the TDC operator, who is the ship's gunnery and torpedo officer, has been watching a stop watch and at the same time turning a crank set low in the face of the director before him. This introduces "spread," causing successive torpedoes to follow slightly diverging tracks. When his stop watch indicates ten seconds after the first fish has been fixed, the TDC operator snaps, "Fire!"

"Fire two!" repeats the firing key operator into his phones, pressing his brass knob.

"Number two fired electrically!" reports the firing key man.

Roger Paine, operating the TDC, waits until his stop watch again indicates ten seconds, and then repeats, "Fire!" Three torpedoes churn their way toward the unsuspecting destroyer.

Cautiously Dick O'Kane runs up the periscope. Suddenly he curses. "They're going aft! The bastard has speeded up!"

At the same moment a report from the sound man: "Two hundred turns, sir!"

"That's eighteen knots," says Morton. Then to Roger Paine, "Let's lead him a bit. Set speed twenty knots!"

"Bearing—mark!" from O'Kane.

"Zero one zero!"

"Set!"

"FIRE!"

A fourth torpedo heads for the enemy.

A cry from O'Kane—"Cease firing! He's seen the fish! He's turning away! Down 'scope!" The periscope starts down.

"Leave it up, by God!" Mush's voice has taken on a new quality, one not heard before by *Wahoo's* crew. A raging, fighting, furious voice—the voice of a man who will always dominate the fight, who will lead and conquer, or most assuredly die in the attempt.

As the periscope starts up again, all eyes in the conning tower instinctively turn toward their skipper. This is something entirely new and unorthodox. *"Why, that will make sure he sees us, and will surely bring him right down on top of us! What can the captain be thinking of?"*

As if in answer to the unspoken thought, Morton speaks again, in the same reckless, furious tone as before. "We'll give that son of a bitch a point of aim all right. Let him come after us! Wait till he gets close, and we'll blast that goddam tin can clean into kingdom come!"

At the full import of these words, the atmosphere in the tiny conning tower is electric. Striving to keep his voice calm, the telephone talker relays the plan of action to the rest of the ship, so that every man is apprised of it, and, of course, aware of the most extreme danger in which it places *Wahoo*. But not one of them falters, not one quails; although some may be mentally saying their prayers, they loyally go through with their skipper all the way.

Morton's plan is indeed unprecedented in submarine warfare, although obviously it has not been thought up on the spur of the moment. *Wahoo* is going to remain at periscope depth, instead of going deep and trying to evade the working over with depth charges she has invited. She will leave the periscope up in plain view—it being broad daylight, remember—to make sure that the enemy destroyer knows exactly where the submarine is. Seeing the periscope, of course, the Jap will also know the exact depth to set on his charges. But as he rushes in to make this apparently easy kill, *Wahoo's* bow will be kept pointed toward him, and at the last possible minute, so that he will not have a chance to avoid it, a torpedo will be fired right down his throat!

This, rather obviously, is a pretty risky way to operate. Four torpedoes already have been fired, and there are only two more ready forward. All four after tubes are ready, of course, but there is no time to turn the submarine around. So Morton is shooting the works with only two fish, and one of them had better hit!

Grimly, O'Kane hangs on to the periscope, watching the Jap ship complete his evasive maneuver—turning away and paralleling the last torpedo, and then, after it has safely passed, turning around once more and heading for the source of the sudden attack. Smoke belches from his stacks as his fire rooms are called upon for full power. Around he comes, a full 180 degrees, until all that O'Kane can see is the destroyer's sharp, evil-looking bow, curiously now rather fat in appearance. Men are racing around the decks, and at least a hundred of them take stations in various spots of the topside, on top of turrets and gun shields, in the rigging, and along the rails on both sides of the bow.

Sweat pours off the face of the executive officer as he stares at what looks like certain destruction. But he does not forget his primary mission. "I'm keeping right on his bow!" he growls. "Angle on the bow is zero! You can get a bearing any time!" Occasionally he twirls the periscope range knob, and a new range is fed into the TDC. All is silent—except for the muttered bearings and ranges of the quartermaster, and the captain's terse commands, and the hoarse breathing of the ten men in the conning tower, and the creak of the hull and the murmur of water slowly passing through the superstructure. O'Kane becomes conscious of a drumming sound and realizes that it is only the racing beat of his own heart.

"One five double oh yards"—from the quartermaster. Paine looks inquiringly at his skipper. Surely he must fire now!

Morton's jaw muscles bulge, and his face assumes even more vividly that prizefighter expression which was to become well known—and even feared—by his crew. But his mouth remains clamped shut.

The dials of the TDC whirl around: 1,400 yards' range!—1,350 yards!—1,300!—1,250!

As the range reaches 1,200 yards, the captain's lips part at last, and a roar bursts from him, as if pent up within him until there is no containing it.

"FIRE!"

Wahoo's fifth torpedo starts its trip toward the rapidly approaching enemy. The men in their cylindrical steel prison feel a tightening of the suspense; the tension under which they are all laboring rises to a nearly unbearable pitch. But O'Kane is still giving bearings, and the TDC dials are still racing. Torpedo run for that fifth fish should be about thirty-two seconds. Morton waits a full ten seconds.

"FIRE!"

The sixth and last torpedo leaves its tube.

Dick O'Kane continues to watch at the periscope. A curious feeling of relief, of actual detachment from the whole situation, wells up within him. He now has the role of spectator, and there is nothing he or anyone else can do to change the outcome of events. He makes a mental reservation to pull the 'scope down if the torpedoes miss, so that the destroyer will not break it off passing overhead.

Two white streaks almost merge into one in the murky water, swiftly draw themselves toward the onrushing Jap. Twenty seconds since the first one was fired. Dick notices much activity on the bridge of the destroyer. He starts to heel to port, as his rudder is evidently put hard a-starboard. The first white streak is almost there now—is there, and goes on beyond, evidently a miss by a hair-breadth. But the second white chalkline is a little to the left of the first—it is almost there now—it is there. My God, we've missed! What?—WHAM! A geyser of dirty water rises right in the middle of the destroyer, breaks him exactly in half, holds him suspended there like a huge inverted V, his bow slanted down to the right. The white-clad figures crowded all over his topsides are tumbling ridiculously into the water, arms and legs helplessly flailing the air. A cloud of mingled smoke and steam billows out of the broken portion of the stricken hull, rises hundreds of feet into the air, a continuation of the original geyser. Then, swiftly, the halves separate, and each slides drunkenly beneath the once-smooth surface of Wewak Harbor, now roiled up by the force of the explosion and the splashes from hundreds of particles of metal and other pieces of gear from the doomed vessel.

Within *Wahoo*'s thick steel hull the force of the explosion is terrific, something like a very close depth charge, as heavy a blow as if the destroyer had actually succeeded in completing his run upon her. Some of the crew, in fact, do believe they have received the first of a series of such depth charges. But in the conning tower there is wild exultation. Always kept ready for an opportunity such as this, the camera is broken out, and several pictures are made of the bow of the enemy vessel, which, for a moment, remains to be photographed.

Then, and not until then, *Wahoo* goes to deep submergence—obviously not very deep in an anchorage—and starts for the entrance of the harbor more than nine miles away. The trip out is punctuated by numerous shell splashes on the surface of the water, sporadic bombing, and the patter of several distant machine guns. No doubt the Japs in the shore batteries would like to cause the undersea raider to lie "doggo" on the bottom until some anti-submarine forces, perhaps the two patrol ships sighted in the early morning, can get to the area. But *Wahoo* doesn't scare worth a damn, and late that evening she surfaces well clear of the harbor.

When asked later how he had managed to keep his nerve in the face of the attacking destroyer, Morton is reputed to have answered: "Why do you think I made O'Kane look at him? He's the bravest man I know!"

So it was that *Wahoo* gave the submarine force her first lesson on one way to dispose of enemy destroyers. Needless to say, that method was seldom sought deliberately, even by the more successful sub skippers, but it is worthy of note that Sam Dealey in *Harder*, Roy Benson in *Trigger*, and Gene Fluckey in *Barb* at one time or another attempted similar shots.

Three days after Wewak, *Wahoo*'s lookouts sighted smoke on the horizon. This was to be a red-letter day.

The minute smoke is sighted, or radar contact made at night, it is necessary to determine the approximate direction of movement of the contact. Otherwise, the submarine might track in the wrong direction, lose contact, and never regain it. So *Wahoo*'s bow is swung toward the smoke, and several successive bearings are taken. This takes time, for it is not easy to determine the direction of motion of a wind-blown cloud of smoke when the ship making it is not visible. You don't want it to be visible, either, for that might enable an alert lookout to sight you.

The smoke resolves itself into two freighters on a steady course, no zigzag—which makes the problem easier. Shortly before 0900 *Wahoo* dives with the two vessels "coming over the hill," masts in line. Then she lies in ambush, her crew at battle stations, torpedoes ready except for the final operations, always delayed until the last possible moment before firing.

Wahoo's plan is to lie a little off the track of the two ships, and fire at both almost at once in a single attack, so that torpedoes fired at the second ship will have nearly arrived before hits in the leading ship might give the second sufficient warning to maneuver to avoid. As the targets finally show up, however, Morton realizes that he is too close to the track to carry out his original intention of firing three of his six bow tubes at each ship. You must allow enough range for your fish to arm and reach running depth. So Mush regretfully reverses course, and now plans to shoot stern tubes. Since there are only four tubes aft, he will have to be content with two fish per ship, and consequently less certain of sinking them.

Closer and closer come the two unsuspecting ships. Submarining is exactly like hunting, for you stalk your prey, lay a trap for him, and then wait for him to fall into it. Granted that merchant ships do not have an equal chance against a submarine, a skillfully handled ship can escape once the submarine has been detected, and an exceptionally well-handled one might even do damage to the undersea craft. Of course any submarine caught on the surface, by no matter what agency, is in trouble. So there is a definite element of danger in the hunt, and it is accentuated if defensive vessels, such as escort ships or aircraft, are about. Tension mounts as the game draws nigh. Periscope exposures become briefer but more frequent, to prevent a chance sighting as the firing point approaches. O'Kane is still doing the periscope work—excellent training for the skipper-to-be of USS *Tang*.

Twenty degrees to go. Since the two ships are nearly in column and not far apart, it is planned to hit the first one just after he has passed astern of *Wahoo*, and immediately get the second just before he crosses her stern. Thus there will be the minimum interval between all fish, and it will be more like a single salvo.

"Make ready the stern tubes! Set depth ten feet!"

"Tubes ready aft! Depth set, ten feet!" The telephone talker repeats the report from the after torpedo room.

"Match gyros aft!" The TDC operator cuts in the gyro regulator for the after torpedo room, and a quick telephone check is made to insure that the angle transmitted from the conning tower is actually being reproduced at the tubes. It is the third time this particular check has been made this morning, but this is the time you want it to count.

"Stand by aft!" Sound indicates there are only a few degrees to go. Plot and TDC indicate the same thing. O'Kane puts the 'scope back up.

"Continuous bearings!" The periscope bearing reader commences a singsong chant:

"One seven nine—one seven nine and a half—one eight oh—one eight oh and a half—one eight one . . ."

"Set—set—set!" from Rog Paine on the TDC.

Mush takes a final look at all dials, checks the bearings,

and pronounces the word they have all carefully avoided saying until this moment:

"Fire!" The first torpedo speeds on its way. Ten seconds later, "Fire!" again, and the second torpedo is ejected, to follow nearly in the path of the first.

"Check fire! Shift targets!" Morton is taking no chances that an excited sailor might shoot off the last two torpedoes aft.

At the same time, from O'Kane on the periscope, "Check fire! Shifting targets!" These two know each other's thoughts, know exactly what is expected and desired. Dick spins his periscope a few degrees to the left, picks up the second target, a somewhat larger freighter.

"On target! Bearing—mark! Continuous bearings!" And the chant resumes:

"One six nine, one six nine and a half, one seven oh——"

"Fire!" and, ten seconds later,

"Fire!"

Total time to fire all four torpedoes has been thirty-seven seconds.

The skipper orders left full rudder and full speed in order to get the bow tubes around in case the stern tubes prove to have been not enough.

Wahoo has barely started her swing to the left, when—

"Whang!" and then, almost exactly ten seconds later,

"Whang!" again. The first ship.

O'Kane had lowered his periscope to avoid being seen. Knowing the approximate time required for the torpedoes to reach the first target, he now raises it just in time to see the two hits, one near the bow of the leading ship, the other in his stern. He swings to the second ship, and sees a thudding hit in the stern of that one also, an instant before the sound and shock wave of that explosion reaches *Wahoo*.

Three hits for four torpedoes. Not bad shooting, Mush. Now let's see if they sink, or if you have to polish these cripples off.

Down periscope again. *Wahoo* continues her swing, to bring her bow tubes to bear. Shortly before the circle is complete, up goes the 'scope, and a sweep around is made, to take stock of the situation.

Wonder of wonders! Now three ships are seen, instead of the original two! The newcomer is a large transport-type vessel, and troops can be seen crowding the decks. He must have been behind the larger freighter, hidden from the limited view of the periscope eye. So there are two damaged ships and one undamaged.

"Stand by forward!" Bow tubes are ready, outer doors opened. There is no time to track this new target—only time to make the tubes ready, put the bearing into the TDC, and shoot. The same speed as for the original targets is used, because there is no information indicating a difference in the transport's speed, until this moment anyway.

"Fire!" after ten seconds. "Fire!" and then "Fire!" for the third time. Three torpedoes flash out toward the transport, and the last two hit him, with the familiar tinny, high-pitched explosion. The sound of water pouring into his damaged hull comes clearly over the listening gear, and his screws can no longer be heard. That will hold *him* for a while. Now back to the other two ships!

A quick look around shows that one is dead in the water, listed to starboard, and down by the stern. Nothing much to worry about there. He's evidently on his way to Davy Jones's locker right now.

But that second target is still under way, and has turned toward *Wahoo*. Give this Jap skipper credit for trying his best to fight his way out of the tough spot he is in. He has turned toward the place where the torpedoes came from, probably in the hope of ramming the submarine, or, at least, of interfering with further shots. He achieves his intention, too, for *Wahoo* is forced to fire two torpedoes quickly at him—another "down the throat" shot—in hopes of cooling off his combativeness. One hit, but even this doesn't stop him. Closer and closer comes the wounded hulk, yawing slightly as the Jap skipper and helmsman try to keep on course. Too late to fire another fish. The range is too close to allow proper functioning, and it would simply be a torpedo wasted. Nothing to do except duck.

"Flood negative! All ahead full!" The orders crack out like a whiplash. "Left full rudder! *Take her down!*"

Down plunges *Wahoo*, to get out from in front of that tremendous bow on which O'Kane has been counting rivets for the past fraction of a minute. Eighty feet, by conning tower depth gauge, and everyone breathes easier. Nothing can reach you down here. And listen to what's going on topside! Explosions, bangings, cracklings, water gurgles, a whirling and a thumping all over the place. *Wahoo* has certainly raised hell with this convoy!

But this is not the time for compassion. The job now is to get the rest of those ships down, and quickly, before they can get help from somewhere. "Up periscope!" Though the submarine is below periscope depth, and the range of visibility under water is not very great, a quick look will tell O'Kane whether they are coming up under the dark hull of one of the ships up there.

The periscope breaks surface to show nothing in sight, and Morton heaves an involuntary sigh of relief.

Only two ships can be seen now, while a large area covered with dirt, coal dust, and debris marks the end of the first target. The freighter which had attempted to ram is still under way, but the transport is stopped dead in the water, his topsides boiling with soldiers. *Wahoo* bores in, lines him up, and shoots one torpedo.

A bull's-eye! The wake heads straight for the target, now looming big in the periscope field, and passes harmlessly beneath him. No explosion. Morton grimly orders another fish fired. It follows the path of the first, but this time the depth mechanism does its job, and the torpedo goes off right under the tall, sooty stack of the doomed vessel. A blast of water momentarily hides his amidships section from view, reaching up higher than the top of the stack itself. Then it subsides, showing the ship broken in half, sinking rapidly by the bow, with men clad in olive drab jumping off into the water, or trying desperately to lower the lifeboats they should have gotten ready long ago.

Two down out of three, and time out is taken to get a few pictures. Besides, the remaining torpedoes have to be loaded into the tubes and checked, a job much better accomplished submerged than on the surface. It is now noon, and *Wahoo*'s crew is sent individually, as they can be spared, to get what food the harried cooks have been able to get up on short notice. In the conning tower, Morton and O'Kane continue to watch the fleeing ship, munching sandwiches and drinking coffee between looks.

Suddenly, a pair of heavy masts is sighted over the horizon. This is beginning to look like old home week for the Japs—and for Davy Jones, too, if the instantly laid plans of *Wahoo* bear fruit. This fellow looks like a warship. So much the better!

There are a few more torpedoes left, and his name is on one of them.

Wahoo proceeds at maximum sustained submerged speed in the direction of the unidentified vessel. Unfortunately, she has so badly depleted her storage battery during the morning's action that she cannot chase at high speed, and hence cannot get into position to attack the new arrival. In the meantime, the crippled freighter has been staggering away from the scene as rapidly as his engines can drive his battered hull. The plotting parties check his speed at about six knots, quite respectable for a ship with two torpedoes in him. You really have to hand it to that Jap skipper.

It is soon obvious that *Wahoo* cannot hope to catch either vessel. She continues to watch through the periscope, and sees the newcomer revealed as a large tanker instead of a warship. He joins up with the cripple, and the two proceed away at the maximum speed of the latter, black smoke pouring from stacks of both ships. All this time the undersea raider watches helplessly, too far away to interfere and too low in battery power to give chase.

There is a hasty council in the conning tower. Morton, O'Kane, and Paine do some rapid figuring. Then, their computations completed, *Wahoo* changes course and proceeds directly away from the fleeing ships as rapidly as her waning battery power will permit. A continuous watch is kept on the quarry until finally the tops of their masts have disappeared over the horizon. Then *Wahoo* commences some maneuvers which are rather strange for a submarine anxious to avoid detection in enemy waters.

The periscope rises higher and higher out of the water as the submerged vessel comes closer to the surface. As the height of the tip of the periscope increases above the surface of the sea, O'Kane and Morton can see farther over the horizon, and sight is thus kept on the escaping ships as long as possible. Finally, with the hull of the submarine only a few feet below the water and the periscope extending a full fifteen feet into the air, contact is finally lost. The periscope twirls around rapidly, scanning the horizon and the skies for any sign of other enemy activity. Then, swiftly, it starts down.

There is a moment's hiatus, and suddenly a long black shadow, visible beneath the waves, becomes sharper and more distinct. A moment later a sharp bow breaks the surface of the water at a large angle, plowing ahead through the waves like the forehead of some prehistoric monster, and within about ten seconds the whole low dark hull, cascading water from her decks and through freeing ports along the sides, has appeared.

Up on the bridge there is sudden activity. The crash of metal on metal is heard as the conning tower hatch is flung open. The head and shoulders of a man appear, shortly to be joined by another.

Morton's robust voice: "Open the main induction!"

There is a loud clang as hydraulic mechanism opens the huge engine air-induction valve. Instantly the exhaust roar of a diesel engine starting explodes into the stillness. Simultaneously, a small cloud of gray smoke pours from a half-submerged opening in the after part of the hull. This process is repeated three times, at rapid intervals, until four streams of exhaust vapor, two from each side, are sputtering and splashing the water which attempts to flow back into the half-submerged exhaust pipes. The speed of the submarine increases through the water. A high-pitched screaming sound can be heard distinctly over all the other noises, as though a hundred cats had caught their tails in a wringer simultaneously. This noise is made by the low-pressure air blower, which is pumping atmospheric air into the ballast tanks, completing the emptying job which had been started submerged by high-pressure air.

All this time *Wahoo*'s speed through the water has been increasing as the diesel engines take the place of the battery for propulsion, and she rises higher and higher out of water as the ballast tanks go dry. Soon she is making a respectable 17 knots—considering that one engine must be used to recharge the nearly empty storage battery so that *Wahoo* will be ready for further action submerged if necessary—which, of course, is exactly Mush Morton's intention.

While other members of the crew are relieved from their battle stations, there is no rest or relaxation for the plotting parties. But not one of them thinks of being relieved, nor would he accept relief were it offered. The plotting parties are busy with a problem which, by virtue of nearly incessant drill, has become second nature to them. You have a target trying to get away from you. You have his approximate bearing, and you have a good idea of his speed. Also, you have a lot more speed available than he has. Problem: Find him. Problem: Keep him from sighting you. Problem: Dive in front of him so that, despite his zigzags, he will run near enough to the spot you select to give you a shot!

So *Wahoo* chases her prey from the moment of surfacing, shortly after noon, until nearly sunset. This is known as the "end around," and is to become a classic maneuver in the Submarine Force. You run with your periscope up, barely maintaining sight of the tips of the enemy's masts, so that he will not have a chance of spotting you, and you run completely around him, traveling several times as far as he does, in order to arrive at a point dead ahead of him.

Half an hour before sunset *Wahoo* dives, once more on the convoy's track. This approach is much more difficult than the previous one. The enemy remember only too vividly the fates which befell their two erstwhile comrades, and consequently are zigzagging wildly. Then, too, *Wahoo* wants to attack the tanker first, since he is as yet undamaged.

Finally, one hour after diving, *Wahoo* sees the tanker limned in her periscope sights in perfect attack position. The old routine procedure is gone through. As always, there is still the same breathless hushed expectancy, the same fierce thrill of the chase successfully consummated, the same fear that, somehow, at the last possible moment, your prey will make some unexpected maneuver and frustrate your designs upon him. And you never forget that your life, as well as his, is in the scales.

O'Kane is at the periscope . . . Paine is on the TDC . . . Morton is conducting the approach, as always, blind.

Bearing! Range! Set—FIRE!

And three torpedoes race out into the gathering dusk. One minute and twenty-two seconds later, "WHANG!"— a single hit. The tanker stops momentarily, then gets under way again, at reduced speed. *Wahoo* spins around for a shot at the crippled freighter, but that canny Jap has already started away from there, and his change of course has spoiled the setup.

It is still fairly light, though too dark to see effectively through the periscope. There are only four torpedoes left in the ship, all aft. A moment's reflection, and Morton gives the command to carry the fight to the enemy.

"Surface!" Three blasts of the diving alarm, the traditional surfacing signal, sound raucously in the confined interior of the submarine. Up comes *Wahoo*, ready to try her luck on the surface, under cover of what darkness there may be.

In this she has the advantage of a much lower, darker hull, and, since there is as yet no moon, the shadows of night grow progressively thicker, concealing her more and more from the Japanese lookouts. Another advantage lies in the fact that the two damaged ships choose to stick together instead of separating. But having torpedoes in the after tubes only is a tremendous disadvantage in a night surface attack and *Wahoo* maneuvers unsuccessfully for two hours, trying to get lined up for a shot.

In desperation Morton even tries to back into attack position, but is frustrated by the submarine's poor maneuverability while going astern. So he must outguess the enemy, despite his radical zigzag plan. *Wahoo* gets directly behind the tanker, which in turn is behind the freighter. Then, as the two Japs zig to the right, *Wahoo* stays on the original course, and when they zig back to the left, the submarine is about a mile on the beam of the unfortunate tanker. Suddenly *Wahoo*'s rudder is put full left, and her port propeller is backed at full power, while her starboard screw is put at ahead full. In this manner Morton is able to twist his ship, get her end on to the broadside of the now-doomed Jap, and let fly two torpedoes.

One hit amidships. The sound of the explosion cannot be heard, but its effects are spectacular. The vessel folds in the middle and plunges from sight almost instantly.

"All ahead full!" Now for that freighter! *Wahoo* has played around with him long enough.

But the skipper of the lone remaining Jap ship has other ideas. He keeps up a continuous fire with his guns and steams in an even more radical and haphazard fashion than before. Now and then he sights the ominous shape of the sea wolf stalking him, and places a few well-aimed shells alongside, forcing her to turn away and once even forcing her to dive.

For an hour this cat-and-mouse game keeps up. Finally, a powerful searchlight beam is sighted over the horizon. An escort vessel or destroyer, probably sent to succor four vessels who had reported being under attack by submarine. *Wahoo* had better do something to end this stalemate fast! Again Morton puts on his thinking cap. What would he do, if he were the skipper of the Jap freighter?

"Well," thinks Mush, "there's no doubt at all what I'd do! I'd head for that destroyer just as fast as ever I could!" And he heads *Wahoo* toward the destroyer, full speed.

Sure enough, the lumbering hulk of the wounded cargo vessel is soon sighted, headed in the same direction. Only *Wahoo* has preceded him, and now lies in wait for him, and two torpedoes come out of the night to put finis to a gallant defense.

Four ships sighted and four down was *Wahoo*'s record for January 27, 1943. The whole one-sided battle lasted thirteen hours, and after its conclusion one Jap destroyer was left fruitlessly searching the area with his searchlight.

Like everything else she did, *Wahoo*'s entrance into Pearl was dramatic, for lashed to her fully-extended periscope was—a broom!

• • •

On her next patrol, which she spent in the Yellow Sea between China and Korea, *Wahoo* ran the entire distance to the patrol area, deep in the heart of Japanese-controlled waters, on the surface, diving only for necessary drills. When the patrol was completed she surfaced, still in the middle of the Yellow Sea, and headed for home, digressing only to track and sink one lone freighter sighted on the way. Only this attack, incidentally, prevented her from making the same "no dives" boast on her return trip as well. During the patrol, which covered nineteen days in the assigned area, *Wahoo* sank nine ships, one trawler, and two sampans, and again expended all her ammunition. Once again the broom was lashed to the periscope.

And again, in April 1943, *Wahoo* and Morton made their third war patrol together, sinking three ships and damaging two.

But she fell upon bad days, and Morton was a stubborn man; to these circumstances, and their unfortunate combination at just the wrong time, we may lay the responsibility for the sad loss of USS *Wahoo* and her fighting skipper.

After Mush Morton's third war patrol in command of *Wahoo*, an inspection of the ship showed that an extensive overhaul was needed to replace the worn-out battery, to repair damages, and to install new apparatus. So the vessel was ordered to Mare Island Navy Yard for two months. While there, the fine team Morton had built up suffered serious injury with the detachment of Dick O'Kane, who received orders to command the brand-new submarine *Tang*, then under construction at the Navy Yard. Roger Paine moved up to the position of executive officer. Mush

Morton, though he regretted the loss of his very capable second officer, was overjoyed to see him finally get the command which he had longed for, and for which he, Morton, had repeatedly recommended him.

In late July 1943, *Wahoo* arrived back at Pearl Harbor, after the completion of her overhaul. Then bad luck struck, for Paine developed appendicitis, and had to be removed to a hospital for an operation. Morton had been deprived of the two officers he depended upon most, but, nonetheless confident, he proceeded on his fourth patrol.

Now Dudley W. Morton was a man of original ideas and independent thinking. Submarine doctrine called for shooting several torpedoes at each target, in a spread, in order to take into account possible maneuvers to avoid, errors in solution of the fire control problem, or malfunction of torpedoes. No quarrel could really be had with this procedure, so long as a submarine was apt to see and be able to shoot only a few ships per patrol. But in three successive patrols *Wahoo* had returned before the completion of her normal time on station, with all torpedoes expended. Morton knew he had the knack of searching out targets where other men could not find them.

If you know you are going to see plenty of targets—so ran his argument—why not shoot only one torpedo at each ship, and accept those occasional misses? If a submarine fires three fish per salvo, and sinks eight ships with her twenty-four torpedoes, is that as effective in damaging the enemy as a submarine which fires single shots and sinks twelve ships with twenty-four torpedoes? Yet in the first case the sub should be credited with 100 percent effectiveness in fire control; in the latter, with only 50 percent. The problem, according to Mush, lay simply in the number of contacts you could make. So he asked for, and received for his fourth patrol, the hottest area there was—the Japan Sea!

The Japan Sea is a nearly landlocked body of water lying between Japan and the Asiatic mainland. It can be reached from the open sea in only three ways—through the Straits of Tsushima, Tsugaru, or La Perouse. The only other possible entrance is through the Tartary Strait, between Sakhalin Island and Siberia, which is too shallow for seagoing vessels and, anyway, under the control of Russia. It was known that the Japanese had extensively mined all possible entrances to "their" sea, and that they were carrying on an enormous volume of traffic in its sheltered waters with no fear whatever of Allied interference.

If *Wahoo* could only get into this lush area, Mush figured, she should find so many targets that she would have an ideal opportunity to try out his theory. He knew the entrances were mined but he also knew that it takes an awfully good mine field to completely close up such a large passage as La Perouse or Tsushima, and that his chances of running through on the surface above the anti-submarine mines (which, of course, would be laid at depths calculated to trap a submerged submarine) would be good. He also was banking on probable laxness and inattention on the part of the Japanese defenders, and on taking them by surprise.

So on August 2, 1943, *Wahoo* departed Pearl Harbor for the Japan Sea, carrying with her a determined captain and an entirely new team of officers, some veterans of her previous patrols, but practically all of them in new jobs as a result of the drastic changes at the top.

On August 14 *Wahoo* transited La Perouse Strait, on

the surface at night, at full speed. Though detected and challenged by the shore station on Soya Misaki, she remained boldly on her course, ignoring the signal, and having done his duty the watcher in the station went back to sleep, leaving all navigational lights burning as though it were still peacetime.

Mush Morton was certainly right about one thing. He entered the Sea of Japan on August 14; that same night *Wahoo* sighted four enemy merchant ships, steaming singly and unescorted. In all, she carried out four separate attacks, three of them on the same ship, firing only five torpedoes in all. And here Fate dealt Morton her most crushing blow! *Faulty torpedoes!*

There is nothing in the world so maddening as to bring your submarine across miles of ocean; to train your crew up to the highest pitch of efficiency and anticipation; to work for weeks getting into a good fertile area; to assume heavy risk in arriving finally at an attack position—and then to have the whole thing vitiated by some totally inexplicable fault in your equipment.

Time after time *Wahoo* sights the enemy's vital cargo carriers and tankers. Time after time she makes the approach, goes through all the old familiar motions which have previously brought such outstanding success—and time after time there is nothing heard in the sound gear, after firing the torpedoes, save the whirring of their propellers as they go on—and on—and on! Once, indeed, the sickening thud of a dud hit is heard, but most of the time the torpedoes simply miss, and miss, and miss!

Desperately, Morton tries every conceivable trick in his book. He does not lack for targets—that he had foreseen correctly—so he has plenty of time to try everything he knows. But he is still stubborn, and mutters savagely something to the effect that there is no use in firing more than one torpedo at any target until he has found out why they don't go off.

For four days *Wahoo* valiantly fought her bad luck, and made, in all, nine attacks upon nearly as many enemy ships. Results achieved, zero! Heartbreaking, hopeless, utter zero!

And then Mush Morton finally broke down. After four nightmarish days in the area, during which he became increasingly silent, moody, and irascible, sometimes venting the smoldering fury which possessed him with outbursts of a fantastic, terrifying rage, Morton decided that there was only one thing left to do. Characteristically, it took him only four days to reach this decision and to implement it. Fate had been able to make him do something no Jap had ever succeeded in doing—cry "Uncle."

A message was sent to the Commander Submarines, Pacific, informing him of the complete failure of the torpedoes of his most outstanding submarine. The reaction from Admiral Lockwood was instant: orders to proceed immediately to Pearl Harbor, and Mush Morton's action was equally decisive: *Wahoo*'s annunciators were put on "All ahead flank," and were left in that position until the submarine reached the entrance buoys off Pearl. The only exceptions to this performance were caused by the appearance of a neutral merchant ship, which was identified as *Wahoo* maneuvered in for an attack; and two Jap sampans, whose captured crews found their final destinations to be somewhat different from what they had expected.

On August 29, only eleven days from the Japan Sea,

Mush Morton and his *Wahoo* stormed into Pearl Harbor and tied up at the submarine base. This time there was no broom tied to an extended periscope, and the booming exuberance with which this sub had been wont to return from patrol was totally lacking. But such was the fame of *Wahoo* and her skipper that there was quite a crowd of men and officers on the dock to greet her and to tender the usual congratulations upon safe return. On this occasion there was a cloud over the normally lighthearted feelings of those present, for all knew that there was something radically wrong. One or two made an effort to say something cheerful to the obviously suffering commanding officer, but nothing they could say or do could allay the fact that Morton, who up to this time had been the most successful skipper of the whole force, had returned from his last patrol empty-handed. As soon as he decently could, Mush strode away from the crowd and hurried to the office of ComSubPac.

Once there he gave voice, in no uncertain terms, to the anger which possessed him. Virtually pounding his fist on the table—after all, you don't pound your fist at an admiral, even one so understanding as Admiral Lockwood—he insisted that something was radically wrong, and that corrective measures had to be taken immediately. The admiral and his staff listened thoughtfully, for this was by no means the only report they had received about malfunctioning of the submarine's major weapon, and Morton was not the first man to cry "Damn the torpedoes!" Half-formed thoughts about sabotage, inefficiency, or improper preparation hovered above this gathering, and the upshot of it was that the Commander Submarines, Pacific Fleet, gave his word to Commander Dudley Morton that he would find out what was wrong with the fish if it killed him. In their hearts, the members of his staff echoed his sentiments—for, after all, every man there was a veteran submarine skipper himself.

The interview with *Wahoo*'s skipper at an end, Lockwood asked the question which Morton had been waiting for: "Well, Mush, what do you want to do?" Knowing his man, the admiral was prepared for the answer he got, but it must be admitted that he would hardly have been surprised had Morton indicated that he had been taking a beating lately, and would like a rest.

A rest was farthest from Mush Morton's mind at that moment. "Admiral," he said, "I want to go right back to the Sea of Japan, *with a load of live fish this time!*"

The two men took stock of each other. Morton saw a seamed, genial face, normally weather-beaten from years at sea, now showing signs of the strain of keeping his boys going and solving their problems for them—of holding up his end of the larger scope of the war plan—of defending and protecting his operations from those who, not knowing of the phenomenal results being achieved, would encroach upon, limit, or circumscribe them. With a small shock, however, he realized that at the moment there were only two emotions showing in the admiral's eyes—worry, over him, and—*envy*.

On his side, the admiral saw a young, virile officer, proud in his profession with the pride that comes only from a sense of accomplishment, and which will support no criticism. A fiery man, a fighter, and a leader. But burning in his steady eyes was the shining light of the crusader, now doubly dedicated, because his latest crusade had failed.

They shook hands. "We'll get you ready as soon as we

can," said Lockwood. Morton stood up gravely, thanked him shortly, and departed. As he watched that straight, tall figure stride out of his office, the thought flashed across the admiral's mind: *"I shouldn't let him go. I ought to take him off his ship and let him cool off a bit. But I just can't do it!"*

So *Wahoo* was given another load of torpedoes, which were most painstakingly checked for perfect condition, and immediately departed for the Japan Sea to redeem her previous fiasco. She stopped at Midway en route, but nothing more was ever heard or seen of her, and what information we have been able to gather, consisting of reports of losses which could only have been due to depredations made by *Wahoo* on her last patrol, has come from Japanese sources. According to these sources, four ships were sunk by *Wahoo* in the Japan Sea between September 29 and October 9,1943. Knowing the Jap tendency to deflate records of losses, it is probable that the actual number of ships sunk was eight or more, instead of four.

Wahoo never returned. Surprisingly, however, among the 468 United States submarines which the Japs claimed to have sunk, there was not one record, or any other information anywhere discovered which, by any stretch of circumstances, could explain what had happened to her. The enemy never got her. They never even knew she had been lost, and we carefully concealed it for a long time, knowing how badly they wanted to "get" *Wahoo.*

Like so many of our lost submarines, she simply disappeared into the limbo of lost ships, sealing her mystery with her forever. This has always been a comforting thought, for it is a sailor's death, and an honorable grave. I like to think of *Wahoo* carrying the fight to the enemy, as she always did, gloriously, successfully, and furiously, up to the last catastrophic instant when, by some mischance, and in some manner unknown to living man, the world came to an end for her.

TRIGGER

5

TIME PASSED, and *Trigger* was a veteran. Her lean snout had explored the waters of the Pacific from the Aleutians to the Equator, and she had sunk ships wherever she went. We had also accumulated our share of depth charges, although none—for chills and thrills—the equal of our first working over.

On the 10th day of June 1943, at about five o'clock in the afternoon, we were once again off Tokyo. We had been there for thirty days, and were due to start for Pearl Harbor at midnight. "Captain to the conning tower!" Benson dashed past me in the control room, leaped up the ladder to the conning tower where Lieutenant (j.g.) Willy Long had the periscope watch. "Smoke inside the harbor!" I heard Willy tell the skipper. "Looks like it's coming this way!"

You could feel *Trigger* draw a deep, hushed breath. Captain Benson ordered me to plane upward two feet, to allow him to raise the periscope that much higher out of the water and thus see a little farther. Then the 'scope came slithering down and the musical chimes of the general alarm, vibrant with danger, reverberated through the ship, and started our hearts beating faster and our blood racing as we ran to our battle stations.

A few swift observations, and the voice of the skipper: "Men, this is the jackpot. We've got the biggest aircraft carrier I've ever seen up here, plus two destroyers. We're going to shoot our whole wad at the carrier."

Men's jaws slackened. This was big-league stuff. Silence answered the captain's announcement.

The carrier's escorts were two of the biggest and most powerful Japanese destroyers. And they were certainly doing a bang-up job of patrolling for submarines. The carrier was coming out of Tokyo Bay at high speed, zigzagging radically, but the tin cans were working on a complex patrol plan of their own, and they were all over the lot. Long before we reached firing position we rigged *Trigger* for depth charging and silent running. We knew we were going to catch it—there was simply no way to avoid it if we did our job properly.

There was even a good chance, the way the escorts were covering the area, that we'd be detected before shooting. For after firing, when a long, thin fan of bubbles suddenly appeared in the unruffled water—well, at the apex of the fan you were pretty sure of finding the submarine responsible.

I can remember how the palms of my hands sweated, and how the flesh crawled around my knees as we bored steadily into firing position. This way and that zigzagged the carrier, and that way and then the other went our rudder as we maneuvered to keep ourselves in position ahead of the task group.

"Make ready all tubes!" Captain Benson is taking no chances, plans to have all ten tubes ready to shoot from either end of the ship. "Stand by forward."

We maneuver for a shot. This boy is coming like hell, and no fooling! Twenty-one knots, we clock him. One destroyer on either bow, the whole trio zigzagging radically.

We twist first one way, then the other, as the carrier presents alternately starboard and port angles on the bow. Evidently we lie on his base course. What a break!

"Up periscope. Bearing—mark! Three five zero. Range, mark! Down periscope. Range, six one double oh. Angle on the bow five starboard. How long till he gets here? What's the distance to the track? Control, sixty-three feet. Right full rudder. New course, zero six zero."

I can hear snatches of the clipped conversation between Steve Mann and the skipper.

"He'll be here in eight and one-half minutes. Zigged three minutes ago, at thirteen minutes. Another zig due about three minutes from now, at nineteen minutes, probably to his right. Distance to the track, five double oh. Depth and speed, Captain?"

"Set all torpedoes depth twenty feet, speed high. Spread them two degrees. What's the time now?"

"Seventeen and one-half minutes."

"We'll wait a minute. Sound, what does he bear?"

"Three five one—Sound."

"That checks, Captain. Better take a look around. The starboard screen is coming right for us."

"Up periscope. There he is—mark! Three five three. Range—mark! Four seven double oh. Looking around—bearing—mark! Three three seven—screen, down periscope! Angle on the bow seven and one-half starboard. Near screen angle on the bow zero. He will pass overhead. Sound, keep bearings coming on light high-speed screws bearing three three seven!"

"High-speed screws, three three seven, sir. Three three seven—three three seven—three three six-a-half—three

three six-a-half—three three six—three three six—three three five—three three oh—three two oh—I've lost him, sir. He's all around the dial!"

The familiar *thum—thum—thum* sweeps unknowingly overhead. We heave a big sigh of relief. He's out of the way for a minute.

"Never mind him now! Sound, pick up heavy screws bearing about three five eight."

"Heavy screws zero zero one sir, zero zero two—zero zero three."

"It's a zig to his left! Up periscope. Bearing—mark! Zero zero five. Range mark! Down periscope. Two two double oh. Angle on the bow thirty starboard. The son of a gun has zigged the wrong way, but it's better for us at that. Right full rudder. Port ahead full! Give me a course for a straight bow shot! Make ready bow tubes! Match gyros forward!"

"One two five, Captain, but we can't make it. Better shoot him on zero nine zero with a right twenty gyro."

"Steady on zero nine zero! All ahead one third. How much time have I got?"

"Not any, sir. Torpedo run one one double oh yards. Range about one eight double oh, gyros fifteen right, increasing. Shoot any time." Good old Steve is right on top of the problem.

I shout for more speed, which we will need to control the depth while shooting. Each torpedo being some three hundred pounds heavier than the water it displaces, we stand to become 3,000 pounds lighter all of a sudden.

"Up periscope. . . . bearing—mark! Three three five! Set! Fire ONE! . . . Fire TWO! . . . Fire THREE! . . . Fire FOUR! . . . Fire FIVE! . . . Fire SIX! . . . All ahead two thirds."

As we in the control room fight savagely to keep from broaching surface, I can feel the repeated jolts which signify the departure of the six torpedoes in the forward tubes. The sudden loss of about eighteen hundred pounds forward makes *Trigger* light by the bow. The increase in speed comes too late, and inexorably she rises.

WHANG! WHANG! WHANG! WHANG! Four beautiful solid hits. The carrier's screws stop. He lists and drifts, helpless. We have time to notice that he is brand-new, has no planes visible, and is of a huge new type not yet seen in action. Little men dressed in white run madly about his decks. His guns shoot wildly in all directions.

We spin the periscope around for a look at the destroyers. Oh, oh! Here they come, and pul-lenty mad! *Take her down!*

We are up to fifty-six feet when finally we start back down. Back to sixty feet, and now we can plainly hear that malignant thum, thum, thum, thum again. Down she plunges, seeking the protection that only the depths can give. THUM, THUM, THUM, THUM—WHAM!— WHAM! WHAM! WHAM! WHAM! WHAM! WHAM! WHAM! WHAM! WHAM! WHAM! WHAM! and so on for forty-seven consecutive bull's-eyes, no clicks at all! It seems inconceivable that any machine, made of man, can withstand such a vicious pounding. The air inside the *Trigger* is filled with fine particles of paint, cork, and dust. Ventilation lines and pipe lines vibrate themselves out of sight and fill the confined spaces with the discordant hum of a hundred ill-matched tuning forks. Everyone is knocked off his feet, clutches gropingly at tables, ladders, pipes, or anything to help regain his footing. A big section of cork is bounced off the hull and lands on the deck alongside the auxiliaryman; as he stoops to pick it up and drop it into a trash can he is knocked to his hands and knees and the trash can spills all over the cork. The lights go out, but the emergency lights give adequate illumination. The heavy steel-pressure bulkheads squeeze inward with each blow and spring out again. Deck plates and gratings throughout the ship jump from their places and clatter around, adding missile hazard to our troubles. The whole hull rings and shudders, whips and shakes itself, bounces sideways, up and down.

Two hundred feet, and still the agony continues, the rain of depth charges, if anything, increases in fury. How can man, made of soft flesh and not steel, stand up under such merciless, excruciating pounding? But stand it we do, with dry lips and nervous eyes.

We are scared, but fear leaves our brains clear, our bodies quick and sure. As usual, the temperature soars, 120 degrees or better. We reach 300 feet, but cannot stop sinking for we are heavy. Forward torpedo room bilges are full of water taken in when we fire the torpedoes. Stern tube packing leaks at this depth, and motor room bilges are filling up. Pump room and engine rooms are taking water more slowly through tortured sea valves and fittings. Besides that, the compression of the hull due to the great depth decreases our buoyant volume. We are heavy by about three or four tons, and we dare not pump, because it would make too much noise, especially bucking sea pressure at this depth.

The depth charges cease, but we can hear the angry screws buzzing around overhead. Maybe they've temporarily lost us. If we can keep silent, creep away, we have a chance of evading. But we sink slowly, although we run with a fifteen-degree up angle. We dare not increase speed over the silent speed, and thus increase

our chances of being heard. Absolute silence. The auxiliaryman and trim-manifold man have their tools laid on
the deck instead of in their usual racks. Some men take
off their shoes. The bucket brigade bails water silently
from the motor room bilges and silently pours it into the
after torpedo room bilges. All hands talk in whispers. The
bow and stern planes and steering have been put into
hand operation instead of hydraulic, and brawny sailors
sweat profusely as they turn the huge wheels. They must
be relieved every five minutes, for they gasp for breath in
the foul air.

We've been breathing this same air since early morning, and now it is night again. Eighty-five men use up a lot
of oxygen, especially when doing hard physical work. We
test the atmosphere—$2\frac{1}{2}$ percent carbon dioxide. Three
percent is the danger line—can knock you out. Four percent will kill you, if you can't get out of it. So we spread
CO_2 absorbent, and release oxygen from our oxygen bottles. That helps. But the heat—nothing can be done about
that. You simply sweat and eat salt tablets. Your clothes
and shoes are soaked. The decks and bulkheads are slip-
pery, and literally alive with water. The humidity is
exactly 100 percent. But you don't notice it.

Slowly *Trigger* sinks. Down, down, far below her safe
tested depth. *Trigger,* if you are worthy of your heritage, if
you can keep the faith of those who built you—who will
never know—and of those who place their lives in
yours—who will know, if only for an instant—keep it
now! We have faith in you, else we'd not subject you to
this test. Vindicate that faith, we pray you!

Far, far below where she was designed to go, *Trigger*
struggles on. Sinking slowly, her hull creaking and groaning at the unaccustomed strain, her decks bulging in the

center, light partition doors unable to close because of the distortion caused by the terrific compression, she finally brings us to the point where it is safe to speed up a little, enough to stop her descent. And so we creep away, finally surfacing to complete our escape.

It wasn't until more than a year later that our carrier was spotted and photographed by a reconnaissance plane. We had set him back a long time, at a critical period. Too bad he didn't sink, but the effect on the Japs of seeing that half-sunken wreck come dragging back on the end of a towline and settle ignominiously into the mud of Tokyo Bay after his brave departure the day before must have been considerable and significant. For we had tagged the uncompleted aircraft carrier *Hitaka* on his maiden trial trip, just as he poked his freshly painted nose outside the torpedo nets.

Later we discovered that our first two torpedoes had "prematured"—exploded just before reaching the target— and that *Hitaka* had in fact received only two holes in his hull, both of them aft. It wasn't our fault that the enemy had had time to tow him back into the shallows, for the four hits we had earned should have taken care of him immediately. Our report did add impetus to the campaign ComSubPac was then waging to get the torpedoes fixed up, however, and had the additional unlooked-for result of starting a rash of stories about the submarine which lay on the bottom of Tokyo Bay for a month waiting for *Hitaka* to be launched. But this was all small comfort.

Trigger had been so badly damaged that it took two months to repair her. During this period Roy Benson, now promoted to Commander, who had commanded her for four patrols, and Lieutenant Steve Mann, who had placed her in commission with me, five patrols before, were detached. Commander Benson reported to the Submarine School at New London, as instructor, and Steve went as exec to the new submarine *Devilfish*, then under construction at the Cramp Shipbuilding Works near Philadelphia. I succeeded Steve as executive officer. Stinky, who by this time was trying to get us to call him "Sinky," took over as engineer.

For a time we wondered who our new skipper was to be, and hoped it would be somebody who had had a lot of experience already as exec of a hot ship. Our hopes were fulfilled to overflowing when, after a short time, we learned that Robert E. Dornin, commonly known as "Dusty," veteran of many patrols in *Gudgeon*, had been ordered to take over *Trigger*. Knowing his reputation, we expected great things of our ship in the next few months, and in this we were not to be disappointed.

6

SEAWOLF

IN THE MEANTIME, *Seawolf* had been long overdue for repairs, and her crew for an extensive rest, so she was ordered to Mare Island Navy Yard for a complete modernization. While in California she received a new skipper, Lieutenant Commander Royce L. Gross, commonly known as "Googy," and Fred Warder left the ship he had commanded for more than three years and for seven war patrols.

When *Seawolf* stood out to sea again, refurbished inwardly and outwardly, she immediately proceeded to demonstrate that she was still the same *Wolf* as of yore. Her first war patrol under Gross lasted twenty-six days in all, from Midway to Midway. Its high point was an eleven-hour battle with a large escorted freighter, as a result of which the freighter's bow was blown off—he sank a few hours later—and Gross learned to his dismay that there was still plenty of room for improvement in torpedoes.

A few days later a damaged ship was encountered, in the tow of a tug, and escorted by a single destroyer. Gross decided that the escort was by far the more valuable target, and attacked him first in hopes of getting up on the surface later and sinking the towed vessel by gunfire. This plan was foiled by the approach of yet another destroyer after the submarine had expended all her torpedoes, but *Seawolf* carried away a series of photographs, later widely publicized, showing the last moments of H.I.J.M.S. *Patrol Boat #39*. And then Roy Gross brought his veteran submarine back to Midway for a fast refit and some more torpedoes.

Googy's second patrol produced only one hit for sixteen torpedoes fired, with the majority of blame definitely going to the recalcitrant fish. Nevertheless, that one hit sank a ship, which is illustrative of what might have been done by our submarines had they had dependable armament. The situation was improving, although at this point no one in *Seawolf* could have been criticized for thinking otherwise.

On her tenth patrol, Gross's third, came the first indications of a new deal for the old *Wolf*. In her assigned area for but five days, she spent the entire time working over a single convoy, sinking three ships in all; and she then attacked and sank two reconnaissance sampans with her deck guns. On her first attack, submerged between two columns of freighters, she fired her bow tubes at the largest ship in the left-hand column, and immediately afterward fired her stern tubes at the largest ship in the right-hand column. Both ships sank. Surfacing after a depth charging, she pursued the convoy, overtook it, made another submerged attack, and fired four torpedoes, none of which hit. Nothing daunted, she resumed the pursuit, made a night surface attack, and obtained one hit in the largest remaining ship, leaving him dead in the water. With four torpedoes left, *Seawolf* bored in on the surface to finish him off, disregarding the salvos of gunfire with which he sought to dissuade her. She fired each of her precious remaining torpedoes independently and carefully—and got two dud hits and two erratic runs. That left her without any torpedoes; so Gross manned the deck guns, closing the enemy slowly, firing deliberately, feeling him out. With the return fire, originally erratic, to be sure, now entirely silent, *Seawolf* continued to close the range. After approximately one hour of target practice, the enemy vessel, hit by more than seventy rounds from the submarine's three-inch gun, rolled over and sank within sight of her gun crews.

The torpedoes were still not perfect, but they were improving, and skill and persistence were still paying off.

Patrol number eleven again saw Gross bringing his ship back to port with no torpedoes remaining, leaving two enemy vessels at the bottom of the China Sea and damaging a third which in all probability also sank, though not seen to do so. Torpedo malfunction had again robbed the *Wolf* of at least one and possibly two more targets, but it was now obvious from other patrol reports that the problem was finally on its way to a solution. Reports of other submarines were indicating a larger proportion of successful attacks, and Skipper Gross was at a loss to explain the heartbreaking misses on his last few attacks. In his self-criticism he failed to appreciate what every other submariner had long since seen. *Only once had Gross brought back torpedoes!* Every submarine skipper was highly respectful of the man who could consistently average two ships per patrol, and that was exactly what Googy Gross had done so far.

On December 22, 1943, the *Wolf* got under way from the submarine base at Pearl Harbor for her twelfth war patrol. Lasting only thirty-six days, it topped all the superlatives earned by that fighting submarine and her amazingly aggressive skipper. Fred Warder had a worthy successor.

On January 7, 1944, *Seawolf* passed through the Nansei Shoto chain, and on January 10 she began a forty-eight-hour battle with a Japanese convoy. Torpedoes expended—seventeen; hits—nine certain and four possible; ships sunk—three. The wheel had finally come around full for *Seawolf*.

Two days later, still patrolling her area north of Formosa, but with only three torpedoes remaining on board, *Seawolf* again sights smoke. This time it is four freighters and two destroyers.

Again *Seawolf* leaps in pursuit. Again the call for the plotting parties, the tedious tracking, the meticulous positioning of targets.

This time Roy Gross is in a dilemma. He cannot hope to do much damage with only three torpedoes, but the convoy is in his area and he cannot let it go by. The only answer is to get help, and quickly. Hastily a contact message is sent out, addressed to any and all submarines in the vicinity. Another message is sent to ComSubPac, in Pearl Harbor.

And all the while *Seawolf* continues tracking. Once again Googy decides on a night attack. He figures he will try to get in submerged just at dusk—and if necessary re-attack on the surface a little later.

No luck on the submerged attack. With the convoy well in sight, the situation progressing nicely, a sudden zig away puts *Seawolf* far out in left field. Gross might have tried a long-range shot, but not with only three precious torpedoes left. Gritting his teeth, he lets them go—but surfaces eight miles astern.

Overtaking on the starboard flank, flying in at full

speed in her attempt to complete the surface attack before moonrise, the *Wolf* is forced to cross astern of the starboard flank destroyer at excessively close range. A precarious situation for a moment, but she is not detected; the ships of the convoy line up for what appears to be a perfect shot—when suddenly they zig away. The combination of circumstances, with *Seawolf* at close range nearly ready to shoot, puts her virtually in the convoy directly astern of the last ship.

Holding his breath, Gross settles down to act like a Jap, hoping that the herding destroyers are not in the habit of looking their sheep over too closely. He closes in a bit more. Lagging too far astern will only attract attention. Furthermore, if you are a little closer there will be a better chance of picking up a chance shot.

Calmly Roy Gross waits his chance, all the while narrowly watching the destroyers patrolling on either beam. They give no indication of noticing anything untoward, and finally a sharp left zig puts one of the target vessels nearly broadside to *Seawolf*'s bow tubes.

A quick setup. Range and bearing by radar, bearing checked by TBT. Angle on the bow estimated from the bridge, checked by plot, verified by TDC. In a matter of seconds comes the welcome word from the conning tower:

"Set below, Captain!"

"Stand by forward!" Another quick bearing from the Target Bearing Transmitter . . . another quick radar setup . . .

"Set!"

"Fire!" *Seawolf*'s last three torpedoes race out into the night, trailing their streams of bubbles. They diverge slightly as their fan-shaped spread reaches out for the left freighter in the starboard column.

Suddenly the forward part of the target bursts into incandescence! A brilliant flame flashes into the sky with straight, streaked fury, razor-edged disaster roaring into the heavens.

Seconds later the after part of the ship also bursts into holocaust. In the brilliant flame which lights up the stricken vessel the fascinated watchers on *Seawolf*'s bridge see a mast topple to one side, the single stack to the other, and then all is blotted out in a screaming, searing flame which guts the entire ship in a single white-hot second.

The noise of the explosion reaches *Seawolf,* drowned in the insanely triumphant uproar of the forces she has released. At the limiting peak of the inferno a black boiling cloud of smoke billows hundreds of feet into the sky.

On the surface of the sea it might well be day. The perpetrator of the outrage and the white faces on her bridge are brilliantly silhouetted in the funeral flames of her victim.

The skipper recovers first. "Right full rudder! All ahead flank!" He shouts the orders down the open hatch at his feet.

A stream of troubled white water flows aft from *Seawolf*'s stern, angling sharply off to starboard under the impetus of the suddenly accelerated propellers and the full rudder. The yammering of the diesels comfortingly reaches the ears of the bridge personnel, and careening to port, the white water glaring and foaming between the wooden deck slats, the *Wolf* dashes away.

Ten depth charges are heard a few minutes later—a good sign—and the submarine checks her headlong rush some five miles away. The thing on Gross's mind now is the remainder of the convoy.

COMSUBPAC FROM SEAWOLF X URGENT X OPERATIONAL X CON-
TACT X CONVOY X THREE FREIGHTERS TWO DESTROYERS BASE
COURSE ONE-FIVE-ZERO SPEED NINE POSIT BAKER FIVE FOUR YOKE
TWO THREE X ALL TORPEDOES EXPENDED X TRAILING BT K

Captain Joe Grenfell, lately of the submarines *Gudgeon*
and *Tunny*, now serving on the staff of ComSubPac,
receives the decoded message. Day after day the officers
on the staff of ComSubPac stand their watches hoping for
just such a break. They have been bound to their desks by
official orders and cannot get out in the boats, yet their
hearts are out on the sea as they watch their friends coming and going. Here is one of the few chances a "staffie"
gets to toss a couple of personal licks at the enemy.
Grenfell does not neglect the opportunity.

Scanning the message, he rises from his desk where he
has been working on next month's submarine disposi-
tions and strides swiftly to the side of the room where a
heavy curtain conceals the entire wall.

A two-handed pull on a pair of cords alongside, and
the curtain slides back, revealing a huge chart of the
Pacific. Studded here and there, concentrated chiefly
about the home islands of Japan, are numerous tiny submarine silhouettes, each bearing a name. This is the Top
Secret disposition chart.

With a long plastic ruler and an equally long pair of
dividers, Grenfell carefully picks off a spot on the chart;
draws a light circle about it with an arrow pointing southeast. He studies the area carefully, noting the locations of
the submarines in the vicinity. A three-ship convoy is a
valuable prize, but not one to justify calling away all submarines in the general area. It is necessary to select one or
two who can best reach the target from their present positions, considering the possible objective of the enemy.

Several hundred miles to the southwest of the convoy's plotted position is a single marker bearing the name *Whale*. To Grenfell's practiced eye there is little doubt that this is the ship which must fall heir to the job.

Again the ruler, measuring. Again the dividers, stepping off distances carefully. A few scribbled figures on a pad of paper. He checks the situation, goes over the distances and the computation a second time. More than one impossible mission has been generated right here. Satisfied, he lays aside the instruments, tears the piece of paper off the pad, draws the curtain back across the chart, and returns to his desk.

FOR WHALE FROM COMSUBPAC X CONVOY THREE SHIPS TWO ESCORTS SPEED NINE X POSIT BAKER FIFTY FOUR YOKE TWENTY THREE AT TWENTY HUNDRED ITEM X COURSE ONE FIVE ZERO X SEA-WOLF TRAILING REPORTING X DEPART PRESENT STATION INTERCEPT X ACKNOWLEDGE X BT K

Off the coast of China, Fred Janney, executive officer of the USS *Whale*, decodes the message and immediately calls the skipper. The two pore over the charts of the area.

After several minutes Commander A. C. (Acey) Burrows lays down his pencil.

"Looks as if we can catch them on three engines, Fred."

"Yessir, Captain," replies Janney, "except that if we take a more northerly course on four engines we might intercept them earlier and be able to make a night attack. Besides, that would give us nearly twenty-four hours longer to work on them."

"Guess you're right. Let's bend on four engines and try it."

Whale, until now patrolling leisurely in the traffic lanes south of Formosa, veers away from her accustomed circuit and speeds to the northeast.

In the meantime. *Seawolf* has been keeping contact astern of the convoy. It is now night, and over a period of several hours she has sent two more contact reports. The trouble with this kind of business is that you never know whether you are getting anywhere. It is up to someone else to perform; all you can do is wait. After the exciting action of the past few days the monotony becomes deadly and is felt throughout the whole ship. Finally the quarter-master of the watch turns to the captain.

"Captain, sir, that ship, the one we blew up a while ago—maybe one of these has got a load of avgas too. Do you think maybe our gun might set it off if we tried it, sir?"

Gross stares unblinkingly at his interlocutor.

"You might have something there, Kuehn," he says. "We ought to wait till it's a little darker, though, before we try it."

After a few more minutes' discussion, in which several other officers and enlisted men express their views, the general alarm rings again, and the announcing system blares forth.

"Battle stations! All hands man your battle stations for gun action!"

Seawolf's three-inch gun is manned, trained out on the starboard beam, and she commences to ease in on the nearest enemy ship. Silently she creeps toward the foe, ammunition and crew at the ready, nerveless fingers twitching the firing keys, eyes straining to pierce the gloom. At a range of approximately two miles, with the water sibilant along the thin side plating of the submarine hull, Gross hoarsely calls out:

"Commence firing!"

Six shots answer him from *Seawolf*'s deck gun and six

tracer streams mark the paths of the shells on their way toward the enemy. Possibly one or two hits are achieved, but there is precious little time to verify them, for all five enemy ships instantly reply with a veritable barrage of shellfire.

Comment in the patrol report: "Considered this a good idea that didn't work . . . continued tracking well clear to port."

Gross orders another contact report to be sent to Pearl Harbor. He has not yet been able to talk directly to *Whale* by radio, though he has received word she is on her way. This is exasperating because a considerable time lag is involved in sending the message to Pearl for decoding, re-encoding, and retransmitting to *Whale.*

Some twenty-eight hours after the initial contact with the convoy, fourteen hours after sinking the vessel, *Seawolf* sights two planes approaching the convoy. Evidently these had been ordered out as air cover, and their arrival forces the submarine to dive. Five hours later she is back on the surface making full power in pursuit—and three hours after that, contact is regained. Lesson: If you drive a submarine under, *keep* him there.

0245 on the morning of January 16, nearly forty-eight hours after the initial contact, *Seawolf* is still trailing, pumping out information every few hours. Finally Gross is able to talk directly to Acey Burrows. Comment in the patrol report: "This was encouraging."

1554: fifty-four hours after initial contact, three explosions are heard in the distance, followed a little later by a fourth.

1807: more explosions; flashes of gunfire in the convoy. Subsequently, for a period of about two hours, *Seawolf* hears sporadic explosions from the direction of the convoy. Some are identified as depth charges and some may be torpedoes. Much gunfire is visible through the elevated periscope but by this time it is night again, and nothing further can be seen.

Seawolf's weary plotting parties now report that the convoy has stopped.

Carefully the *Wolf*'s radar checks over each enemy ship. All five are still visible, but only one appears to be under way, and he is leaving the area of action at full speed. The indications are that *Whale* may have hit and damaged two of the freighters, and perhaps is occupied at the moment by the two destroyers. Under these circumstances, she will never get another shot at the last ship—unless, somehow, the fleeing freighter can be induced to turn back after a suitable interval.

Despite mute signals of exhaustion which he detects in himself and his companions, the thought, in Gross, is father to the deed. Once again the terribly fatigued *Wolf* swings into action. The plotting parties, by now quite expert, resume their interminable chore.

About two and a half hours later: "This ought to be long enough! If *Whale* is going to get out from under those tin cans she'll have pretty well accomplished it by now. Time to turn this fellow around! *Battle stations—gun action!*"

Gross sees the answering gleam of assent in the eyes of his men. Once again *Seawolf*'s tiny deck gun is manned, and the submarine ghosts in toward the fleeing enemy. The gun crew is on deck, the ammunition is standing by. The radar is giving steady ranges to the sight-setters. All is desperate readiness.

Nervelessly the low-lying sub closes in on her much larger antagonist. The mettle of the latter had been shown not long ago, when *Seawolf* had made her earlier attempt at gun action. When a surface ship has been alerted to the presence of a submarine, the greatest advantage of the undersea vessel—the factor of surprise—is taken from her. In this case, of course, there can no longer be any surprise, except perhaps at the temerity of the submarine skipper.

Googy Gross, for all his daring tactics, is not the man to pass up any possible advantage which he might be able to garner. He jockeys carefully for position, hoping to open fire from such a direction that the enemy's stack smoke at least partially blankets the expected return fire. The moon is about to rise, however, and Gross realizes that its additional light will enable his adversary to see him and probably reply effectively, at the necessarily short range he would have to employ should he open fire now. And so the *Wolf* glides along, keeping parallel course with, but just out of sight of, the Nipponese freighter.

Then the moon rises, and *Seawolf* maneuvers to silhouette the target against the frosty light in the east.

Unlike the previous gun attack, this time the object is not necessarily to sink the vessel—though that outcome, of course, would be welcomed—but to cause him to reverse course and drive him back toward *Whale*. It is a gigantic bluff Gross is acting, one worthy of his well-known poker prowess. At a range of about two miles the *Wolf* commences rapid fire, pumping out her shells as fast as they can be loaded.

The reaction from the enemy is twofold and immediate. Apparently he has been keeping his guns manned for just this possibility, although he probably has not divined the ulterior motive behind this second gun attack. Instead of changing course, he instantly returns the fire with two heavy guns—both considerably larger than that of the submarine—plus several machine guns.

Noting that the Jap return fire is wild and erratic, Gross holds to his initial program, and keeps his crew at it. The hotly served gun on the submarine's deck registers several hits before the Nip gun crews manage to find the range. Then, with shells whistling overhead and plunging into the water not far away, Googy is forced to shear sharply and break off the action.

Feelings of bitter disappointment fill the skipper of the *Wolf.* He has exposed his ship and crew, in their badly fatigued state, for nothing gained. Yet there was little else he could do, under the circumstances—so run Captain Roy Gross's thoughts as he hears a report from one of the lookouts:

"Target has changed course!"

And so he has; but he isn't heading back toward *Whale* yet. Rather, it develops, he is steaming in large circles, apparently puzzled as to which direction to choose. Gross stations his ship to southeastward of him, vowing to have another go at him if he needs it.

But he doesn't. With the *Wolf* dogging his heels at the more respectable range of about four miles, he heads back in the direction he came from, zigzagging radically, but heading northwest for sure. Her purpose accomplished, *Seawolf* follows along, sending periodic contact reports to *Whale.* Every time the Jap edges a little too far one way or the other, accidental "sighting" of a submarine shadowing him in that quarter sends him back in line again.

Proof that Acey Burrows is back on the surface—*Whale* replies to the first report instantly. Position, course, and speed of the enemy are radioed to her, in each case answered with the cryptic "R." According to plot she and the remainder of the convoy are approximately fifty miles to the northwest. As Gross sends Burrows the necessary information as to enemy movements, Burrows will try to position himself for interception.

Every time the Japanese skipper zigs or zags, a new message crackles through the ether:

FROM SEAWOLF TO WHALE BT ZIG X NEW COURSE 350 SPEED SAME K

It is almost as if a sheep were being herded to slaughter—and indeed he is. You can imagine the Jap skipper's state of mind at this point. Everywhere he has turned he has run into a submarine. He must think there are dozens of them in the area, never dreaming that eleven of the twelve submarines are one and the same—the *Seawolf*—and without torpedoes.

0524 on the morning of January 17, 1944, three torpedo explosions, followed by the reverberations of gunfire from the Jap. Possibly one fish hit him.

0600: plot reports the ship has stopped.

0620: in the growing light the Jap ship has evidently sighted *Seawolf* still prowling in the distance on the surface, keeping well clear of possible erratic torpedoes. Since this is the only enemy he can see, he opens fire again. *Seawolf* does not even bother to dive.

0623: one terrific explosion in the target. Smoke, spray, and steam rise high in the air, and the ship settles by the bow.

0635: the target has sunk, a victim of at least two torpedoes from *Whale*. *Seawolf* is on her way back to port, with the skipper, the exec, the plotting party, and the communication department utterly exhausted after seventy-two hours on their feet under the most grueling strain.

When *Seawolf* returned to Pearl Harbor with her report of four ships sunk, plus one "assist," she was again received with wild enthusiasm—a not unusual thing for the *Wolf.* Characteristically, Gross gave the credit for his fifth ship to *Whale*, who had actually sunk it. Acey Burrows, on the other hand, stated that the credit belonged to *Seawolf.* There was glory enough for all.

The career of the grand old submarine was just about over. She went back to San Francisco and for the second time was modernized. But progress is rapid in war, and she was an old ship—as fighting submarines go. She neither carried the number of torpedoes nor possessed the thick hull skin of later vessels. With full recognition of her valiant record to date, *Seawolf* was confined to secondary missions. She had sunk her last ship.

The remainder of the saga of the *Seawolf* is quickly told. Under the command of Lieutenant Commander A. L. Bontier she left Australia on what was to be her fifteenth patrol.

On October 3, 1944, a Japanese submarine attacked and sank USS *Shelton* (DE407) not far from *Seawolf's* reported position. Maddened, *Shelton's* comrades fanned forth in all directions to hunt the Nip submersible.

On that same day, as luck would have it, *Seawolf*, *Narwhal*, and two other United States submarines were also in the vicinity, in an area in which no attacks on any submarines whatsoever were permitted.

USS *Rowell* (DE403), anxious to avenge the sinking of

Shelton, pressed her search hard, and finally detected a submerged submarine. Either not having been informed or having forgotten that he was in a "no attack" zone, her skipper immediately ordered attack with all weapons. He later reported that the submarine behaved in a peculiar manner, making little attempt to escape, and continually sending a series of dots and dashes over the sonar equipment. After several attacks, debris and a large air bubble came to the surface. A probable "kill" was credited, and a submarine silhouette was painted on *Rowell*'s bridge.

Seawolf had been contacted by *Narwhal* at four minutes of eight on the morning of October 3. She did not answer an attempt to contact her next morning, nor was she ever heard from thereafter. It has since been established that the Japanese submarine which sank *Shelton* experienced no countermeasures, and was able to return to Japan. There is no Japanese report of attack on an American submarine which could possibly account for the known circumstances of *Seawolf*'s disappearance.

Investigation disclosed what looked like certain though circumstantial proof that the submarine sunk by *Rowell* had been *Seawolf*. The fact that the trapped submarine had sent sonar signals, instead of evading, provided the final argument. Personnel of the American destroyer strenuously insisted that the signals were not in the correct recognition code, but mistakes had been made in them before.

Sooner or later it was bound to happen. There had been instances of our own forces firing on United States submarines—one of the most inexcusable occurring near San Francisco in 1942 when USS *Gato,* escorted by one of our destroyers, was bombed nevertheless by a blimp which totally ignored the frantic signals sent by the escort. There had been many other cases of United States planes attacking friendly submarines during the war, and a few of surface forces firing on them. Indeed, the whole problem of submarine recognition had long been a perplexing one. Elaborate systems for safeguarding our submarines had been built up, and those lapses which did from time to time occur could be explained, usually, as unfortunate errors in the heat of battle. A few times, however, what appeared to be a lack of the rudiments of common sense had tragic results.

And so, alone and friendless, unable to defend herself, frantically striving to make her identity known to her attacker, the old *Wolf* came to the end of the trail. Who can know what terror her crew must have tasted, when it became plain to them that the American destroyer escort above them, specially built and trained to sink German submarines, was determined to sink them also? Who can appreciate their desperation when they realized that the genius of their own countrymen had, by a monstrous miscast of the dice, been pitted against them?

And who can visualize the hopeless, futile, unutterable bitterness of the final disaster, when, combined with the shock of the frame-smashing depth charges, came the rapier-like punch of the hedgehogs, piercing *Seawolf*'s stout old hull, starting the hydrant flow of black sea water, and ending forever all hopes of seeing sunlight again.

TRIGGER

7

TRIGGER SPENT EIGHT WEEKS being ripped apart and then put back together again by the Pearl Harbor Navy Yard. Dornin relieved Captain Roy Benson, and I was sent off on three weeks' leave in the States. When I got back to Pearl, I carried in my heart the knowledge that I had met my bride-to-be, and had seen my father for the last time. A mountain of work instantly engulfed me.

One day toward the end of the overhaul, Stinky sought me out.

"We want to install an ice-cream freezer on board," said he without any preliminaries.

"You mean one of those wooden hand-cranked jobs?" He nodded.

"Who in hell ever heard of an ice creamer in a submarine?" I demanded.

"Well, we think we know where we can get one. Besides, wouldn't you like a nice cool dish of ice cream sometime when it's good and hot, like right after charging batteries or running silent for half a day—like two months ago when those two tin cans were after us?"

"My God, man, you're fat enough already. How are you ever going to lose weight with an ice creamer on board?"

Stinky grinned. "Speak for yourself. But just think how good a big heaping bowl of cool raspberry ice or peach melba would taste. All you have to do is push the pantry button, and in comes Wilson with a big double scoop of it on a dish, all round and firm and cool, just starting to melt a little on the edges, maybe with a dab of whipped cream and a cherry on top—"

I could taste the saliva starting to drool into my mouth. "Sounds swell," I growled. "Just where do you think you're going to stow this contraption, and where will you get the ice, and who's going to turn the crank—you? Or will you put a special man on watch?"

"It's going to be automatic. We'll take the motor off the ship's lathe—"

"The hell you will!"

"—and we'll hook it up to the ship's main refrigerating system so we won't have to bother either with ice or cranking it."

Submariners are born gadgeteers, and if anyone could rig up this kind of contraption, they could. I felt myself weakening.

"If you connect it to the refrigerating system, it will have to be permanently installed—just where have you planned to put it?"

Stinky's self-assurance for the first time appeared to wane a little. "Well," he confessed, "the only place we could think of where there's enough room is on deck between the periscopes—"

My outraged bellow nearly blew him from the ward-room, but he continued doggedly:

"So we thought maybe you would help us find a place for it."

The vision of the skipper carefully stepping over the

ice-cream freezer while he made a periscope observation was too much. My thought must have been mirrored in my face, for Stinky quickly went on:

"We've already got it half finished, if you'd care to see it."

I might have known it. One submarine had already been reputed to have dismantled a jeep and stowed it away belowdecks just before starting patrol. I myself had once connived at stashing away the essential parts of a motorcycle behind the main engines. By comparison an ice-cream freezer was a cinch.

Sincavich led me to the forward engine room, where there was a steel worktable and vise. Five sailors, among them the chief of the boat—the senior enlisted man on board—were crowded about the two-by-three-foot bench. At our approach they showed us what they had been doing with a delighted conspiratorial air.

When we set out for *Trigger's* sixth patrol, in an out-of-the-way corner of the control room rested the fruit of Stinky's efforts. My first sample of its product had the distinct flavor of hydraulic oil superimposed on that of the ice cream, and I noticed particles of metal in it from the grinding of the gears. But neither oil nor metal filings reduced our pleasure. We ran the machine almost continuously, and had ice cream at least once a day.

It was a good thing, too, that the installation happened to be in the control room, within sight and supervision of the chief in charge of the control room watch. In addition to his primary duties of handling the hydraulic main vent manifold, rigging the bow planes in and out when surfacing or diving, opening and shutting the main induction, keeping a watch on the condition of the "Christmas

Tree"—as we termed the panel of red and green lights indicating whether our principal hull openings were open or closed—checking the trim of the ship hourly, and supervising the radar watch standers, this worthy now inherited the extra chore of making sure the ice creamer was properly operated. Such extra duty he took on without complaint, for it also included testing the product—in soup bowls.

We soon found that as the ice cream slowly froze into the desired consistency, the paddles became harder and harder to turn, while the motor ran slower and slower. Without careful supervision, there would obviously come a time when the motor could turn no more.

Strict instructions were issued about ice-creamer operation, including names of qualified operators. Nevertheless, about a week after we had left Pearl Harbor the daily ration of ice cream suddenly stopped, and Stinky—now known as Officer in Charge of Ice Cream—was immediately called on the carpet by the skipper. His crestfallen explanation was that someone had neglected to watch the machine, and the ice cream had become so hard that the motor had finally stopped. The first indication of trouble had been the odor of burning insulation, and now, with or without the ice cream, the motor refused to turn at all.

The strain of unanimous and vocal disapproval by the whole ice-cream starved crew was obviously heavy. At mealtime in the wardroom Stinky sat silent—for him—and developed the habit of bracing himself when the dessert appeared. Someone was sure to make some pithy comment.

"If we hadn't filled all our storerooms with that damned ice-cream mix, we wouldn't have to eat this lousy farina"—as whatever concoction our poor cooks dreamed up was almost invariably called.

"Your sparktricians don't seem to have any trouble with the main motors of this bucket; why in the all-fired hell can't they fix a simple thing like an ice-creamer motor?"

When Dornin had first been informed of the casualty he had summarily ordered a general court-martial on Stinky, and every day, with evident relish, he recited the cruel and original punishments he expected the court to adjudge.

Stinky fought back desperately, but every day we threw out his arguments as specious, irrelevant, and without foundation. The harried look on his face daily became more pronounced.

Then one day, just before dessert was due, Sincavich suddenly excused himself from the table and squeezed his way out of the wardroom. His departure threw a damper on our spirits, and our consciences twinged us. No dessert came for a few uneasy minutes, and then in came Stinky, carrying a huge baking platter from the galley, in the center of which reposed grandly a tremendous baked Alaska!

We found out that a modification had been made to the ice creamer. Fastened securely to the bulkhead nearby was a large ammeter, to indicate how much electricity the motor was using, and hanging on a hook below it was a card containing a lengthy set of typed instructions.

Once again ice cream was on our daily menu, and the charges and specifications preferred against Stinky were all dismissed. But our joy was short-lived. Someone coming off watch at 0400 had tried to make a can of ice cream while we were charging the ship's main storage batteries, and had forgotten about the higher voltage existing at such times. Grim-faced electrician's mates again dismantled the burned-out motor and took it, the useless instruction sheet, and the ammeter back into the recesses of the engineering spaces. Our morale drooped once more.

Days passed. The hunted look reappeared on Stinky's face, and all the once-quashed specifications against him were revived, with some additional ones. We wondered how we could mete out the punishment he deserved immediately, without waiting until we got back to port— a general court-martial required more officers on it than we could supply. It was then suggested that we could easily constitute half a court, and, after hearing all the evidence and finding the defendant guilty, adjudge precisely half of the deserved penalty.

It took longer than the first time to fix the motor, because, as Stinky said, "the motor armature was much more thoroughly burned out." But finally came the day when he again disappeared just before dessert was due—and, as our mouths dripped in anticipation, brought in a second baked Alaska, if anything, larger than the first.

Our electrical gadgeteers, realizing the fault with the ice creamer was basically that its safety precautions were overcomplicated, had gone all out for simplification. From that day on the ice-cream machine was an unqualified success.

The ammeter was still there, but the face of its dial now bore only the legend, Condition of Ice Cream. At the one end of the needle's travel was the single typewritten word: Soft. Slightly past the center of the arc was the statement, printed by hand in large red letters: Hard Enough.

And we discovered in a day or so that Stinky had left strict written orders that no matter what the circumstances, the time of day or night, even if the captain himself had ordered it, permission to start a battery charge had to be obtained first from the Officer in Charge of Ice Cream.

8
HARDER

HIT 'EM AGAIN, _HARDER!_ No one in the Submarine Force will ever forget that battle cry. It is ringing still in the halls of Dealey Center, New London; at deserted Camp Dealey, on Guam; and at the submarine base, Pearl Harbor. For the USS _Harder_ was a peer among peers, a fighter among fighters, and, above all, _a submarine among submarines._ And when she and her fighting skipper were lost, the whole Navy mourned, for her exploits had become legendary. It was characteristic that she gave her life to save one of her fellows, for she interposed herself in front of an attacking ship to give another submarine an opportunity to escape, and in so doing received the final, unlucky, fatal depth charge.

Harder's record, after only three patrols, was already one to conjure with in the Pacific Fleet. Built in Groton, Connecticut, at the Electric Boat Company, she first appeared at Pearl Harbor in June 1943, and for uniformly outstanding results, dogged courage, and brilliant performance, soon had few equals in our Submarine Force. Her record speaks for itself: First patrol, three ships sunk and one damaged; second patrol, four ships sunk and one damaged; third patrol, five ships sunk.

On *Harder*'s fourth patrol Sam Dealey carried off an exploit unprecedented in submarine warfare, an operation epitomizing the competence and daring of the magnificent ship he had molded. *Harder* was detailed "lifeguard" submarine for an air strike on Woleai Atoll, one of the hundreds of small Pacific islands taken over by the Japs after World War I. To save a downed aviator, Dealey deliberately ran his ship aground, sending three men, including Lieutenant Logan, his torpedo officer, ashore in a rubber boat to effect the rescue. Since the flier was only exhausted and not injured, Sam assigned him a bunk in Officer's Country, and *Harder* continued on patrol.

When Dealey brought *Harder* into Fremantle, he had sunk one destroyer and one freighter and damaged and probably sunk a second destroyer. As he indicated in his patrol report, his ship now had the pleasure of seeing her total tonnage record of enemy ships exceed the 100,000 tons' mark—a distinction attained by only a few of our undersea fighters. That it was due entirely to his own efforts, Sam would have indignantly denied, pointing to the outstanding officers and men who served with him, who, he said, were responsible for making *Harder* what she was. Frank Lynch, his executive officer, and Sam Logan, his torpedo officer, were his two mainstays, and to them he invariably tried to shift the credit. Frank, a behemoth of a man, had been regimental commander and first-string tackle at the Naval Academy. He combined qualities of leadership and physical stamina with a keen, searching mind and a tremendous will to fight. Sam, slighter of build, less the extrovert, was a mathematical shark and had stood first in his class at the Academy. Under pressure of the war years, he had discovered a terrible and precise ferocity which always possessed him whenever contact with the enemy was imminent. To him, operation of the torpedo director was an intricate puzzle, to be worked out using all information and means at his command, divining the enemy's intentions and anticipating them, working out new techniques of getting the right answer under different sets of conditions.

"With those two madmen pushing me all the time," Dealey would say, "there was nothing I could do but go along!"

It was, however, *Harder*'s fifth war patrol which fixed her position, and that of Sam Dealey, in the annals of the United States Submarine Force for all time.

On May 26, 1944, *Harder* departed from Fremantle, Australia, on what many have termed the most epoch-making war patrol ever recorded. It must be remembered that Sam Dealey, Frank Lynch, and Sam Logan were by now experts who had long served together. Their ship was a veteran, and organized to the peak of perfection in fighting ability. Who can blame Dealey, with this sort of help, for deliberately selecting the most difficult of accomplishments?

Your submarine is primarily a commerce destroyer. While it will attack any moderate-to-large warship it encounters, its principal objective is the lifeline of the enemy—its merchant carriers. The submarine will spend long hours lying in wait in sea lanes frequented by enemy cargo vessels, and her personnel will spend longer hours trying to outguess their adversaries, to determine where they are routing their ships in their effort to evade submarine attack. The submarine will, of course, similarly try to intercept enemy war vessels. But the destroyer or escort vessel is the bane of the sub's existence, for it is commonly

considered too small to shoot successfully and too dangerous to fool around with. Besides, sinking a destroyer was
not ordinarily so damaging to the enemy's cause as sinking a tanker, for example. Sometimes a destroyer would
intercept a torpedo intended for a larger vessel, and sometimes you had to shoot at one in desperation—and sometimes one would give you a shot you simply couldn't pass
up. But ordinarily you avoid tangling with one.

Sam Dealey, ever an original man, had a new thought. It
was known that the Japanese Navy was critically short of
destroyers of all types, first-line or otherwise. Intelligence
reports were to the effect that those few they had were
being operated week in and week out, without pause for
even essential repairs, in their desperate effort to keep
their sea lanes open. Add to this the tremendous screen
necessary for a fleet movement and the probability that
it could be hamstrung—or at least rendered extraordinarily vulnerable—if the number of destroyers or escort
ships could be substantially reduced. In short, Dealey
decided that the war against merchant shipping was
entirely too tame for his blood, and he asked and received for his operating area the waters around the
major Japanese Fleet Operating Base of Tawi Tawi in the
Sulu Archipelago. He reasoned that once he revealed his
presence there, which he planned to do in the time-
honored submarine manner, there would be no dearth
of destroyers sent out to track him down. And if there
were too many in one bunch, he could avoid them; if
they came out by ones and twos, he'd deliberately tangle
with them.

And tangle he did. Shortly after sunset of the first day
in the area, a convoy was sighted and *Harder* gave chase.
The moon came out during the pursuit, the convoy

changed course, and events soon confirmed the submarine's detection by the enemy. The nearest destroyer emitted clouds of black smoke, put on full speed, and commenced heading directly for her—and there was nothing left to do but run for it.

At full speed *Harder* could barely exceed 19 knots, and it soon was evident that the tin can astern was clipping them off at 24 or better. The range inexorably reduced to 10,000 yards, then 9,000, then 8,500—at which point Sam pulled the plug out from under his ship and dropped her neatly to periscope depth.

The moment the ship was under water, Dealey called out, "Left full rudder!"

Obediently the submarine altered course to the left, drawing away from the path down which she had been running. A tricky stunt, this, fraught with danger. If the DD up there had enough sense to divine what had occurred and suspect the trap laid for him, things would be tough. He'd have little trouble in picking up the submarine broadside with his supersonic sound equipment, and probably could do plenty of damage with an immediate attack.

But he suspected nothing, came on furiously down the broad wake left by the sub, blundered right across her stern, and was greeted with two torpedoes which hit him under the bow and under the bridge, and broke his back.

With his bow torn nearly off and gaping holes throughout his stricken hull, the Jap's stern rose vertically in the air. Clouds of smoke, spray, and steam enveloped him, mingled with swift tongues of red flame which feverishly licked at his sides and decks. Depth charges, normally stowed aft in the depth charge racks ready for immediate use, fell out the back of the racks and went crashing down upon the now-slanted deck. Some of them, reached by the flames, went off with horrifying explosions which effectively nullified any chance survivors the holocaust might have had.

Less than two minutes after the detonations of the torpedoes, the long black hull of the submarine boiled to the surface. Sam Dealey was not one to give up the convoy that easily, and *Harder* took off once more at full speed after the enemy. But further contact was not to be regained with this particular outfit.

"Radar contact!" Another destroyer, and not far away. From the speed with which the range diminishes, it is obvious that he is heading directly for *Harder!*

Battle stations submerged! A few hurried minutes of tracking. No doubt about it: this fellow is a comer! Perhaps he has seen the submarine—although that seems hardly possible, or maybe he has radar information—we've suspected the Japs of this for some time. Or maybe he's merely running down the most probable bearing of the submarine, based on previous information. Whatever the cause, he certainly deserves 100 percent for effort so far, and *Harder* had better get out of the way.

"Take her down! Dive! Dive!" There may still be a chance to go after the convoy, but this new fellow requires attention first. Again the approach. Not so easy as the last time. This bird is wary, and zigzagging. He's alert, no question of it, and no doubt is fully aware of what happened to his buddy. On he comes, weaving first one way, then the other. It is now fairly dark. Broken clouds obscure the moon and deprive Sam Dealey of the light he sorely needs to make accurate observations. The destroyer is a dim blur in the periscope. Ranges are inaccurate and estimations of enemy course difficult to make. Finally, with the best infor-

mation he can set into the TDC, Sam gives the order to fire. Six torpedoes flash out toward the oncoming destroyer.

Sound listens intently for the sound of the proper functioning of the deadly fish. A white-faced operator turns to the skipper. "Can't hear the first two!" he gasps. "Last four seem to be running O.K.!" Two sinkers! Damn those undependable torpedoes! But four out of six are still all right. They should do the trick, barring extraordinary luck and skill on the part of the Jap.

We've simply *got* to see what he's doing. Up with the periscope again. Time stands still for the members of the fire control party—as it does, indeed, for every man aboard. You have no way of knowing what is going on except through the eyes of the captain. From his attitude and his actions, plus what few words of description he might remember to say, you make up your own picture of the topside.

This time they do not have long to wait. Dealey's figure stiffens. "He's seen them! He's turning this way! Take her down!" As the submarine noses over in obedience to the command, Sam gets a last sight of the enemy ship twisting radically as he avoids the torpedoes. Almost inaudibly he mutters, "Good work, you son of a bitch!"

And that is as far as Sam Dealey's accolade of the enemy's maneuvers goes, for he has much to do and a very short time in which to do it. *Harder* is immediately rigged for depth charges and for "silent running."

The sound man has suddenly become the most important man in the ship. All hands hang upon his words, as he deliberately turns his sound head control wheel. "Target is starting a run!" You might have thought the sound operator was reporting a drill instead of a life-and-death battle. "Target," indeed!

"He's shifted to short scale." The enemy destroyer has speeded up his pinging, shortened the interval between pings as the range closes. All hands unconsciously brace themselves, awaiting the first shock of the depth charges. It doesn't take long.

Harder is just reaching deep depth as five depth charges explode in her face. This veteran ship and crew have received many depth charges in the past, but a depth charge is something you never get used to. The whole ship shudders convulsively as the explosions rain upon her, and the vibration of the hull swiftly fills the air with clouds of dust particles and bits of debris from broken light bulbs and other fragile fixtures.

In the control room a new man is on the stern planes. This is his first patrol and he is doing the best he can, straining perhaps a bit too hard in his anxiety to have everything perfect. The stern plane indicators stop moving. He instantly deduces that the electrical control for the stern planes has been damaged. Quickly he shifts into hand power, nervously tugging at the slow-moving change gear. Then, panting heavily and a little flustered, he rapidly spins the wheel—the wrong way! It takes less time to do than it does to tell about it. The power to the stern planes had not been lost—merely the indicating circuit. And as *Harder* reaches maximum submergence, she has full dive on her stern planes instead of full rise.

In a second everyone realizes that something is wrong. Instead of gradually decreasing its angle, the ship tilts down even more, as though going into an outside loop. The deck slants at an impossible angle and the depth gauge needle goes unheedingly past the 300-foot mark.

"All hands aft on the double!" The diving officer's harsh command starts everyone moving, with the exception of those who are required to remain at their stations. In the meantime he quickly checks the situation, and reaching across the struggling stern planesman's shoulders, flips a tiny switch which cuts in the emergency stern plane angle indicator—which should have been energized previously. The emergency indicator shows Full Dive. Grasping the wheel, the diving officer puts his whole body into countering the frenzied effort of the now-frightened stern planesman, wrests the wheel away from him and commences to spin it counterclockwise. He works silently with the furious speed of urgency. When he finally has the planes corrected to full rise, he turns them back over to the trembling sailor who has been the cause of the trouble.

"Watch this," he says, pointing to the emergency angle indicator. No time now for investigation or instruction. The angle is coming off the ship. She finally levels off, far below her designed depth, and then commences to rise again. Forty-odd men huddled in the after parts of the ship create a rather large, unbalanced weight. The stern planes in hand power are slow to turn, the bow of the ship continues to rise, and the deck now tilts again in the opposite direction. The men sent aft understand what is going on and stream forward as soon as the ship commences to rise, but it is not until she is halfway back to the surface that she is finally brought under control.

In the meantime, the destroyer has reversed course and returned to the vicinity, and lets fly with another severe hammering.

You have to hand it to this destroyer. He has taken the initiative away from the submarine and has effectively protected his convoy. Sam Dealey's only thought by this time is to get away from him. It takes a few hours to do so, but finally *Harder* comes to the surface several miles away from the scene of the attack. These have been an eventful four hours.

Late forenoon of the next day *Harder*'s crew is still resting from the strenuous previous evening. The ship is patrolling submerged, and everything appears to be calm and peaceful, when the musical "Bong! Bong! Bong!" of the general alarm shatters the quiet of the sleeping crew. The word flashes almost instantly through the ship: "Another destroyer!"

This is a fast one. There has been a slight haze on the surface and the range at sighting is 4,000 yards, angle on the bow port twenty. *Harder* turns and heads toward the enemy, preparing all torpedo tubes as she does so. At 3,000 yards the destroyer turns and heads directly toward the submarine as though he had sighted the periscope in the glassy smooth sea. He commences weaving, first to one side and then to the other, and increases speed rapidly as he roars in. No question but that he has detected the submarine. Sam will have to fire right down his throat in order to get him. If he misses—well, he'd better not. If the destroyer catches the submarine at shallow depth, things will be pretty tough.

The range closes quickly—2,000 yards; 1,500 yards— Sound has been listening intently to the target's screws coming in and speeding up as he does so, but, like all good sound men, he trains his gear from side to side to check on all sectors. Suddenly he sings out, "Fast screws bearing zero nine zero, short-scale pinging!"

This can mean only one thing, but there is no time to look now. Keep calm, keep cool, one thing at a time, this bird up ahead is coming on the range. Get him first and worry about the other later.

One thousand yards. Stand by forward! Stand by one! Angle on the bow ten port, increasing. Wait a second until he has come to the limit of his weave in that direction and is starting back. Angle on the bow port twenty, range, 700 yards. He stops swinging.

"Bearing—mark," snaps the skipper. "Stand by!"

Sam Logan on the TDC makes an instantaneous but careful check of his instrument and observes that the generated target bearing on the TDC is exactly the same as the periscope bearing.

"Set!" he snaps back at his skipper.

"Fire!" Logan takes up the count at the TDC, spacing his torpedoes deliberately so that they cannot possibly run into each other and so that they will diverge slightly as they race toward the destroyer. One after the other two more torpedoes stream out toward the careening destroyer.

"Right full rudder, all ahead full," Dealey hurls the orders from the periscope as he stands there, his eyes glued to his instrument, watching for the success or failure of his daring attack.

Suddenly he shouts, "Check fire!" Almost simultaneously a heavy explosion is felt by everyone in the submarine. There is no need to pass the word to explain what that was. They have heard plenty of torpedo explosions by now.

With full speed and full rudder *Harder* has already started to gather way through the water and turn away from the destroyer. Dealey continues watching, however, and is rewarded by seeing the third torpedo smash into his stern. Clouds of smoke, steam, and debris rise from the stricken enemy high over the tops of his masts. He is so close that he continues coming, although his directive force and power are both gone, and *Harder* must get clear.

Suddenly there is a tremendous explosion, far more violent than the others. The submarine trembles from stern to stern and the noise is almost deafening. Surprisingly, there is less cork dust and debris tossed about inside in spite of the seemingly much-greater-than-usual shock. The destroyer's magazines have let go at a range of 300 yards, and within a minute after first being hit, his gutted, smoking remains sink beneath the waves. From time of sighting to time of sinking has taken nine minutes.

But what about this other set of screws on the starboard beam, which Sound has been nervously reporting for the past two minutes? The skipper starts to swing his periscope to that bearing but is interrupted by the sound man's cry:

"Fast screws close aboard! He's starting his run!"

With her rudder hard over, *Harder* rushes for the depths. She has not quite reached her maximum submergence when the first depth charges go off.

This new chap is pretty good, too, and he doesn't waste many. Twisting and turning, always presenting *Harder*'s stern to the Jap and endeavoring to make away from the area of the attack, Sam Dealey matches wits with the enemy. After four long hours he manages to shake him loose, and the submarine returns to periscope depth. Then, for the first time in more than six hours, Dealey has a chance to leave the conning tower.

In less than an hour he was back at the periscope with two more destroyers in sight. As Dealey scanned the horizon he sighted a third one, then a fourth—then a fifth, and then a sixth! All six were in line of bearing headed for *Harder*!

When Sam Dealey reached this point in his patrol report, he could not resist inserting the comment: "Such popularity must be deserved."

It is on record that *Harder*'s captain was now torn between two emotions: the desire to go after the enemy and tangle with them in hopes of getting one or two more, and a much more prudent and sensible decision to beat it. In the end, the latter judgment prevailed.

But all was not over yet. Two days later, shortly before dawn, *Harder* was detected and bombed by a plane, the bomb exploding close aboard as she was on her way down. It is strongly suspected that the subsequent sighting of two destroyers to the westward shortly before noon was a result of a report made by the pilot. Once again, what with air cover and the glassy smooth sea which existed in the locality, *Harder* decided to play it safe and evade.

But not so that night. Shortly after sunset, while the submarine is running on the surface off Tawi Tawi, one of the bridge lookouts sights two destroyers dead ahead. Now conditions are a little more to Dealey's liking, and the odds not so uneven.

The battle stations alarm is sounded again, and in a few minutes the submarine slips silently beneath the waves. The destroyers are on a line of bearing, and Dealey hopes to get them both with a single salvo.

Twenty minutes after being sighted the two destroyers pass in an overlapping formation across the bow of the submarine at a range of about one thousand yards. This is the moment Dealey has been waiting for. He plans to shoot at the nearest destroyer. Any torpedoes that miss will have a chance of hitting the second target.

"Stand by forward."

They do not have long to wait. Four torpedoes, evenly spaced, run toward the enemy. Dealey stands staring through his periscope. The first torpedo passes just ahead, and misses. The second torpedo hits near the bow, and a few seconds later the third hits under the bridge. The fourth torpedo misses astern.

At this juncture Dealey swings his ship with hard right rudder, getting ready for a setup on the second destroyer if that should prove to be necessary. The first destroyer, now burning furiously, continues on his way but slows down rapidly as simple momentum takes the place of live power from his propellers. Behind his stern Dealey can again see the second vessel, just in time to see the fourth and last torpedo crash into him. It is instantly apparent that no additional torpedoes will be needed for either ship.

Gripping the periscope handles, Dealey swings the 'scope back to the first destroyer which by this time is only 400 yards away, broadside to. He is just in time to observe another explosion take place amidships in the unfortunate ship. The destroyer's decks buckle in the center and open up with the force of the blast, just under the after stack. Momentarily everything is blotted out, but Dealey gets the impression that the stack has been blown straight into the air.

In a moment the force of the explosion hits *Harder* with sufficient strength to make her heel over. But Dealey swings back quickly to the second destroyer, observes an even more powerful and, in the gathering darkness, totally blinding explosion from under his bridge. The explosion in the first destroyer had probably been a boiler reached by sea water; that in the second was evidently his magazines.

Within a matter of minutes both ships have disappeared, and *Harder* is once more on the surface, sniffing about at the scene of destruction, and then clearing the area at high speed in the event that planes might be sent from Tawi Tawi to investigate the sudden disappearance of two more tin cans.

Next morning *Harder* was a few miles south of Tawi Tawi, reconnoitering the anchorage. At about 0900 two destroyers were sighted, evidently on a submarine search. Perfectly willing to oblige them, Sam Dealey commenced an approach. The enemy's search plan evidently did not include the spot where the submarine lay, and they passed on over the horizon.

In the late afternoon a large Japanese task force, consisting of several battleships and cruisers, was sighted, escorted by half a dozen or more destroyers and three or four aircraft circling overhead. *Harder* was out of position for an attack, but it appeared that here was an opportunity for a contact report which might enable some other submarine to get into position to trap the task force later on.

While watching the largest battleship, which appeared to be one of Japan's two mystery ships—huge 60,000-ton monsters—Dealey saw him suddenly become enveloped in heavy black smoke, and in a few moments three distant explosions were heard. It was possible that one of our other submarines already had made an attack.

Suddenly a destroyer darted out of the confused melee of ships and headed directly for *Harder*. Perhaps her periscope had been sighted!

Battle stations submerged!

At maximum full speed the destroyer's bow is high out of water. His stern squats in the trough created by his own passage, and black smoke pours from his stacks, to be swept aft by the wind of his passing. *Harder* turns and swings her bow directly toward the onrushing vessel; lines him up for a shot directly down the throat.

Things are deathly quiet in *Harder*'s conning tower. There is no problem to solve by TDC or by plotting parties, except the determination of the approximate range at which to fire. The target's bearing remains steady. The torpedo gyros remain on zero. The target's angle on the bow remains absolute zero, and he is echo ranging steadily, rapidly, and right on.

The range closes with fantastic speed. Dealey makes an observation every thirty seconds or so. The periscope is almost in continuous motion. The sweat peels off his face, drips off the ends of his fingers as they grip the periscope handles—everything else in the conning tower is stock-still, as though time had ceased to function, except for the range counters on the TDC, which steadily indicate less and less range.

Range, 4,000 yards. Only a few minutes to go. The sound man, intently listening to the approaching propeller beats, reports, "He has slowed down."

Through the periscope it is obvious that he has indeed slowed down. His bow wave is smaller, and he now appears to be digging his bow deeper into it as the stern rises somewhat.

From the sound man: "Turn count fifteen knots!"

Wily fellow, this. He knows he is approaching the submarine's position, and plans to search the area carefully.

On he comes. Still no deviation in course, headed directly for the submarine's periscope. Probably he has seen it, and he no doubt plans to run right over it as he drops his depth charges. Not being a submarine man, he probably fails to realize that that periscope has been popping up and down in nearly the same place entirely too precisely and entirely too long. Perhaps he doesn't realize that the submarine is obviously making no attempt to escape.

In *Harder*'s conning tower the range dials on the TDC have reached 1,500 yards; target's speed is 15 knots, angle on the bow zero, relative bearing zero, torpedo gyros zero.

"Stand by to shoot! Up periscope!"

The periscope whines softly as it rises out of its well. At this moment another report from Sound: "Fast screws! Close aboard starboard beam!"

Another ship! Destroyer, of course! The thought flashes through Dealey's mind with a small shock. He has been so intent on laying a trap for this fellow dead ahead that he has neglected to look about for others who might be coming.

"Too late to worry about him now," Dealey mutters to himself, squatting before the periscope well. Aloud he says, "To hell with *him!* Let's get this son of a bitch up ahead."

"Bearing—mark!" The periscope starts down. "No change," barks out Dealey, meaning that the situation is exactly as it should be.

"Set!" from Sam Logan on the TDC.

"Fire!" from Lynch. As assistant approach officer, Frank Lynch is responsible that all details of the approach have been correctly executed and the proper settings made on the torpedoes. The ship lurches; one torpedo is on the way. Sam Logan deliberately waits five seconds, then he turns a handle on the face of the TDC a fraction of a degree to the right and quietly says again, "Set."

"Fire." A second torpedo speeds on its way. Logan turns the handle again, this time to the left.

"Set."

"Fire." *Harder* shudders for the third time as a torpedo is ejected.

There is no time to waste looking around. Not even time to try to identify the source of the extra set of screws on the starboard beam.

"Take her down! All ahead full! Right full rudder." If the torpedoes miss, *Harder* will have two minutes to gain depth before the destroyer is on top of her.

Lynch has a stop watch in his hand. Logan is intently watching the face of his TDC, where a timer dial is whirling around.

The suspense is unbearable. *Harder* has already tilted her nose down and is heading for the protection of the depths at full speed, but she has not, of course, moved very far yet.

"How long?"

"Forty-five seconds, Captain! Should be hitting any second now!"

"Fifty seconds!" You'd think Logan was timing a track meet.

"Fifty-five seconds!" And precisely as the words are uttered there is a terrific detonation. One torpedo has struck home.

"Sixty seconds!" Logan is still unperturbed. At that instant another terrific explosion rocks the submarine.

Two hits for three fish. Dealey smiles a tight smile of exultation. That's one son of heaven who won't be bothering anyone for a while.

But there is no time to indulge in backslapping. *Harder* has reached only eighty feet in her plunge downward and is passing right beneath the destroyer. This is an excellent move, for it will confuse and interfere with the author of that other set of propellers. However, Dealey has not reckoned with the tremendous effect of his torpedoes. Just as the submarine arrives beneath the enemy ship there is the most deafening, prolonged series of rumblings and explosions anyone on board has ever heard. Either the enemy's boilers or his magazines have exploded. In fact, the noise and shock are so terrific that quite possibly both boilers and magazines have gone off together.

But this merry afternoon is just starting, for the other set of propeller beats now joins in the game and proceeds to hand out a goodly barrage of depth charges as *Harder* still seeks the shelter of deep depths. He has evidently radioed for help also, and it isn't long before Sam Dealey is able to distinguish a different sort of explosion amid the rain of depth charges. Aircraft! And soon after, two more ships also join the fray. For a couple of hours numerous depth charges and bombs were heard and felt, but, in the words of *Harder's* skipper, "no one was interested in numerical accuracy at that time."

Some hours later, after darkness had set in, the submarine surfaced. In the distance astern a single lighted buoy burned, marking the location where the fifth Japanese destroyer in four days had been sunk by this one sharpshooting submarine.

Of the beating he had taken, Sam Dealey, characteristically, said very little. One paragraph in his patrol report merely stated: "It is amazing that the ship could have gone through such a terrific pounding and jolting around with such minor damage. Our fervent thanks go out to the Electric Boat Company for building such a fine ship."

However laconic and matter-of-fact Sam Dealey may

have been about the patrol just completed, our own Submarine Force Commander and indeed the Supreme Commander of Allied Forces in the area recognized an outstanding job when they saw one. They had one advantage over Dealey, in addition to the latter's natural unassuming modesty. They had been sitting on the sidelines, reading the dispatches and noting the Japanese reaction. Reports had come from all sides, wondering what the Americans had turned loose off Tawi Tawi. The Jap radio had blared unceasingly that a submarine task force of unprecedented magnitude had been operating off that fleet base, that several submarines had been sunk, but that they had, of course, themselves sustained some losses. Each time a submarine sinking had been claimed, Admiral Christy and his staff had mentally crossed their fingers; each time events proved that *Harder* was still very much alive, they had sighed with relief. And finally, when Sam Dealey had reported "mission accomplished" and started for home, their jubilation knew no bounds.

A huge delegation met *Harder* on the dock when she arrived: Admiral Christy, the submarine force commander in that area, himself coming to Darwin to do honor to this ship, and embark for the trip back to Fremantle. The ship was met in Australia by another delegation, including General Douglas MacArthur, who awarded Captain Dealey the Army Distinguished Service Cross on the spot.

The officers and crew were also subsequently recognized by suitable decorations, and when the news arrived in the United States, accompanied by the unanimous recommendations of all responsible officers, President Roosevelt awarded the Congressional Medal of Honor to Sam Dealey and the Presidential Unit Citation to *Harder* herself. Frank Lynch was promoted to command of his own boat, and Sam Logan moved up to the post of executive officer.

But although *Harder* and her skipper survived the deeds for which this recognition was accorded, the awards themselves were made posthumously. Sam Dealey's widow received the Medal of Honor in his name, and the United States Submarine Force reverently accepted the Presidential Unit Citation in trust for the day when another ship shall be built bearing the name *Harder*.

For neither survived the next patrol.

Usually when a submarine fails to return from patrol, there are surmises, rumors, wild theories, sometimes a Japanese claim of a sinking, but rarely anything concrete to explain what happened. Sometimes survivors returned from the unspeakable brutalities of Jap prison camps after the war to tell what caused the losses of their ships, but these cases were very few in number. *Harder* was an exception, for she operated in a wolfpack during her sixth and last patrol, and another vessel actually witnessed and reported the circumstances of her loss.

On the morning of August 24, 1944, *Harder* dived off the west coast of Luzon, in company with USS *Hake*. Being the senior skipper, Dealey had decided to make a reconnaissance in this area in hopes that it might yield results comparable to those he had achieved only three days before when, as commander of a five-boat pack, he had engaged two convoys in a fierce, close-range battle, sinking in all ten ships, and driving the rest into harbor where they huddled for protection from the subs ranging back and forth before the entrance.

Shortly after daybreak on the fateful August 24, echo ranging was heard, and two escort-type vessels of about one thousand tons each were sighted. Both submarines immediately commenced approaching for an attack. However, the larger of the two ships suddenly zigged away and entered Dasel Bay. The other stayed outside, and at this time *Hake* broke off the attack, feeling the remaining target was hardly worth the torpedoes it would take to sink him, *Harder*, however, held on, and *Hake* sighted her periscope crossing in front, passing between *Hake* and the enemy vessel. *Hake* by this time had commenced evasive maneuvers, for the Jap was echo ranging loudly and steadily in her direction. Exactly what was in Sam Dealey's mind is, of course, not known; his previous record indicated that he would have had no hesitancy in tangling with this chap if he thought it worthwhile. Furthermore, he had more or less got *Hake* into this spot, and may have felt that he owed it to the other submarine to get her out again. But, whatever his motives, he maneuvered *Harder* between the other two vessels with the result that the Jap, naturally enough, took off after him instead of after *Hake*. According to the latter's report, the enemy vessel showed some confusion, probably because of the two targets where he had suspected no more than one.

Sam Dealey was perfectly capable of an act of self-abnegation such as his maneuver appears to have been. It must be pointed out, however, that the enemy vessel was a small anti-submarine type, and that Dealey had several times previously come off victorious in encounters with much more formidable ships. Of the two submarines, *Harder* was doubtless the better trained and equipped to come to grips with this particular enemy. It was simply the fortunes of war that, in this case, Fate dealt two pat hands—and Sam's wasn't good enough.

With *Hake* a fascinated spectator, the Jap made his run. Possibly *Harder* fired at him, though *Hake* heard no torpedo on her sound gear. The enemy came on over Sam Dealey, and suddenly dropped fifteen depth charges. *Harder*'s periscope was never seen after that, nor were her screws heard again.

According to the Japanese report of the incident, the periscope of a submarine was sighted at about two thousand yards, and a depth charge attack was immediately delivered. After this single attack, a huge fountain of oil bubbled to the surface, and considerable quantities of bits of wood, cork, and other debris came up and floated in the slick.

So perished a gallant ship, a gallant captain, and a gallant crew. All of Sam Dealey's skill and daring could avail him not one iota against the monstrous fact that the enemy's first depth charge attack, by some unhappy stroke of fate, was a bull's-eye.

9

TRIGGER

TRIGGER MADE HER NAME with a rush. She began her career as a night fighter, and it was on the surface at night, retaining the initiative with speed and mobility, that her rapier-like thrusts wrought the greatest damage upon the enemy. In her ensuing four patrols she sank a total of nineteen ships and damaged four. Six times, single-handed, she engaged enemy convoys far outmatching her in escort vessels. By this time I was the only officer left of the original commissioning gang, and *Trigger* and I understood each other pretty well, although frequently she surprised me.

We didn't have long to wait before Dusty Dornin took *Trigger* into action. On September 8, 1943, we left Pearl Harbor bound for Formosa, and maintained full speed all the way, not even submerging when passing Wake Island. Dusty's philosophy was to carry the battle to the enemy at all times; make him show how good he was before we pulled the plug. And on September 23, having just arrived in our area, we sighted a fat target.

We are submerged off Formosa, patrolling what our calculations indicate should be a Jap shipping lane. For two days we have been here, and nary a sign of ships have we seen. Maybe we've guessed wrong. But not this time, for at about 1600 of the second day smoke is sighted. A convoy, running for Japan.

Battle stations submerged! We start the approach. This time, however, we are not lucky, for we are so far off the base course of the ships that we are forced to watch help-lessly while they steam by well out of range. But we take a good look; six ships in two columns; in the near column three big fat tankers, the leader a new modern 10,000 tonner; in the far column three average-size freighters. What a plum! Never mind the plane we see buzzing above the convoy. These birds are our meat! We secure from bat-tle stations, but follow at maximum sustained submerged speed, keeping our quarry in sight as long as possible, waiting for dark.

With the last rays of the setting sun we are on the sur-face, all ahead full on four engines, running down the track after the vanished convoy. No engines to spare for a battery charge. Give them all to the screws. Put the auxil-iaries on the battery. You can't get anywhere by halves in this business.

The chase is tense and thrilling. We have an estimate of target course and speed, but if he's smart he'll change radically at dark. Our game is to dash up and regain con-tact quickly, before he gets very far from his original track. If we miss him, we suspect he'll have turned to his left, but that's just a guess, and cuts down our chances 50 per-cent. Best bet is to go like hell, which we do.

It pays off, too, for this particular son of heaven didn't even bother to change course. We pick him up dead ahead, right on his old track—and he's stopped zigzag-ging. This is murder.

And so it proves. We draw up on the starboard bow of

the convoy, out of sight, then stealthily creep in. Slowly the biggest tanker lumbers into our sights. Angle on the bow, starboard seventy-five. Range, 1,500 yards. Bearing, 335. Target speed checks perfectly, at 7 knots. Surely this big *Nippon Maru*-class tanker can do better than 7 knots. The Japs have tied him down with a bunch of slow boys—too bad for him! On he comes, filling our binoculars with his huge, heavily laden bulk. Looks good—looks perfect! We plan to fire three fish at the first tanker, three at the second, then spin on our tail and shoot four at the third one. They won't know what hit them.

Stand by forward! He's coming on. Bearing—mark! We're keeping the sights on him now—a few more degrees. Come on—come on—Fire ONE! . . . Fire TWO! . . . Fire THREE! . . . Check fire! Shifting targets—second ship. Bearing—mark—set—Fire FOUR! . . . Fire FIVE! . . . Fire SIX! . . .

Left full rudder! All ahead full! Stand by aft!

Trigger leaps ahead, swings steadily left. She has nearly one hundred eighty degrees to swing, and it takes a long time. She is only halfway around, broadside to broadside with the leading tanker, range about one thousand yards heading in opposite directions, when suddenly, cataclysmically, the darkness of the night is thunderously shattered with light. A sheet of brilliant white flame shoots 1,000 feet into the air! The leading tanker must have had a load of aviation gasoline, for he has burst into incandescence.

Momentarily blinded by the terrific fire, we recover to see the whole scene as bright as day. On the deck of the doomed tanker scores of little white-clad figures rush helplessly across his decks to the bow, where the fire has not yet reached. It must be awfully hot over there. We shift our eyes to the second tanker and see a torpedo hit with a flash of flame right amidships. A fire starts, but he steers around the brilliantly blazing pyre of his leader and continues on his course. The second ship in the far column is hit with a soundless catastrophe. He folds in the middle into a big V and starts down. Evidently he caught a torpedo which missed the first or second tanker. We had figured on that, hoped it would happen. Three ships hit, two down for sure, in the first salvo!

In the meantime, the Japs obviously can see *Trigger*'s black hull, too, and their ready guns begin to bark. A few shells scream overhead, but not very close. They are probably too excited to settle down, and we ignore them, intent on getting our stern tube salvo off. But the third tanker pulls a joker and shears out of line directly toward us. By this time we are running directly away from him, and he is coming, bows on, 700 yards away. We are still increasing speed, but so is he, and he's gaining on us with his initial advantage of speed. A gun on his forecastle opens up, and this time the shells whistle fairly close. One or two drop alongside, not too close yet, but no doubt he'll improve.

Maybe he thinks he has the drop on us; he cannot know that we have the drop on him too. We could dive, but *Trigger* is stubborn. Stand by aft! Continuous aim. Angle on the bow, zero. Range, 700 yards. We're starting to hold our own now, as we pick up speed. Fire SEVEN! . . . Nothing happens. Fire EIGHT! . . . Nothing. We must hit him! Check everything carefully. It must be the tumultuous wash of our straining screws throwing the torpedoes off. Fire NINE! . . . Still nothing. Now we are in the soup. One torpedo left aft. It has to be good. He is coming much too close with his shells now. Give him one more, then dive! Fire TEN! *"Clear the bridge!"* "Honk, honk!" goes the diving alarm. *"Dive! Dive! Take her down!"*

Down we plunge, listening for that fateful crack which tells us he's found our pressure hull with a five-inch shell before we could get her under. We pass forty feet and breathe easier. Startlingly a voice squeaks over the welcome gurgle of water and the drumming of *Trigger*'s superstructure: "Where's the captain?"

No answer. We look about. "Did anybody see him get off the bridge when we dived?"

No answer. Fear lays an icy hand over us. Just then a stream of furious curses shocks our ears and warms our hearts. There is Dusty, inside the periscope well, supporting himself on the edges by his elbows, struggling to climb back out, cussing a blue streak. He has reason to cuss, too, for the quartermaster has his big feet firmly planted on the skipper's hands and is calmly and nonchalantly lowering the periscope! End of tableau.

About this time, as we pass seventy-five feet, a good loud WHANG reverberates through the water. We had almost forgotten the target in this novel emergency, but get back to business quickly. "Target's screws have stopped!" This from the sound man. "Breaking-up noises."

"Control! Sixty feet!" The order snaps out, and feverishly we get *Trigger* back to periscope depth, put up the 'scope and take a look. Wonder of wonders! There floats the stern of the tanker, straight up and down! So we surface, hoping to catch one of the two remaining ships with our last few torpedoes.

We find one. We track him. As usual he doesn't see us—or so we think, until he opens fire with both his deck guns. While we think over this development, another ship—the only other ship—opens fire behind us. Then, as shells from both parties scream overhead, we realize the truth. They are shooting at each other. We are still undetected; so we make four separate attacks on this bird up forward, use up all six of our remaining torpedoes, and get only two hits. Finally we are forced to leave him, sinking slowly by the bow.

We find the last ship, too, but we can't hurt him. So we turn *Trigger's* bow east and shove off. As we go, we pass close by our first tanker, by this time nearly consumed, his steel hulk red-hot from end to end. In the distance another fire flares up and bursts into brilliant flame. We take a look there, and find to our delight the second tanker stopped, abandoned, and ablaze from bow to stern. We verify his complete destruction, and depart at last after one of the shortest patrols on record.

Score for the night's work: three big tankers sunk, one freighter sunk, one freighter probably sunk. Total, five out of six, and a very unhappy good evening to you, Tojo!

Less than a month after leaving Pearl Harbor, *Trigger* was back at Midway, with a cockscomb of five miniature Jap flags flying from her extended periscope. The usual crates of fresh fruit, leafy green vegetables—lettuce and celery especially—ice cream, letters from home, and assorted bigwigs, were on the dock awaiting us.

This business of welcoming a submarine back from war patrol had been started as a sort of morale booster, and to say that it hit the mark is putting it mildly. After having been deprived of these things for about two months we were almost as avid for fresh fruit and leafy vegetables as we were for the mail—and it was not at all uncommon to see a bearded sailor, pockets stuffed with apples and oranges, reading letter after letter in quick succession, and munching on a celery stalk at the same time.

There was one submarine, however, which, so the story ran, was always welcomed somewhat differently. It seems that months before the war started, USS *Skipjack* (SS184) had submitted a requisition for some expendable material essential to the health and comfort of the crew. What followed was, to the seagoing Navy, a perfect example of how to drive good men mad unnecessarily. For almost a year later *Skipjack* received her requisition back, stamped "Cancelled—cannot identify material." Whereupon Jim Coe, skipper of the *Skipjack*, let loose with a blast which delighted everybody except those attached to the supply department of the Navy Yard, Mare Island, California.

This is what he wrote:

USS SKIPJACK

SS184/L8/SS36-1   June 11, 1942

From:	The Commanding Officer.
To:	Supply Officer, Navy Yard, Mare Island, California.
Via:	Commmander Submarines, Southwest Pacific.
Subject:	Toilet Paper.
Reference:	(a) (4608) USS HOLLAND (5184) USS SKIPJACK reqn. 70-42 of 30 July 1941.
	(b) SO NYMI cancelled invoice No. 272836.
Enclosure:	(A) Copy of cancelled invoice.
	(B) Sample of material requested.

1. This vessel submitted a requisition for 150 rolls of toilet paper on July 30, 1941, to USS HOLLAND. The material was ordered by HOLLAND from the Supply Officer, Navy Yard, Mare Island, for delivery to USS SKIPJACK.

2. The Supply Officer, Navy Yard, Mare Island, on November 26, 1941, cancelled Mare Island invoice No. 272836 with the stamped notation "Cancelled—cannot identify." This cancelled invoice was received by SKIPJACK on June 10, 1942.

3. During the 11 1/4 months elapsing from the time of ordering the toilet paper and the present date, the SKIPJACK personnel, despite their best efforts to await delivery of subject material, have been unable to wait on numerous occasions, and the situation is now quite acute, especially during depth charge attack by the "back-stabbers."

4. Enclosure (B) is a sample of the desired material provided for the information of the Supply Officer, Navy Yard, Mare Island. The Commanding Officer, USS SKIPJACK cannot help but wonder what is being used in Mare Island in place of this unidentifiable material, once well known to this command.

5. SKIPJACK personnel during this period have become accustomed to the use of "ersatz", i.e., the vast amount of incoming non-essential paper work, and in so doing feel that the wish of the Bureau of Ships for reduction of paper work is being complied with, thus effectively killing two birds with one stone.

6. It is believed by this command that the stamped notation "cannot identify" was possibly an error, and that this is simply a case of shortage of strategic war material, the SKIPJACK probably being low on the priority list.

7. In order to cooperate in our war effort at a small local sacrifice, the SKIPJACK desires no further action to be taken until the end of current war, which has created a situation aptly described as "war is hell."

J. W. COE

It is to be noted that Jim Coe was wrong in one particular—it had been only ten and a quarter months. But his letter, carrying in it all the fervor and indignation of a man who has received a mortal hurt, achieved tremendous fame.

We also heard that it had achieved rather remarkable results back in Mare Island, although this was mostly hearsay. But one result was extremely noticeable indeed: whenever *Skipjack* returned from patrol, no matter where she happened to put in, she received no fruit, no vegetables, and no ice cream. Instead, she invariably received her own outstandingly distinctive tribute—cartons and cartons of toilet paper.

Jim Coe, a most successful submarine commander and humorist to boot, is no longer with us. After three patrols in command of *Skipjack*, he returned to Portsmouth, New Hampshire, to place the new submarine *Cisco* in commission. On September, 19, 1943, *Cisco* departed from Darwin, Australia, on her first war patrol, and was never heard from again.

• • •

Our orders said, "Refit at Midway," which didn't please us particularly since the only things of interest on Midway were gooney birds and whisky, the former of which became very boring after an hour or two. That evening at the Gooneyville Tavern I met Don Horsman, who had been repair officer during the overhaul of the month before. Don had been trying his best to get into a submarine on patrol, and I was glad to see that he had finally broken away from the Pearl Harbor Navy Yard.

We had much to talk about—mutual friends; his cute family of three little girls; and the performance of various items of equipment in *Trigger* which we had worried over together. In the midst of the conversation a thought struck me.

"Don," I said, "what's the dope on the *Dorado?* She should be due in Pearl any day now, shouldn't she? We heard from Penrod that his wife christened the ship, and that his father was also there when she was launched. That was several months ago."

The grin faded from Don's moonlike face, and he put his drink down. "She's down, Ned," he said.

It didn't hit me at first. "Down where?" I asked naïvely. "Didn't they send her straight to Pearl?"

"I mean—down—gone. Penrod never even got to the Panama Canal. One of our own planes claims to have sunk a German submarine at the time and place where she was supposed to have been."

I pressed Horsman for more details, and the noise and confusion of the first day back from patrol faded from consciousness. But that was all Don had heard.

ARCHERFISH

10

SOME OF THE STORIES of World War II can never be fully told. Some will live only in the hearts of men who took part in them, who will carry their secrets silently to their graves. Some stories will not be told at all, because the only men who could tell them lie at the bottom of the sea. And some are part of our naval heritage, and will go down in history with stories of *Old Ironsides*, Thomas Truxton and his *Constellation*, John Paul Jones and *Bon Homme Richard*, *Enterprise*, and many others.

Such a story is the story of *Archerfish*, the ship which broke the heart of the Japanese Navy.

The keel was laid for USS *Archerfish* in Portsmouth, New Hampshire, on January 22, 1943. Exactly one year later she sank her first ship. And on November 28, 1944—but let's start at the beginning.

The story really begins in 1939 in Yokosuka, Japan. The Japanese Naval Ministry was holding secret sessions. The probability of becoming involved in the European war was growing greater and greater; the probability of then finding their nation pitted against the United States was almost a certainty. How, then, to assure Japan of a telling superiority? How to fight that great American sea power in the Pacific? And how to do away with the London Naval Treaty, which limited Japan to an ignominious three-fifths of the war vessels allowed the United States?

There was only one answer. The treaty already had been violated—tear it up. Start building in earnest for the war they know is coming.

Secret instructions were sent to the largest shipyard in Japan. Millions of board feet of wood came from the forest reserves, and thousands of carpenters were employed to build a gigantic yard. Houses for 50,000 people were requisitioned and these, too, were fenced in around the fenced Navy Yard. Finally, one day in 1940, an order was issued from the commandant's office: "From this date henceforth no one leaves the Navy Yard." And so was born the battleship *Shinano.*

By the summer of 1942 she was not quite half finished. This super-battleship with two sisters, *Yamato* and *Musashi*, was bigger than any war vessel ever before constructed in the history of the world. Bigger than *Bismarck*, the German behemoth of 50,000 tons. Almost three times as big as *Oklahoma*, lying bottom-up in the mud and ooze of Pearl Harbor. Armor plate twenty inches thick. Engines of 200,000 horsepower. Guns throwing projectiles eighteen inches in diameter.

Then at the Battle of Midway, in June 1942, the flower of the Japanese naval air force met destruction. *Akagi, Kaga, Soryu,* and *Hiryu*—all first-line carriers—were sunk. The attack on Midway was turned back, a complete failure. The Naval Ministry met again in secret session, and decided that completion of new aircraft carriers was paramount. So *Shinano* was redesigned. Some of the tremendous armor plate was removed from her side. Her huge barbettes, turrets, and eighteen-inch guns were never installed, and the weight thus saved was put into an armored flight deck made of hardened steel four inches thick. Under this flight deck were built two hangar decks, and below them another armored deck, eight inches thick. She was capable of storing 100 to 150 planes, and could land them and take them off simultaneously from an airfield nearly one thousand feet in length and 130 feet in width.

But all this took time, and as 1944 drew to a close, the need of the Japanese Navy for its new supercarrier became increasingly acute. Finally, in November 1944, *Shinano* was nearly completed. The commissioning ceremonies were held on November 18; a picture of the emperor in an ornate gilded frame was ceremoniously delivered to the vessel, and she was turned over to her commanding officer.

Then the bad news arrived. Japanese strategic intelligence reports indicated that air raids on the Tokyo area would become increasingly severe, with a good possibility that the brave new ship would be seriously exposed at her fitting-out dock. There was even a possibility that United States forces would discover the existence of the huge vessel and make a special effort to destroy her before she could get to sea. This could not be permitted. The Tokyo area was too vulnerable. The ship must be moved to the Inland Sea.

Now the Inland Sea is the body of water formed between the islands of Honshu, Shikoku, and Kyushu. It has three entrances: two, the Bungo and Kii Suidos, into the Pacific, and one, Shimonoseki Strait, into the landlocked Sea of Japan. It is an ideal operating base for an inferior navy which must depend upon being able to hide when it cannot fight.

But *Shinano* is not ready to go to sea. True, she is structurally complete, her engines can operate, and she floats, but she is not quite ready. Her watertight integrity has not been proved. Air tests have been made of only a few of her hundreds of compartments. Many holes through various bulkheads have not yet been plugged. Watertight doors have not been tested, and it is not known whether they can be closed; furthermore, even if they can be closed, no one knows if they are actually watertight. Electrical wiring and piping passing through watertight bulkheads have not had their packing glands set up and tested. Cable and pipe conduits from the main deck into the bowels of the ship have not been sealed. The pumping and drainage system is not complete; piping is not all connected. The fire main cannot be used because the necessary pumps have not been delivered.

Most important of all, the crew has been on board for only one month. They number 1,900 souls, but few have been to sea together. Many have never been to sea at all, and *none have had any training whatsoever on board* Shinano. They do not know their ship. *They are not a crew. They are 1,900 people.*

But it is decided, nonetheless, that *Shinano* must sail to safer waters immediately. To do so she must pass out of Tokyo Bay, steer south and west around the southeastern tip of Honshu, and enter the Kii Suido, a trip of only a few hundred miles. But about half the trip will be in waters accessible to United States submarines. That risk she must take. Give her an escort of four destroyers, and send her at high speed so that the submarines cannot catch her. Make the move in absolute secrecy, so that there will be no possibility of an unfortunate leak of information.

The die was cast, and on the afternoon of November 28,

1944, *Shinano* set sail with her four escorting destroyers. Sailors and workmen crowded about her decks, and the gilded frame glittered in the late afternoon sunlight on the flying bridge. From within the frame, the image of the Son of Heaven beamed happily on this mightiest of warships.

Thus was set the stage for the greatest catastrophe yet to befall the hapless Japanese Navy. Work for four years building the biggest ship of its kind that has ever been constructed by man; put 1,900 men on board; install a picture of the emperor on the bridge, and send her out through a few miles of water exposed to possible operations of American submarines.

There was nothing particularly portentous about the laying of the keel of *Archerfish*. She displaced 1,500 tons, or one-fiftieth the tonnage of the huge vessel fated to be her adversary. She was only one-third the length of *Shinano*, and her crew of eighty-two men and officers was about one-fortieth of the 3,200 estimated fully designed complement of the Japanese ship.

Leaving New London, *Archerfish* zigzags southward through the center of the broad Atlantic, in waters infested by her enemy sisters. Do not think that a submarine is not afraid of other submarines. We are probably more afraid of them and more respectful of them than any other type of vessel would be. A submarine cruising on the surface is a delicious morsel. It almost always travels alone, and its only defense is its own vigilance. Zigzag all day and even at night, if the visibility is fairly good. Keep a sharp lookout and radar watch. Tell yourselves over and over again, "Boys, don't relax. We are playing for keeps now."

The weather becomes perceptibly warmer. Finally, land is sighted, and *Archerfish* slips through the Mona Passage into the Caribbean Sea. Here the waters are even more infested with German submarines than are the wide reaches of the central Atlantic. *Archerfish* puts on full speed and dashes across the Caribbean to Cristobal, at the Atlantic end of the Panama Canal. She arrives early in the morning and proceeds immediately through the great locks, and through Gatun Lake to the submarine base at Balboa on the Pacific end of the Canal.

No danger here from German subs. No time, either, for any rest for the tired crew, for they have lost the edge from their training and must be brought back "on the step" again. One week is all that is available. *Archerfish* is issued nine practice torpedoes, and fires them again and again. Target convoys are provided. Day and night exercises are conducted. Rarely does the crew turn in before midnight, and all hands are always up at 0500. *Archerfish* does not even stop for lunch, but instead distributes sandwiches to all members of the crew, making up for it with a good breakfast and a good dinner.

One week of this; then, her crew once again in fine fettle, *Archerfish* sails across the broad Pacific, on the final and longest leg of her journey to Pearl Harbor. She and her crew have had a pretty steady go of it. They have been training strenuously and incessantly for the past two months with practically no rest, but they cannot be allowed to relax.

They know that the competition in the far western Pacific is mighty tough, so they drill steadily, on every maneuver of which the ship is capable, except the actual firing of torpedoes. *Archerfish* cannot fire torpedoes, because she is transporting a full load of "war shots." One of the most convenient ways of getting torpedoes to Pearl Harbor was to send them by submarine.

Finally land is sighted. A PC boat signals through the early dawn to *Archerfish*, "We are your escort," and swings about to lead the submarine to Pearl Harbor. This is the last stop. Belowdecks all hands are feverishly cleaning up the ship and themselves. They intend to make a good entrance into Pearl; they are proud of their ship, and will not willingly allow her to suffer by comparison with any other in looks or efficiency.

Finally *Archerfish* gently noses into a dock at the submarine base, Pearl Harbor, where a small group of officers and enlisted men await her. Admiral Lockwood, the Commander Submarines, Pacific Fleet (also known as "Uncle Charlie"), is on hand to greet this newest addition to his forces. With him is an array of talent: the squadron commander, the division commander, the officer in charge of the repair department, the submarine supply officer, a submarine medical officer, an electronics officer, and a commissary officer.

The enlisted men are evidently a working party. As *Archerfish* approaches the dock, they scamper to catch the weighted heaving lines thrown by members of her crew. Pulling in swiftly on the "heevies," they haul heavy hawsers from the deck of the submarine to the dock. Others stand by with a narrow gangway and, when the submarine finally comes to rest alongside the dock, bridge the gap between dock and ship with it.

The moment the gangway has been placed, Admiral Lockwood, followed by his train of experts, walks aboard to greet the skipper, who by this time has jumped down from his station on the bridge. Asking if there are any outstanding emergency repairs or other troubles, Uncle

Charlie chats for a few moments. Like a man who has just had a new automobile delivered to him, he is interested in all the new wrinkles and gadgets on board. Then, bidding the skipper good-bye until lunch, to which he has been invited at Uncle Charlie's mess, the admiral leaves the ship.

This is the opportunity the rest of his staff have been waiting for. Each one of them searches out his opposite number on board and makes arrangements for necessary repairs. In addition, there are several last-minute alterations which must be accomplished before the ship can depart. The workmen—all Navy men—who are to perform these operations are to a large extent already en route to the dock with their tools and equipment. By this method of making alterations virtually on the fighting front, so to speak, our submarines always went into battle with the very latest and finest equipment.

Meanwhile, the enlisted men who had come on the dock with the admiral, and who had handled lines for the ship, have not been idle. Three or four bulging mail sacks, a crate of oranges, a box of nice red apples, and a five-gallon can of ice cream were brought down with them on a handcart. These they now passed over the gangway to the eagerly awaiting crew of *Archerfish*.

On December 23, 1943, while *Shinano* was still building, *Archerfish* departed Pearl Harbor on her first war patrol. Too bad she could not have stayed for Christmas, but orders must be obeyed, and operations seldom take notice of such things. Besides, her crew had been brought up to the fever pitch of enthusiasm. Christmas or no, she was eager to be on her way.

On January 8, 1944, *Archerfish* entered her assigned area, near Formosa. If any of her crew expected even this final lap of her 13,000-mile voyage to war to be a rest cure, they must have been disappointed, for every day of this two-week period was utilized for drill. Practice makes perfect.

To some extent a submarine is a weapon of opportunity. You cannot attack ships which do not arrive. If the seas are too rough, you have the devil's own time keeping an efficient periscope watch, for if you run too close to the surface in order to increase your effective periscope height and see over the wave tops, you stand grave danger of "broaching"; that is, surfacing involuntarily as a result of wave action.

On her first patrol *Archerfish* and her disgusted crew fought heavy weather for two solid weeks, but finally she reported radar contact with four large and five smaller ships heading in the general direction of Formosa. The leading ship was attacked and sunk and *Archerfish*'s patrol report stated, "We had celebrated the first anniversary of our keel laying in right smart fashion."

Months passed, and she was a veteran. The vast Pacific was her playground and her no man's land. Then, as Joe Enright, her skipper, recorded in the fifth war patrol report of *Archerfish*, on November 28, 1944, she was patrolling submerged to the south and west of the western entrance to Sagami Nada, or outer Tokyo Bay. No ships had been sighted. No contacts of any kind (except fishing boats) had been made thus far in the patrol, which had begun twenty-nine days before.

At 1718 she surfaced, the visibility having decreased to such an extent that surface patrolling was feasible and desirable. With no premonition of the events which were to give him an enviable place in our naval history, the commanding officer ordered the regular routine of night-time functions. A radar watch had of course been established the instant the ship broke water. Two engines were put on battery charge and one engine on propulsion at leisurely speed. Air compressors were started, and garbage was assembled, ready to be thrown over the side in burlap sacks. The crew settled down to the routine of alert watchfulness, which is a concomitant part of night surface submarine operations in enemy waters.

At 2048 Fate finally uncovered her hand and brought together the characters she had been coaching for so long. Four years for *Shinano* and almost two years for *Archerfish*—time means little to the gods. How she must have sat back in her big, soft, easy chair, and chuckled. Having brought the two major characters of her play together, now she would leave it up to them, and see what would happen.

"Radar contact!" These words never fail to bring a shiver of anticipation to the submariner. From the size of the pip, the range, and the speed which the first few hasty moments of plotting show this target to be making, there is no doubt whatever in the minds of any of the crew of *Archerfish* that she is really on to something big. The word passes almost instantaneously throughout the ship, "Something big and fast!"

With the ease and sureness of long practice, tracking stations are manned. On the first word of radar contact, the officer of the deck had turned the bow of *Archerfish* directly toward the contact, and had stopped. This gave the plotting party an immediate indication of the direction of target movement. As soon as this had been determined, *Archerfish* roared off in hot pursuit, not directly at the target, but on such a course that she might have an opportunity of getting ahead of him. The main engine still on battery charge was replaced by the auxiliary engine, and all four great nine-cylinder diesel engines were placed on propulsion. Within minutes after the initial contact, *Archerfish* was pounding along at full speed, 18 knots, throwing a cloud of spray and spume from her sharp knifelike bow as she hurried across the sea.

This is where the long, monotonous labor of patrol starts to bear fruit. Plotting and tracking the target is no simple matter. Every minute a range and bearing; every minute the singsong "Stand by, stand by, *mark!*" Every minute plotting parties plot the ship's course and its position at the instant of the "mark"; then, from that point, they draw range and bearing, and thus locate the position of the enemy ship at the same instant. Your own ship twists and turns in the dual effort to gain firing position and to keep range to the target so that he will not sight her, or get radar contact on her, but keep close enough so that her radar will have no difficulty in keeping contact on his much larger bulk. After a few minutes of chase, the target's course is determined to be roughly 210. The target's speed is 20 knots; he is zigzagging, and by the size and strength of his radar pip is mighty big and mighty important. Radar also indicates four smaller vessels: one ahead, one on either beam, and one astern.

Joe Enright is climbing all over his ship like a monkey. First up to the bridge to be sure all is under control, then down to Plot to get an idea of what it is doing. Next, a quick look at the radar scope for a personal evaluation of what the operators have on there; then a quick look at the TDC; then back to the bridge. Then the whole thing over again.

The well-drilled crew are responding beautifully and

solving the problem like clockwork, but all the information collected by his attack party must be transmitted to the captain. It must be weighed in his mind; he must collect all the tiny details, any one of which might suddenly assume tremendous proportions. In no type of vessel is the commanding officer so personally responsible for the actual handling of his ship as in a submarine.

What is the state of moon and sea? It is better to attack with the moon silhouetting the targets instead of the submarine. But torpedoes run better if fired down the hollow of the waves rather than across them. The two considerations must be evaluated; the best decision reached. Not content with the mere reports of progress from junior officers and crewmen working below, the captain has to be personally sure that they are not making mistakes. In his climbing up and down from control room to conning tower to bridge, it is necessary that he protect his night vision, as it would not do to have him partially blinded on the bridge when the crucial moment comes. Therefore, all belowdecks control compartments are blacked out. No lights are allowed except the dim red glow of plotting party lights and the orange and green lights of the radar. All is silent in the control party, except the hushed reports which are continually going back and forth.

Archerfish is logging only 18 knots. This will not be sufficient. The call goes down from the bridge: "Maneuvering, make all the speed you can! All ahead flank!"

Watching their dials carefully, the electrician's mates in the maneuvering room slowly increase the rheostat settings, and the thrashing propellers increase their speed another 20 r.p.m. The pitometer log registers now a little more than 18½ knots.

Again word from the bridge, "Control, give her a five-

minute blow! Blow safety! Blow negative!" The scream
and grind of the low-pressure air-blowing pump fill the
interior of the ship. This low-pressure pump is used in the
latter stages of surfacing when a large volume of air is
required to complete emptying the ballast tanks of water.
In this case, the intention is to blow out what residual
amounts of water night remain or have leaked back in, in
order to speed up the ship. Negative tank and safety tank
are always kept full of water in order to carry out their
designed purposes. Negative tank is so built that when it is
full, the submarine properly compensated, and the ballast
tanks flooded, the sub has negative buoyancy and will
sink. Thus she dives faster. Safety tank, on the other hand,
is used to give the ship quick, positive buoyancy, if she
should need it. Altogether, these two tanks carry approximately thirty-six tons of sea water. Emptying them, while
it decreases the safety factor with which the ship ordinarily operates, also decreases the amount of weight she has
to drag around with her and hence increases her speed.

But in spite of these measures, *Archerfish*'s speed quiv-
ers around 19 knots or possibly a shade more. Still not
enough. A third time from the bridge comes the order:
"Maneuvering, give her all you've got! To hell with the
volts and amps! Watch your motor temperatures, but *give
me more speed!*" Shaking their heads—this is foreign to
their training and upbringing—the electrician's mates
carefully manipulate their rheostats once more. By means
of the engine remote-control governor linkage, the r.p.m.
of the four huge main diesel engines have already been
increased to the maximum, and they are racing just as
fast as they possibly can. Doubtfully the generators are
loaded a bit more, and the amperes flowing to the four
straining motors increase a trifle. The propellers increase

their speed by another five or six r.p.m. *Archerfish* has done all she can, and the pitometer log dial now indicates 19½ knots.

At about this point, approximately one hour after the initial contact, the patrol report states, "Saw the target for the first time, an aircraft carrier! From here on it was a mad race to reach a firing position."

It is every submarine skipper's dream to find himself in hot pursuit of such a target. *The jackpot—an aircraft carrier!* The biggest game of all! *Archerfish*, the huntress. Can she bring this monster down in his own environment?

The skipper is all over the ship again, and visits the control stations at frequent intervals. He calls for Lieutenant Rom Cousins, the engineer officer, sends him back into the engineering spaces with instructions to squeeze out every possible extra turn on the laboring screws. He sends Dave Bunting to be sure that all last-minute adjustments are made on his torpedoes. There might even be time to pull and check all fish. When you stick your neck in the mouth of the dragon in hopes of getting a shot at him, you want that shot to be good.

The communications officer comes in for his share of attention. Joe Enright jots down a message on a piece of paper and hands it to him. Gordon Crosby disappears into the radio room, codes the message, and then stands watch on the radioman as he transmits: *"NPM V W3TU—K . . . NPM V W3TU—K . . . Radio Pearl from Archerfish, I have an urgent message. . . . Radio Pearl from Archerfish, I have an urgent message."*

Straining their ears, the radiomen listen to the welter of dots and dashes filling the ether. Radio Pearl is busy; a lot of ships are calling it, and it is receiving a steady stream of messages. *Archerfish* must wait her turn. The answer from NPM says, *Archerfish from Radio Pearl, Wait.*

But this won't do. *"NPM V W3TU OOO K. . . . Radio Pearl from Archerfish, this message is really urgent!"* There must be some means whereby a ship with an excessively important message can demand and receive immediate attention. Only in this way can any semblance of communication and traffic discipline be maintained.

Radio Pearl comes back immediately with a procedure sign to *Archerfish*. "Go ahead, we are ready."

FROM ARCHERFISH TO COMSUBPAC AND ALL SUBMARINES IN EMPIRE AREAS AM PURSUING LARGE AIRCRAFT CARRIER FOUR DESTROYERS POSITION LAT 3230 N LONG 13745 E, BASE COURSE 240, SPEED 20.

NPM answers simply and very specifically, "R," which means "Received, I assume responsibility, will forward this message to proper authority."

By this time it is early morning at Pearl Harbor, but Admiral Lockwood has left orders with the duty officer to call him no matter where he may be, upon receipt of such a message. He hurries down to the office with his operations officer. It isn't often that one of his submarines latches on to a prize of this kind. Together, with the large wall chart of the Japanese Empire before them, they lay plans to insure the destruction of *Archerfish*'s target. In less than an hour messages pour forth from Radio Pearl. The position, course, and speed of *Shinano* are given. All submarines which might be in a position to intercept her are ordered to proceed to various strategic points and there to lie in wait. Then a further message to *Archerfish*: KEEP AFTER HIM JOE YOUR PICTURE IS ON THE PIANO. The levity in this dispatch is not misplaced. Uncle Charlie knows his boys, and his boys know him.

On and on, on and on, straining every nerve, *Archerfish*

pursues her quarry. The carrier is tracked at 20 knots. *Archerfish* can do no more than 19 or possibly a shade better. But the carrier is zigzagging. If *Archerfish* can detect his base course and parallel that, disregarding the zigs, she may be able to overtake him in spite of the disparity in speeds. But this is tricky, too, because on a zig toward *Archerfish*, the target group might approach close enough for one of the flank escorts to sight the laboring submarine. Conversely, a zig away might lead them out of radar range, where a course change would result in *Archerfish*'s pursuing in the wrong direction. So *Archerfish* cannot blindly charge ahead, but must conform to maneuvers of the target; she cannot lose him, nor can she let him get too close. With these considerations, resisting every move which might tend to increase the distance she must run, *Archerfish* doggedly sets about making an end around. Theoretically, it is possible to get around a target going faster than you are. It *is* possible, but mighty damn hard to do!

One hour before midnight the target group zigs toward, not enough to give *Archerfish* an opportunity to dive and attack on this leg, but sufficiently so that one of the flanking escorts approaches perilously near the submarine—6,000 yards. Determined to take every conceivable, practicable chance to avoid being forced to submerge prematurely, the skipper orders all bridge personnel below, except for Lieutenant (j.g.) John Andrews, the officer of the deck. If *Archerfish* receives gunfire on the bridge, there will be only himself and Andrews up there to worry about.

But the escort ignores the submarine, and Joe Enright calls his lookouts back to the bridge.

At midnight the carrier force makes another big zig, to

the west. *Archerfish* had expected that he was probably headed for somewhere in the Pacific, and therefore had chosen the left or southern flank of the convoy to trail from. A change of base course in the most probable direction, to the south, she hoped would drop the whole outfit into her hands. But such was not to be. The zig to the west puts the submarine even farther out in right field, but doggedly she digs in and continues the chase.

For two and a half hours the pursuit goes on. Racing to crawl up the left flank of the task group, *Archerfish* finds that her top speed is just barely allowing her to pull ahead. But there is obviously no chance of attaining a firing position before dawn. Regretfully, the skipper composes another message.

URGENT—FOR COMSUBPAC AND SUBS IN AREA X TARGET COURSE 275 SPEED 20 X AM TRAILING LEFT FLANK X DO NOT EXPECT TO REACH FIRING POSITION BY DAWN X CONTINUING CHASE.

The answer is prompt. ARCHERFISH FROM COMSUBPAC X KEEP AFTER HIM JOE X ALL SUBMARINES IN THE FORCE ARE PULLING FOR YOU AND ARE BACKING YOU UP.

They are keeping a sleepless vigil at the operations office of ComSubPac, fortified by much coffee and Coca-Cola. But their encouraging message is never received by *Archerfish*.

For at 0300 the sands run out for *Shinano*. Base course is changed again, this time to nearly due south, and incredulously *Archerfish* finds herself almost dead ahead of the target. Fate picks up her dice and stows them away.

"Right full rudder!" The submarine changes course rapidly, heeling to port as she does so. At last *Archerfish* heads for the enemy.

Ah-oooh—gah! Ah—oooh-gah! The diving alarm seems more piercing than usual. *"Dive! Dive!"* *"Flood negative!*

Flood safety!" "Battle stations submerged!" A few men dash through the ship to their battle stations, but most are already there.

"Hatch secured, sir!"

"Shut the induction!"

"Green board, sir!"

"Bleed air in the boat!" "Eight degrees down bubble!" "Easy on the bow planes!" "Blow negative!" "All ahead one third!" "Fifty-five feet!" Expertly each man does his job, and *Archerfish* smoothly slips beneath the waves. Radar gets a final range as the antenna goes under water: 11,700 yards, closing fast.

"Up periscope!" The long, shiny tube hums out of the periscope well. Squatting on his haunches before it, hands poised to catch the handles the moment they emerge, Enright resembles an ageless devotee of some obscure occult religion. Perspiration stands out unnoticed on his forehead, his face is immobile, his eyes staring. You would say he is in a trance, and in a trance he is, for his eyes do not see the crowded darkened conning tower around him. His eyes and mind already are on the surface of the ocean, watching the enemy task group as it comes closer—and closer. . . .

Finally the periscope handles appear. Capturing and unfolding them with both hands, the skipper applies his right eye to the eyepiece and swiftly rises with the periscope to a standing position. He has become so accustomed to this procedure that he is entirely unconscious that he has performed quite a neat little stunt—for from the moment the periscope eyepiece appeared out of the periscope well he has been looking through it, has risen to a standing position with it, and has stopped rising smoothly as the eyepiece reached its upper limit. He slowly rotates the periscope from side to side, searching through the faint predawn light.

"Down periscope! Target not yet in sight. What range do you have on the TDC?"

Since it still lacks more than an hour until dawn, the conning tower and control room are still darkened in order to make it possible to see through the periscope. The radar has been secured, and only the faint red glow of the TDC dial lights, the torpedo ready lights, and the sound gear dial lights are permitted. Dave Bunting consults the TDC range dial. "Range, eight oh double oh, Captain. Bearing two nine five."

"Up periscope! Put me on two nine five!" The captain snaps the command to his exec, "Bobo" Bobczynski, now functioning as assistant approach officer. As the periscope comes up, the latter places his hands beside the captain's on the handles and swings the 'scope until the etched hairline stands at 295. The skipper looks long and hard, and infinitesimally rotates the periscope from one side to the other.

Throughout the ship the men are waiting for the answer to their unspoken questions: "Have we dived in the right place?" "Have we really outguessed him?" *"Does the captain see the target?"*

Finally, in a low voice which hardly expresses conviction, and which certainly is far from showing the relief he feels, the captain speaks. "I see him."

The word flies through the ship. Men look at one another and smile, some a little shakily, but most, a tight-lipped grin of relief and pride. *"We have him in the periscope!"*

The captain's voice now comes a little stronger. "Bearing—mark! Down 'scope! No range yet!"

"Two nine five," Bobo sings out the bearing. Bunting checks his TDC. Down below in the control room, Plot gets the bearing, plots it. There has been a temporary hiatus, while the ship pulls itself together for the final effort, but it is over now.

"Up periscope! Bearing—mark!"

"Two nine six!"

"Range—mark! Down periscope!"

"Six five double oh!"

"Angle on the bow. Starboard five degrees!"

Things are really clicking now. At 20 knots the target will travel the distance between himself and *Archerfish* in nine minutes and a few seconds. It is time to maneuver to gain a favorable firing position as he goes by.

"What's the distance to the track?" The captain can't be bothered with doing this calculation himself.

Bobo does it for him by trigonometry, multiplying the sine of the angle on the bow by the range. He has what amounts to a slide rule to make the computation, and the answer is almost instantaneous. "Five five oh yards!"

Much too close! The submarine is also headed toward the target's projected track. At minimum submerged speed of 2 knots, in nine minutes she will have traveled 600 yards, and will be almost directly beneath the target as he goes by. These thoughts and computations flash across Joe Enright's mind in a split second, even as he gives the order to mitigate the situation. "Left full rudder! Left to course zero nine zero!" By turning her bow more toward the target, *Archerfish* will be enabled to fire torpedoes a little sooner, thus catching *Shinano* at a reasonable range; also, she will not close the track so quickly.

All this time *Shinano* is pounding on to his doom. As soon as *Archerfish* steadies on the new course, her periscope rises above the waves once more, remains a moment, then disappears. Range, bearing, and angle on the bow are fed into the TDC and plot. Her skipper's mind is functioning like lightning. There are three things which *Shinano* may do: Continue on his present course, which will put *Archerfish* in the least favorable firing position, necessitating a sharp track shot ahead of time. Or, zig to his right, causing the submarine to shoot him with stern tubes. Most favorable would be a zig of about 30 degrees to his left, which would leave him wide open for a square broadside shot from the bow tubes.

"How much time?" rasps the skipper, motioning with his thumbs for the periscope to go up.

"He'll be here in two minutes!"

The periscope rises out of the well. "Zig away, to his own left! Angle on the bow starboard thirty!" The TDC dials whirl as the new information is fed into it.

"Bearing—mark!"

"Three four eight!"

"Range—mark!"

"Two oh double oh!"

Swiftly the captain spins the periscope, making a quick scan of the situation all around. Suddenly he stops, returns to a bearing broad on the port beam.

"Down 'scope! Escort passing overhead!"

The periscope streaks down. For the first time they are conscious of a new noise, a drumming noise—propeller beats—coming closer. With a roar like that of an express train, the high-speed destroyer screws sweep overhead.

"This is a shooting observation! Are the torpedoes ready?" Unconsciously, the captain's voice has become clipped and sharp. This is the moment they have worked for all night. He must not fail!

"Shooting observation. All tubes are ready, sir, depth set fifteen feet. Range one five double oh, angle on bow starboard eight five. We are all ready to shoot, sir!"

The cool, self-possessed voice of Sigmund Bobczynski surprises both himself and the captain. There is no wavering, no lack of confidence here. A quick look of affectionate understanding passes between these two who have traveled so far and worked so long together.

"Up periscope! Looks perfect! Bearing—mark!"

"Zero zero one!"

"Set!"—from the TDC officer.

And then that final word, the word they have been leading up to, the word they have all studiously avoided pronouncing until now. *"Fire!"*

At eight-second intervals, six torpedoes race toward their huge target. Mesmerized, the skipper of *Archerfish* stands at his periscope watching for the success or failure of his approach. Forty-seven endless seconds after firing, the culmination of *Archerfish*'s efforts is achieved.

"Whang!" then eight seconds later, "Whang!" Two hits right before his eyes! But there isn't time to play the spectator. That destroyer who just passed overhead will be coming back, and the trailing escort will surely join the party in short order.

A quick look astern of the carrier. Sure enough, here he comes, and less than five hundred yards away. *"Take her down!"*

Negative tank is flooded and the planes put at full dive. Over the rush of water into and air out of negative tank, four more solid, beautiful hits are heard.

The next thing on the docket after a torpedo attack is usually a depth charge attack, and this case proves no exception. But after their glorious experience, it will take a lot of depth charges to dampen the spirits of these submariners. The patrol report actually indicates surprise that the depth charging was not more severe, and merely states, "Started receiving a total of fourteen depth charges," and a little later, "Last depth charge. The hissing, sputtering, and sinking noises continued."

And what of *Shinano* all this time? *Archerfish* made but one mistake in her report. Her target did not sink immediately, as she believed, and, as a matter of strict truth, it would not have sunk at all had its crew possessed even a fraction of the training and indoctrination of its adversary. After all, *Shinano* was theoretically designed to survive twenty or more torpedoes. If she had been properly handled by her crew, and if she had been properly built, she could have made port in spite of *Archerfish*'s six torpedoes.

But water poured from damaged compartments into undamaged ones via watertight doors which had no gaskets; through cable and pipe conduits not properly sealed off and stuffing tubes not packed. The Japanese engineers attempted to start the pumps—and found they had not yet been installed, the piping not even completed. They searched for the hand pumps, but the ship had not yet received her full allowance of gear, and only a few were on board. In desperation, a bucket brigade was started, but the attempt was hopeless. The six huge holes in *Shinano*'s side and the innumerable internal leaks defied all efforts to cope with them.

And then her organization and discipline failed. The men drifted away from the bucket brigade by ones and twos. The engineers gave up trying to get part of the drainage system running. The officers rushed about giving furious orders—but no one obeyed them. Instead, fatalistically, most of the crew gathered on the flight deck in hopes of being rescued by one of the four destroyers milling around their stricken charge. Faint, pathetic hope.

Four hours after she had received her mortal wound, *Shinano* had lost all power, and was nothing but a beaten, hopeless, disorganized hulk, listing to starboard more heavily every moment, a plaything of the wind and the sea. There was only one thing left to do.

The emperor, in his gilded frame, was removed from the bridge and, after being thoroughly wrapped, transferred by line to a destroyer alongside. Then the work of abandoning ship began.

Shortly before 1100 on the morning of November 29 *Shinano* capsized to starboard, rolling her broad flight deck under and exposing her enormous glistening fat belly, with its four bronze propellers at the stern. For several minutes she hung there, lurching unevenly in the moderately rough sea.

Here and there the figures of several men who had not leaped into the sea with the others stood upon the steel plates, silhouetted against sea and sky. Evidently they had climbed around the side and the turn of the bilge as the ship rolled over. Whatever their reasons for not abandoning the ship, they were now doomed, for none of the four destroyers still holding the wake dared approach closely enough to take them off. And the suction of the sinking vessel was certain to take them down with it.

Slowly the massive rudders and propellers started to dip under the seas splashing up toward them. A trembling and a groaning communicated itself to the whole giant fabric, and it began to sway noticeably, swinging the afterparts and the foreparts under alternately. Each time an end dipped, the sea gained a little, and the trembling and groaning increased.

Finally, during one swoop, the stern failed to reappear. Startlingly and suddenly, the bow rose partly out of water, displaying a single eye formed by one gigantic hawse pipe, as if *Shinano* desired a final look at the world she was about to leave. Swiftly then she slid under, stern first, and the last thing seen was the broad bulbous bow, like the forehead of some huge prehistoric Moby Dick, accompanied by the blowing, bubbling, and whistling of air escaping under water.

For several minutes there was considerable turbulence and bubbling to mark her grave, but *Shinano* was gone from the ken of men.

She had known the open sea for less than twenty hours.

11

TRIGGER

TRIGGER WAS A ROARING, brawling, rollicking ship, and she loved the sound of her torpedoes going off. There was the night she and two sister subs took on a seventeen-ship convoy, with the result that there were but nine ships next morning. This was quite a story, for none of the other submarines knew of the presence of *Trigger*, and *Trigger* actually and unwittingly stole two fat targets right out from under the nose of one of her sisters.

It was a night in November. We had penetrated the Nanpo Shoto the night before, and had been hurrying along on the surface all day long, diving twice for inquisitive Jap planes, hoping to get across to the Nansei Shoto and through that chain of islands in short order, en route to our area. We were about one hundred and thirty miles south of the Bungo Suido of unpleasant memories as dusk fell, and with it a pleasant surprise.

Radar contact! The clarion call from Yeoman First Class Ralph Kom on the radar brings us all to the alert. "Big convoy, sir! Five or ten ships, maybe more. Radar interference, too, sir."

That last complicates matters. We've been expecting to run into Jap radar-equipped escorts for quite a while, and apparently we've got one this time. This is going to take some doing, all right, and we ought to have an interesting time of it. In the first place, we figure our radar is probably better than his. In the second place, our small silhouette is harder for a radar to detect than that of a freighter or destroyer. So our tactics are to keep just barely within our radar's range of detection, and we hope that by so doing we'll be outside of his radar range.

Once again we begin tracking and plotting. Our scheme works pretty well, and soon we have his course and speed down cold. We would like to start in from the port flank of the convoy now, but cannot, because that triple-damned radar escort is in our way. Laboriously we work our way across the bow of the zigzagging convoy— we have counted by this time seventeen ships on our radar screen, though we cannot see them at all in the dark—and prepare to start in from their starboard flank. No soap! The five times sincerely damned radar escort has crossed to the starboard side too!

Cussing heartily, we work around to the port side again, hoping the escort's movements were more coincidental than premeditated, and that he is as yet not aware of *Trigger*'s presence. Once on that side the mystery seems explained, because we now find two radar-equipped vessels, one on each side of the convoy. However, this chap on the port side evidently doesn't know his job, and has allowed himself to get way out of position, well out on the port bow of the convoy.

O.K., chum. You slipped up that time. Here we go! *Trigger*'s four murmuring diesels lift their voices in a devouring roar. She swings sharply right and races for the leading ship of the convoy. "Make ready all tubes! Angle on the bow forty-five port. Range, three eight double oh."

The port escort is still unsuspiciously maintaining his station well outside of us.

"All tubes ready, sir! Range, three oh double oh. Angle on the bow sixty port." We can see them clearly from the bridge now. Formless, cloudy masses, a little darker than the dark sky. As we watch them narrowly, they suddenly seem to lengthen a trifle; a zig away! We must shoot right now! "All ahead one third!" The roar of the diesels drops to a mutter. "Stand by forward! Range, two four double oh. Angle on the bow ninety port. Fire ONE! . . . Fire TWO!! . . . THREE! . . . FOUR! . . ."

Four white streaks bubble out toward the convoy, and a large dark shape moves unknowingly and inexorably to meet them. Though we've seen it time and again, this moment is always the most thrillingly portentous one of all. It is the climax of training, of study, of material preparation, and of tremendous, sustained, perilous effort. The lure of the jumping trout, the thrill of the hunt, stalking the wild deer, or even hunting down the mighty king of beasts—none could hold new and unknown thrills for those of us who have watched our torpedoes as they and their huge target approach each other and finally merge together.

The seconds are hours, the minutes days. Target and torpedo wakes are together now. The first torpedo must have missed. Count ten for the second. . . . WHAM! . . . WHAM! Two flashes of yellow light stun the secret darkness. Two clouds of smoke and spume rise from alongside our target. Swiftly he rolls over, men appearing magically all about, climbing down his sides, crawling over his bottom, instinctively postponing their inevitable doom.

In the meantime, all is confusion in the rest of the convoy. Our other two torpedoes, missing the ship they were aimed at, have struck home in some unfortunate vessels beyond him. We hear the explosions and see the flashes—rather to be expected, too, because of the tightly packed crowd of ships—but other than a high cloud of smoke we have no positive proof of damage in more than one other.

Just at this moment, with *Trigger* wheeling madly about under right full rudder and all ahead flank, three shapes detach themselves from the milling mass of freighters and tankers and head for us, bows on. We knew it was too good to last. Destroyers!

A quick decision, regretfully made, for it leaves the rest of the convey free to scatter unhindered. *Take her down!*

Down we go, and just in time, for we pass 100 feet when the first depth charges go off. There are propellers churning all about us, depth charges close aboard snaking *Trigger*'s solid ribs and pounding her tough hide, while we grit our teeth at 300 feet and take our licking. Damn them! Damn them! Damn them!

Suddenly the depth charges cease, and we hear three sets of screws leave us rapidly. Well! A break! Maybe we'll get some more of those bastards! *Fifty-five feet!* Let's go, Control—let's get up there!

Up we come to fifty-five feet, take a good look around through the periscope. All clear. *Surface! Ready on four engines! All ahead flank!* Course one six oh.

High-pressure air whistles into *Trigger*'s tanks. Maneuvering room answers the flank speed bell by giving the motors all the battery has to offer. The screws bite into the water. Engine rooms get standby on all engines. *Trigger* is making 10 knots when she hits the surface. As soon as the conning tower hatch pops out of water we are on the bridge.

Open the main induction! We are answered by the clank

of the induction valve and instantly the starting song of the engines. Four clouds of blue-white smoke pour from *Trigger*'s exhaust pipes and are whipped away by the wind. We are up to 13 knots by this time, and mingled with the whistle of the wind, the splashing rush of the waves, and the deep bass of the diesels, we hear the screaming of the low-pressure blower down in the pump room, completing the job of emptying the main ballast tanks.

A jumble of discordant noises—but to us they are *Trigger*'s eager battle cry.

Without slackening our speed, the diesels are connected to the motors and the battery taken off. *Trigger* continues to accelerate, and two minutes after surfacing she is making 18 knots. As her tanks go dry she increases speed to 20 knots, angrily burying her snout in the waves as she hurries heedlessly through them or over them.

We pick course 160 because this was the base course of the convoy. Before we dived our impression was that the Japs had scattered, but common sense indicates that they'll probably try to continue in the same general direction.

Sure enough, one hour later we find a lone merchantman. In a hurry now, we bore in and fire immediately. One hit, but he's a tough customer, and that's not enough for him. He opens up with two deck guns, tries futilely to stay on *Trigger*'s low, dark form.

Furious now, *Trigger* rushes past him, turns on her heel, and comes charging back. She really bores in this time. To hell with his guns—he's all over the ocean with them! In we go, till his side looms as big and broad as a barn. WHAM! . . . WHAM! That finishes him, and he goes down like a rock.

Course 160 once more, and we run for another hour, pick up another ship, a tanker this time. Once again we hardly alter course. He steams across our bow at 1,000 yards, and is greeted with three crashing torpedo hits, sinking so fast that as we, without changing a thing, pass across where his stern used to be, all we see is his tall stack sticking out of the water, slightly canted forward, smoke still pouring out of the top of it for all the world as though nothing had happened.

We looked around for more ships, but dawn broke, and none were in sight. The sequel to the story was not told till later, when patrol reports were submitted. The second radar-equipped escort, which we had so neatly avoided in our initial attack, was our good friend the USS *Seahorse*, herself the nemesis of many Japs, who was even then in the process of drawing a bead on the same chap we'd sunk.

That *Seahorse* was somewhat disturbed at our intrusion on a convoy she had tracked for nearly twenty-four hours is putting it mildly. But she kindly verified the sinking of two ships plus the probable sinking of a third from our attack, then went on to sink three more herself. In the meantime another United States sub, having trailed the convoy for two days, finally caught up and knocked off one for herself. Total: eight sunk, nine left, probably all escorts.

Wonder what that escort commander told Tojo?

12

TANG

ON JULY 20, 1943, USS *Wahoo* completed her overhaul in Mare Island Navy Yard, and departed for Pearl Harbor, carrying her skipper, Mush Morton, into his last action with the enemy and to his final resting place somewhere in the Sea of Japan. But before *Wahoo* left, her executive Officer, whom Morton had once characterized as "the bravest man I know," was detached and given command of the uncompleted *Tang*, then building at Mare Island. The two men separated with visions of meeting in the not-too-distant future—perhaps to carry out combined operations together. Less than three months later Mush Morton and his *Wahoo* were dead.

Now, O'Kane was not an oversentimental man, and he was as ready as the next to accept the trials of war and the losses that inevitably must come with them. But only one who has experienced the extinction of a whole unit of comrades without trace can fully appreciate the icy fingers which must have clutched around his heart when he received the grim news back in the temporary safety of Mare Island. The effect, perhaps, was not fully evident, since he simply went on with his preparations to ready *Tang* for war. Only O'Kane himself—and perhaps even he did not fully realize how deeply the iron had entered into his soul—could have given a hint of his dedication. For *Tang* and Dick O'Kane had a mission of vengeance to carry out.

They finally headed for Pearl Harbor, impatient to complete their training, and on January 22, 1944, six months after O'Kane had bid farewell to *Wahoo*, three months since that ship had become overdue, *Tang* set her prow westward to seek revenge.

Tang had only one skipper and her whole life was encompassed within the short span of one year—1944. During this period *Tang* and O'Kane reached the top of the Submarine Force Roll of Honor, and the most outstanding record of damage and destruction to enemy shipping ever credited to one submarine was established. The Joint Army-Navy Assessment Committee has the officially documented and incontestable proof of twenty-four vessels sunk. It is well known that *Tang*'s total score was much higher than even that imposing figure, and that a round sum total of thirty would be nearer the truth, for the Japanese tendency to save face resulted in concealing or minimizing many losses, and the confusion into which their merchant marine was thrown by the continuous depredations of United States submarines upset their whole accounting system, until they themselves had not the slightest idea which of their ships remained afloat.

It is early morning, February 17, and *Tang* draws her first blood. *Radar contact!* Man tracking stations! *Tang* stops zigzagging, steadies on course at constant speed while the well-trained though as yet unseasoned plotting parties go to work.

The problem has been gone over many times in drill

after drill, and O'Kane's insistence for perfection now bears its first fruit. Within a matter of minutes, Plot has the answer: enemy course, 100, speed 8, zigzagging about forty degrees every ten minutes. This is all that is needed for the moment. All ahead full! Obediently the electrician's mates on watch in Maneuvering signal to the engine rooms to start the two idle diesels and at the same time increase the loading of the two diesel-generator sets already in operation. *Tang's* easily turning propellers increase their beat as the rheostats are turned up, and soon she is making full speed for the two engines. When the ready signal for the other two engines is received, the electrician's mates bend over their main control board and pull and push the control levers back and forth in rapid succession—seemingly haphazardly but actually in strict accordance with certain rules of procedure—for what they are doing is simply bringing two more generators up to voltage, paralleling them with those already on the line, and then increasing the loading on all four to the maximum rated power output. Sounds simple, but an error might result in burning out one or more motors, or arcing sufficient to cause a bad fire—and there goes your submarine! The nonchalance of these young men—most just boys in their early twenties, some still in their teens—as they unconcernedly race through the motions they have learned, belies the significance of the whole thing.

Plot tells the anxious skipper that their calculations show they will get in front of the convoy well before daylight and have plenty of time for several night attacks.

Dick O'Kane and Murray Frazee, his executive officer, have made night attacks many times before in other submarines. It should be old stuff to them, of course, but it isn't. In the first place, both have been rather a long time away from the war, and the unspoken worry crosses their minds that they may have lost their touch, that the life of ease and safety they have been leading back in the States may have softened them up—that, in short, they may have lost their nerve. Besides, this is Dick's first command. He is burning with the desire to make good, and he wonders whether he really has what it takes, or whether the test will prove that Mush Morton was carrying him along. Likewise, Murray has never been an exec before. Although he has complete confidence in his skipper, and shows it in every move, he, too, has his small secret worry. And *Tang* herself, what about her? Is she not a neophyte? Is she not also burning with the desire to prove herself, to join the ranks of the Dragon Slayers? Or will she join the unhappy company of tired ships, who somehow never found the war?

The symphony of four roaring diesels has a hypnotic effect, to which is added the song of the waves gurgling in the superstructure and the moan of the wind sweeping across *Tang*'s narrow bridge. The vibration communicated to the soles of your feet sets your pulses jumping and your heart beating faster, and it all adds up to the anthem of the chase, which drums in your mind, growing ever louder and more powerful, beating in an ever-rising tympanic crescendo which drugs your senses and drives you beyond normal capabilities, which takes possession of you, wipes out all external considerations, and makes itself the undisputed master of your soul. On and on you run, an irresistible juggernaut which even you could not turn back, if you would. And as they proceed with the chase, both O'Kane and Frazee realize that things have not changed for them, and that it will always be thus.

0200. The convoy has been pretty well identified as consisting of eight ships: two large ones, a medium-sized one which might be a destroyer, and five smaller vessels, probably small anti-submarine patrols. *Tang* is almost in position ahead, and O'Kane is about to give the order to start in for attack, when suddenly one of the flanking escorts appears out of the night, closing rapidly. Only one thing to do—dive!

Ah-ooh-gah! Ah-ooh-gah!—The automobile horn blasts of the diving alarm resound twice throughout the submarine. Alert men in the control room swiftly open the hydraulically operated vent valves, thus releasing the air entrapped in the main ballast tanks. The lookouts tumble down from the bridge. One of them presses the button which causes the bow planes—housed against the superstructure while on the surface—to rig out, and stands by to operate the planes the instant the indicator light glows. Another takes over the stern planes, places them immediately on full dive.

In the maneuvering room, a lever in the overhead of the compartment has been pushed, causing all four engines to stop immediately by action of compressed air on the governors, and the "ampere hounds" quickly rearrange their control switches and levers to put the ship's main storage battery on propulsion in place of the generators.

In the engine rooms the four straining engines are shut down by hand, individually, upon the first notes of the diving alarm. There is always rivalry between the machinist's mates and the electrician's mates as to just who caused the engines to stop in any given instance, and of course there is no answer which either side will accept. But the engines stop, and the engine crew races around the two engine room compartments, shutting outboard exhaust valves, inboard exhaust valves, and inboard air induction flapper valves. Circulating water lines and such lesser openings which do not communicate directly with the interior of the ship may be left for a moment or two, but they, too, are closed quickly.

Meanwhile the chief of the watch in the control room has been watching the engine indicator lights closely, and as soon as all four go green, indicating that the engines are no longer pumping air overboard through their exhaust lines, he pulls toward him a handle which operates the main air induction valve, thirty-six inches in diameter—nonclosure of which was responsible for the loss of USS *Squalus* in 1939—and closes it hydraulically with a sharp thump. He also has been watching the depth gauge, and would have closed the valve before it went under even if there were still an engine running, on the theory—considered incontestable in informed submarine circles—that an insufficiency of air is much more to be desired than a superabundance of water.

All this while men have been jumping down below from the bridge of the submarine. The last man down is the officer of the deck, who is responsible for the proper closing of the upper conning tower hatch and for seeing that no one is left languishing topside. As he leaves the bridge, water is already lapping over the main deck, and he mentally checks off the thump of the main induction as he and the quartermaster of the watch dog the hatch down and inspect it.

It has taken *Tang* less than a minute to dive completely beneath the surface of the water, but she doesn't stop there. If the escort has sighted her, he must mean business, and the thing to do is to put as much black water between the sub and his keel as possible. *Tang* is still in a headlong dive for the friendly depths when the first depth charge goes off, to be followed closely by four more.

But evidently this fellow is not sure of his contact, because he drops his five halfhearted depth charges and goes on his way—fatal error. The moment Sound reports the screws going away, up comes *Tang*. Free of further disturbance by this little man, she bores surely in to firing range, remaining submerged to periscope depth to avoid detection.

0300. The medium-sized ship is positively identified as a destroyer, as he moves unsuspectingly across the bow of the submerged sub. Dick withholds fire, much as he'd like to get this one, for the heavily laden freighter not far astern of him looks like the more valuable target. With so many escort vessels running around, O'Kane feels that his chances of getting off more than one shot are not too good, and his chances of getting an immediate depth charging excellent. The convoy is in rather loose formation, and the ships are too far apart for a simultaneous shot at more than one. That was one of *Wahoo*'s favorite stunts, and how O'Kane would have liked to start *Tang* off with a double bang. But wisely he figures that a sure sinking is far better than two possibles. *Tang*'s first salvo is going to be cold, deadly, and calculated.

0330. The leading freighter lumbers into view. *Tang* has already fired forty-three torpedoes in drill and the efficiency of her fire-control party has been proved. But this time every man on board feels a tightening of nerves, a tenseness of atmosphere, a feeling that these, of all fish, must be good. The range is 1,500 yards; the TDC shows that torpedoes fired now will strike the target exactly broadside on—a perfect setup. Everything is ready.

Here's the first one, Mush.

"Stand by aft!"

The men in the after torpedo room watch closely the gauges and instruments for number-seven tube, and prepare to fire it by hand if the electrical firing mechanism fails. In the control room, the diving officer motions for the chief on the vent manifold to open the vents so that any gases from a depth charge going off directly beneath would pass right through the ballast tanks, rather than being entrapped therein. It is hard enough to keep from surfacing after the sudden loss of weight when a salvo of fish are fired, without adding an entirely unpredictable factor to the problem.

"Bearing—mark!"

"Zero one three!" calls out the quartermaster.

"Set!" from the TDC operator.

"FIRE!" The word lashes out from Dick O'Kane's lips. *Tang*'s first war shot is on the way.

The TDC operator takes over the remainder of the salvo. He waits ten seconds, sings out, "FIRE!" Then ten seconds, "FIRE!" and again, "FIRE!"

Now comes the wait. One minute. Can something have gone wrong? Can we have made some mistake? O'Kane watches anxiously through the 'scope. A lot depends on this, *Tang*'s first target!

"WHANG!" The first torpedo explodes exactly at the point of aim, the target's screws. A flash of light momentarily blocks the vision and swiftly subsides to show a large column of dirty water flung high above the poop deck of the hapless vessel, falling heavily all about his afterparts.

"WHANG!" The second fish strikes home, about one third of the way forward. Another flash of light, and another column of water. The speed of the stricken ship already becomes perceptibly slower, as the sudden braking effect of two jagged holes in his once-smooth skin, as well as the loss of his propeller, destroy his forward motion. He has sunk lower in the water already, in the ten seconds between explosions, and has begun to list.

"WHANG!" A third hit from the pitiless torpedoes. This one is fairly far forward, in the bow of the ship, and it decisively completes the job. His forward motion now completely disrupted, he slithers agonizingly to a stop, and the fourth torpedo, which *Tang* had aimed at his bow, misses ahead.

A quick turn about with the periscope shows the submarine skipper that he is clear of escorting vessels and can spare a moment or so to verify the sinking. The stern single eye of the *Tang* swings back to the doomed Japanese freighter. There is not the slightest doubt that this ship is a goner, but it has been a long time since Dick O'Kane stood at *Wahoo*'s periscope and saw one of her victims go down; besides, this is his—and *Tang*'s—first, the start of his plans for a long vendetta.

To only a few men is the opportunity given to watch a big ship sink, and there is a certain sadness, combined with a sort of fierce, unholy joy and glee, in watching one which you yourself are responsible for.

Another quick look around with *Tang*'s periscope shows that one of the escorts is headed in her general direction, and the sound man reports that he can hear pinging from that direction. Obviously, the Nip is trying the natural and logical tactic of running down the torpedo wakes in hopes of picking up their source. No sense in the source hanging around any longer. Besides, there is no chance of getting the other freighter, for he never had been close enough for a shot, and he is now headed directly away from the area as quickly as he can. So the periscope is pulled down all the way, and the boat is secured for deep depth and depth charging. This promises to be an all-around day for *Tang*: Her first depth charges have already been received, her first attack has been carried out successfully, her first ship has been seen to sink, and now she is due for another working over.

But this Nip destroyer doesn't have his heart in his work, either, and he merely unloads a few charges and goes on his way. *Tang* chalks up practically a free ride, and is back on the surface an hour and a half later, as dawn breaks.

By the time O'Kane was ready to return to port he had added four more scalps to *Tang*'s belt—one a huge naval tanker carrying a crew estimated at more than three hundred men. When she arrived at Midway after that first run, the Submarine Force, Pacific Fleet, knew that spiritually as well as actually it had received the replacement for *Wahoo*. Not only was Dick O'Kane the logical man to inherit Morton's crown as the most successful submariner—he had also earned it. At least he was well on the way to earning it, if he could only keep up his record.

In passing, it is a curious commentary on O'Kane to note that not once in any of his patrol reports did he capitalize the word "Jap" or "Nip." To him they were "japs," "nips," and "other debris," if he bothered to mention them at all.

On her second run, no enemy vessels were sunk, for the simple reason that none were sighted, despite *Tang*'s utmost efforts. About the only thing worthy of note in that line was her meeting with *Trigger* off Palau, during the latter's ninth patrol, and supplying her with necessary spare parts after a terrific beating absorbed a few days before. This fortunate encounter was instrumental in *Trigger*'s being able to remain on station and finally discover a large convoy which she all but wiped out. Though gratifying, however, this was not doing any ship sinking herself, and O'Kane might have been excused for being a bit peeved. However, a chance for action of another kind came, with orders to the Truk area to perform lifeguard duties for an air attack scheduled for that enemy base.

It was a characteristic of O'Kane—as well as of Morton before him—that the most thorough and meticulous preparation was always made for any mission, and this one was no exception. Employing daring tactics, using to the fullest extent all available assistance such as search planes, special radio circuits, and the like, and bombarding the shore batteries whenever he found (or made) the opportunity—usually during the height of an air raid, thus confounding the enemy all the more—*Tang* proceeded to the rescue of twenty-two aviators who had been forced to land in the water. For this most remarkable feat, performed in seven different pickups close to the reef at Truk, usually under enemy gunfire, *Tang* and her skipper won the plaudits of the whole Submarine Force, and the heartfelt gratitude of the carrier task force. This was one of the rare instances in which a sub returning from patrol with no scalps to add to her belt needed no excuses, and actually added to her reputation.

And on her third run *Tang* sank ten ships, for a total of fifteen. O'Kane still seemed to be possessed of a fierce driving urge to sink more Japanese ships, his mission of vengeance not yet accomplished, his search for perfection not yet satisfied. By the time *Tang*'s third patrol was completed, however, the lure of the chase seemed uppermost in O'Kane's mind, and the desire for revenge, and the dedication of all victims to the old *Wahoo*, was no longer the primary motivation. In other words, *Tang* was now working for herself.

While she sank only two ships on her fourth patrol, this was the toughest one to date, for *Tang* was bothered with excellent anti-submarine forces and poor torpedo performance. Shades of poor old Mush Morton! But the trouble was not so serious as *Wahoo* had experienced, and effective results were achieved in spite of it.

On August 11, O'Kane had selected a spot off the coast of Honshu known as Miki Saki for a submerged patrol. It soon became evident that he had correctly gauged a hot spot, for a modern gunboat, which he described as "loaded with depth charges," cruised in the area, while a nondescript motorboat wandered about with six lookouts keeping a sharp watch. All day was spent in avoiding these two characters, but at about 1500 the motorboat, by great good luck, sighted the periscope of the questing submarine, and tailed her from then on.

Not good, this, but *Tang* is not one to give up just because a little boat latches on to her. Surfacing and giving him a quick going over would not be advisable because of the gunboat which had been sighted earlier and the possible presence of planes. Apparently the motorboat is not positive about its contact, for no heavier anti-sub forces come out to help, so *Tang* nonchalantly keeps patrolling the area, although this little fellow is annoying.

Shortly before 1700 smoke is sighted. *Tang* starts the approach, and the smoke resolves itself into two heavily laden ships, escorted by the gunboat, and another escort. Both ships are running as close to the beach as they dare,

and *Tang* goes right on in after them, followed by the ubiq-
uitous motorboat. The approach develops normally, and it
is not long before O'Kane finds himself just where he
wants to be, broad on the leading target's beam, ready to
shoot. Just then there is an excited report from the sound
man:

"Fast screws, Captain! Bearing two one five!" The
sound man has been obeying the standing order for torpedo approaches to search continually all around unless
specifically directed otherwise. These screws are on the
port quarter; the targets are on the port bow, coming up
on the firing point.

O'Kane spins the periscope around for a quick look.
Damn that motorboat anyway! He has evidently warned
the gunboat, and that worthy is now charging down on
Tang with a bone in his teeth and a look of fury suffusing
his sleek hull. A minute and a half to get here. There is
time—barely—to fire the fish.

Tang's periscope turns back to the enemy. The situation
has suddenly changed dramatically, for the worst! There
may be just enough time to shoot the torpedoes, but, oh-
h-h-h, are we going to catch it! Dick O'Kane is a marvel of
concentration. Although the tension has suddenly leaped
up to a terrific pitch he calmly goes through all the many
motions associated with firing torpedoes. But his voice is
clipped, short, and sharp. He expects every man to get it
the first time, and no repeats.

"Stand by forward!"

"Final setup!"

"Bearing.—*mark!*"

"Set!" From the TDC operator.

"Fire!" Three torpedoes, properly spaced, are fired at
the leading ship.

"Shift targets! Second ship! Bearing—*Mark!*"

"Three four one!"

"Set!"

"FIRE!" Even before the second fish of this three-torpedo salvo is on its way, O'Kane turns back to the gunboat, just in time to see him charge across the stern at full speed. Evidently he had misjudged the sub's direction of motion, which is a lucky break. Another minute free, at least. In the meantime, as soon as the last torpedo is fired, the word is passed through the ship: "Rig for depth charge!"

Back goes the periscope toward the targets. Many a man would have pulled his down in this juncture, but not O'Kane. He simply *must* see these targets sink! "Take her down!" he orders, but he keeps the scope up.

"Come on! Come *on!*" He has only a few seconds left to see the hit—he must see it—WHANG! Right in the middle. It must have caught his old-style boilers, for the ship virtually disintegrates. Dick has time to see the explosion, and the ship breaking into two pieces, before the periscope goes under as *Tang* seeks the shelter of the depths.

Two more explosions are heard. One of the members of the control party is assiduously logging the times and characteristics of all explosions—proper evaluation of results requires that some record be kept—and these are later identified as the fourth and fifth torpedoes striking into the second freighter. But the log of the attack merely lists two explosions, ten seconds apart, which "sounded like torpedoes."

But this is by no means all for this merry afternoon. The Jap gunboat has quickly realized his mistake and has reversed course. Sound carefully keeps on him, and soon his bearing is steady. His screws slow down—he is listening and probing with his echo-ranging gear. The high-pitched ping of his sound gear coming in over *Tang*'s receiver—*Peep—peep—peeeeeeep—peeeep*—searches relentlessly this way and that, growing louder when he is on the bearing, diminishing when he is off.

There is a loudspeaker mounted near the sound console, but it is not used. The frenetic bleeps of the enemy apparatus are audible throughout the conning tower from the operator's earphones. Since contact has been so recently lost, it does not take long to regain it, and soon the horrid *"Peep, peep, peep!"* noise is coming in regularly. It won't be long now!

"Screws have speeded up!" suddenly reports Sound.

All at once it becomes obvious to everyone that the interval between successive pings has decreased. The sound man's report—"Shifting to short scale!"—is totally unnecessary. As the enemy approaches, the time necessary for an echo to return from the submerged submarine of course decreases, its length determining the range. But as it decreases, it then becomes possible to send out more *peeps*, and thus get more echoes. The gunboat's shifting to a more frequent ranging interval indicates that he has an excellent contact and that he is coming in for the attack.

"Stand by! He's starting a run!" The word is whispered over the ship's sound-powered telephones, as though the use of full voice might help the enemy in locating the sub.

Tang has not been idle in the short time since the firing of the torpedoes. Preparations for receiving a beating are more or less standard among the submarine force, and it took less than a minute for the well-drilled crew to rig ship for depth charge attack.

The effect upon the various members of the crew

would be revealing, were there any way to detect it. Some men secretly pray as they go about their tasks. Others feel a sort of masochistic pleasure, secure in their own private fatalistic concepts of life and death. All essay a nervous little smile, and watch furtively to see how the others are taking it.

Up in the conning tower, Dick O'Kane has not been idle either. Evasion, like attack, is the skipper's responsibility in a submarine. He has been twisting and turning, presenting the smallest possible target to the probing fingers of the enemy sound gear. At the same time he has been endeavoring to move away from the coast of Honshu, out to sea, where *Tang* will have deeper water and more room to maneuver.

But try as he may, the enemy gunboat has far too good a contact to be shaken so easily. The menacing propellers come ever closer, and their beat is speeded up gradually as the attack is developed. *Tang* has received depth charges before, but never from such a deliberate fellow.

Closer and closer come the malevolent screws, and the bleat of the echo-ranging signals are one continuous "*Peep, peep, peep, peep, peep, peep, peep*" until it seems that the mind must reel. Beads of sweat roll down the forehead and cheeks of the concentrating sound man, curving into the corners of his mouth, and occasionally his nervous tongue licks at the salty taste thus produced. Murray Frazee once wipes off his forehead and the back of his neck, but Sound shakes his head uneasily, and the exec lets it go.

"Coming on the range now!" The report is muttered as though in meditation. "Coming on the range . . . *He's dropped the first one!*" The sound man has caught the splash of the depth charge dropping into the water.

"How fast do Jap depth charges sink?" The question hangs pregnantly in midair. Frazee tries to remember his destroyer days: about ten feet a second—200 feet—that's as deep as we can go—twenty seconds—hope he hasn't got the depth set right . . .

"*He's dropped six of them!*" The report sounds oddly loud in the confined conning tower, and O'Kane realizes with a start of sympathy that this operator—his best—has been on duty for two strenuous hours without once removing his earphones.

"Ten seconds more, Captain!" Frazee tries to assume the disinterested voice of an observer at a target practice.

WHAM! . . . WHAM! . . . WHAM! . . . WHAM! . . . WHAM! . . . WHAM! The shock is beyond all expectation, beyond reason. With a scream of agony, the sound man jerks off his earphones and stands up trembling before his instrument. The poor fellow had forgotten to turn down his gain control before the charges went off, and is really in severe pain. Dick O'Kane clutches the steel hoist cable of the periscope to keep from falling down, and with his free hand supports the shuddering sound man, who has been flung off his balance by the succeeding blows. Several cigarette receptacles are flung to the furiously vibrating deck plates of the tiny compartment. The explosions resound throughout the ship like pile-driver blows. The atmosphere is filled with a strumming many-pitched roar, produced by the sudden vibration induced in the bulkheads and all the pipes and fittings. Occasionally a piece gives way with a peculiarly explosive noise of relief which only adds to the discordant uproar.

Several men are knocked off their feet by the intensity of the barrage. The air within *Tang*'s tough steel hull is filled with flying bits of dust and specks of paint, plus larger items such as sections of cork insulation and other material not firmly nailed down.

Frazee and O'Kane look at each other with dismay. This birdie certainly has the range, all right. Wonder how much of this kind of pounding good old *Tang* can stand. So far, not much serious damage, but there's no telling when one of these blockbusters will be a bull's-eye.

Regaining control over his jumping reflexes and somehow quieting the ringing in his ears to at least bearable level, the sound man returns to his listening equipment, and immediately picks up the gunboat's screws on *Tang*'s port bow, where he is heard to slow down, apparently waiting for possible results to his first attack, and no doubt planning another.

The captain speaks to the conning tower telephone talker. "Check and report all compartments!" The crisp command goes out to all the eight other watertight compartments of the ship, and the reports come back immediately, indicating that the men in each have already taken stock of their situation. So far all is reassuring, although no one in the ship can recollect ever having received a barrage as close as this one before.

O'Kane's mind is a boiling mass of ideas for evasion; so is Murray Frazee's, and the two hold hurried counsel. It is probable that the enemy will try to box *Tang*, in shallow water, against the not-too-distant coast of Honshu.

By this time it is deathly quiet again, even the prolonged swishing noise produced by the depth charges having died down and the querulous *Peep . . . peep . . . peep* can again be heard by the people in the conning tower. O'Kane would like to take a sounding, but dares not, since the signal of his depth finder would furnish the Jap with precisely the information he is seeking—the location of *Tang*. But after a moment's thought Dick has the answer for that one. The operator of the depth-finding equipment receives instructions to take one sounding in the middle of each depth charge barrage, and to leave the gear turned off otherwise. The scheme is instantly obvious to all, for naturally the Jap sound man will not expect to hear anything while the depth charges are going off—while *Tang*'s operator, knowing when to expect the return echo, can probably catch it through the terrific uproar of the explosions. A neat dodge, and one requiring considerable skill.

"He's turning this way!" The sound man in the conning tower diagnoses the maneuver heralding the arrival of a second attack, the one which Dick O'Kane has been waiting for, during which he will put into effect the evasive maneuver he has planned.

"Here he comes! Shifting to short scale! Screws speeding up!"

"Right full rudder! All ahead full!" Until this moment *Tang* has been creeping along at evasive speed, which is as slow as she can go and, of course, running as noiselessly as possible, which can only be accomplished effectively while at creeping speed. This full-speed business will surely be detected over the Jap sound gear, though the enemy's own speed will make this more difficult. But O'Kane is figuring on completely outwitting him. *Tang* turns quickly and heads straight for the Jap gunboat. Perhaps Dick has remembered something which Mush Morton did one time, in a similar situation when brought to bay by a Nipponese destroyer—only difference now is that *Tang* has had no opportunity to get any torpedoes ready forward. And Dick's plan proves to be a modification of the one Morton had used in *Wahoo*, for *Tang* rockets along, figuratively laying her ears back alongside her head, and runs at full speed directly beneath the onrushing Jap.

But though this unorthodox maneuver has caught him somewhat by surprise, the Jap skipper is not napping, and unloads a full cargo of ash cans as the submarine passes beneath him. The deliberate attack he had planned is frustrated, but he makes with a mighty good one, nonetheless.

Sixteen depth charges this time. Because of her high speed, *Tang*'s sound gear is unable to pick up the splash of the depth charges dropping in the water, and there is therefore no warning as to how many to expect. It is just WHAM WHAM WHAM WHAM WHAM WHAM WHAM WHAM WHAM WHAM WHAM WHAM WHAM WHAM WHAM WHAM! One prolonged, unpunctuated, smashing, shattering cataclysm! Nearly everyone in *Tang* is knocked off his feet by the fearful pounding! Deck plates are hurled about, the very frames ring, and the bulkheads and built-in fixtures resound in a hundred different keys. *Tang* shakes throughout her length, seems to whip convulsively in fishtailing fashion, every part of her jumping around weirdly and frighteningly. The unfortunate men handling vital equipment, such as the bow planes, stern planes, and steering, grip their large stainless-steel wheels with white knuckles and bloodless joints, for they have come alive in their hands as though electrified, transmitting a shivering vibration into the very marrow of their bones. In the maneuvering room, where the full power of the battery is being fed into the straining propellers, there is continual arcing and flashing in the control cubicle, the heart of the electric-propulsion equipment. If some of those huge switches should fly open, or if an unusually heavy arc were to fuse some errant piece of copper or steel into a dead short circuit, the whole place would go up in smoke. The battering and pounding are terrific, but the electrician's mates, knowing their lives depend upon it, are holding the most crucial levers and switches in by hand—and lucky is the man who has asbestos gloves.

O'Kane and Frazee, having had perhaps more warning than the others, have hung on where they were, still on their feet. It seems to both that *Tang*'s last moments must have come, for how can a simple steel shell, no matter how strongly and honestly built, withstand a succession of near bull's-eyes? But the unholy barrage finally stops, and a breathless quiet suddenly envelops the ship.

The Jap had been so thrown off balance by *Tang*'s sudden maneuver that he was unable to regain contact, and searched fruitlessly in the wake left by her mad dash for deep water. Thirty-eight minutes after the torpedoes had been fired, *Tang* was back to periscope depth, to see her recent antagonist still searching and depth charging the area, planes circling overhead, and the other escort, which had never been involved in the action, cruising about slowly, picking up survivors. There was nothing else in sight.

Eleven days later *Tang* was back at Miki Saki, with unpleasant memories of the depth charge expert she had encountered there. But the hunting had been poor elsewhere, and now that the area might be presumed to have cooled off a bit, she was back to try her luck once again. Shortly after midnight the sleek submarine rounded Miki Saki and quietly poked her nose into Owase Wan, a small bay nearby, in quest of a ship. Since by this time it must have become plain to the Japs that they had incurred their worst losses at night, it was logical that at least some of their ships would anchor in a more or less sheltered anchorage to ride the night out, and thus accept the relatively lesser risk of a daylight submerged attack. *Tang's* idea was to knock off one of these sitting ducks.

Sure enough! Anchored right in the middle of Owase Wan, unmistakably pointed out by radar, was a ship, rather small, but certainly worth torpedoes.

O.K., chum. *Battle stations surface torpedo!* The call rings throughout the ship, brings all hands out of their bunks or away from whatever else they might have been doing—it was not unusual for submariners to "turn night into day," so far as their sleeping habits were concerned when on patrol, and this particularly was the case with *Tang,* who made most of her fame at night. All hands go to their stations, and a picked crew of gunners mounts to the bridge, there to make ready the twenty-millimeter guns in case it becomes necessary to shoot their way out of shallow water.

First the plotting parties track the ship, to make sure he is at anchor. Correct—speed zero. Then *Tang* noses in slowly, cautiously. It is necessary to get a look at him, to line him up for a broadside shot, so Dick O'Kane takes his ship completely around the enemy, looking him over away from the dark land background. When finally revealed, his silhouette brings a thrill to the skipper. There is no mistaking that long, low shape. This is the gunboat which had given *Tang* that tooth-shaking barrage of depth charges on her last visit to this area!

Boys, we're going to get this bastard! He has it coming to him! Tang twists on her heel, presents her stern to the enemy. One electric torpedo is set for an absolutely straight stern shot, aimed carefully, and fired. It leaves a phosphorescent wake in the water, by which its progress may be followed, but the wake stops after 100 yards of travel, and a loud rumble is heard over *Tang*'s sound gear, indicating that it has suddenly dived to the bottom. One wasted.

Two minutes after the first one, a second electric torpedo is fired, also from the stern. Surely the Japs must be keeping a watch of some kind. But no sign, and the second phosphorescent wake heads straight for the target and passes exactly beneath him. Two wasted, and *how can he fail to notice what is going on?*

Something wrong with the electric fish? Maybe he had better quit shooting them, check them over again. Besides, O'Kane wants to keep the three he has left aft for a full salvo against some other ship. So *Tang* circles, brings her bow around to bear. She is less than half a mile from the target now, but there is still no sign of life on board.

A steam torpedo is made ready in one of the bow tubes. *Tang* is carefully lined up, absolutely steady in the water, and the torpedo is fired. *Damn!* It takes a large jog to the left, then runs properly, and roars past the target, missing to the left by only a few feet. A steam torpedo puts out a most extensive and visible wake under normal circumstances, and the phosphorescence makes it even more visible. Besides, it is a much faster torpedo than the electric, and makes a high-pitched sewing-machine noise which can easily be heard at some distance. But still no reaction from the enemy. *Tang* has been in the harbor now for half an hour, shooting torpedoes from about nine hundred yards, and *still* he sleeps.

Another steam torpedo is made ready, and fired as before. At last, this one settles down right for his middle, draws its greenish-white pencil line unerringly into the belly of the enemy.

KERBLROOM! A pillar of fire shoots out of the amidships section of the stricken ship! Five hundred feet in the air it is topped by a regular Fourth-of-July fireworks, tongues of flames shooting out in odd directions—rockets, pinwheels, and several more explosions. Of the gunboat there is absolutely nothing left.

Every man of *Tang*'s crew now feels much better about that gunboat. The score has been settled, and he won't be around to heckle any more hard-working submariners trying to do their jobs. Sage heads are wagged belowdecks over the inevitable coffee and acey-deucey games. Most indubitably he has been taught a lesson he will never forget.

Tang's bag of two ships on her fourth patrol boosted her total to seventeen. Although you would have thought her outstanding performance rated a rest, that was not the way Dick O'Kane saw it. As a matter of fact, the normal refit time was cut short by four days in order to enable him to get back on the firing line. The coming Philippine campaign promised many action possibilities in the form of Japanese reinforcements sent to help the defenders, and *Tang* intended to be in on the fun. It was known that the favorite route was inside of Formosa, where the Japs evidently hoped that United States submarines would not be able to enter or dare to patrol. Ceaseless coverage, flying both from Formosa and the mainland, plus strategically located and extensive mine fields, was intended to cut down the efficiency of such operations and to increase their hazard.

It is not recorded in history, but the story as known in the Submarine Force is to the effect that Dick O'Kane called his crew together shortly before getting under way, and informed them that he had volunteered *Tang* for the toughest assignment ComSubPac had to offer. He could not tell them where it was until the ship was under way, but he promised them all that there would be plenty of targets. Although the risks were to be many, the rewards would also be many, measured in terms of damage done to the enemy. It is a matter of pride in our service that not one man requested to be transferred out of that intrepid crew. Some, of course, had already been transferred or detached, for rotation of some personnel between patrols was one of the standard policies of the Submarine Force. The biggest loss was that of *Tang*'s executive officer, Murray Frazee, who had received orders to command USS *Gar*, and was already on leave awaiting availability of his first command. Frank Springer, who had been the third officer, moved up to exec, and on September 24 *Tang* departed from Pearl Harbor on what was to be her last and most glorious patrol.

On the night of October 10 *Tang* moves into the Straits of Formosa. Dick's predictions and expectations begin to bear fruit, for in the early morning a ship is sighted. *Tang* tracks him, maneuvers ahead of him, and with dawn about to break, dives on his track. The ship comes on unsuspectingly, and is greeted with three torpedoes, fired in standard salvo fashion. The first two hit exactly as aimed, and the Jap blows up with a thoroughly satisfying explosion. The third would have hit also, had the enemy ship been there to receive it—as it is, it passes just slightly ahead of the suddenly stopped hulk, which is even then in the process of blowing sky-high.

One down, and Dick O'Kane has further evidence that if the fish are working right—and it now seems they might be—one torpedo would have sufficed to dispose of this ship, and the other two were wasted. Well, maybe he'll put the matter to the test next time.

Next time does not long delay in coming, for another ship is sighted several hours after daybreak. O'Kane could attack immediately, but the water is shallow and air cover excellent; consequently he tracks the ship all day submerged. Only a combination of the slow speed of the prospective target and the fact that he follows the shoreline religiously, evidently in the hope that by so doing he is avoiding attack, makes this possible, for ordinarily a submarine is a target of opportunity, and must do all its chasing and end-arounding at night on the surface, or else well out of sight of possible air cover. This time, however, *Tang* has no difficulty in keeping up with the enemy submerged, and after dark a long, dripping shadow silently surfaces 4,000 yards astern of him.

With murmuring diesels, the gray wraith ghosts on past the unsuspecting freighter. There are two small patrol vessels up ahead of the oncoming ship, apparently maintaining a permanent anti-submarine barrier. *Tang* avoids these neatly, gets dead ahead of the enemy ship, then turns off the track and lies to in the wallowing seas, deck aft awash with spray and spume whipped across it by the wind. She has selected her position so as to be only 500 yards away as the target comes by astern. Three torpedoes are ready aft, but this time Dick O'Kane decides to try Morton's idea. Undoubtedly there will be many ships through this area before *Tang*'s time here is over. This is a straight run-of-the-mine freighter; and anyway, if the torpedo does miss him, *Tang* will go on up ahead of him once more and try again.

But no further attacks prove necessary, for the one single torpedo fired does the trick, hitting the target exactly in the middle with a terrific explosion. Two down.

The next few days are uneventful, but in the early morning of the 20th a small task force, consisting of a cruiser and two destroyers, is sighted headed south at high speed. Even though they cut down their speed made good by a radical zigzag plan, *Tang* barely is able to overtake them, racing along the surface using all available power. A normal attack from the usual position on the target's beam is manifestly impossible, since there is not a chance of getting there before dawn. The only possible shot is one up the tail, and *Tang* nearly breaks her neck getting into position. Since the target is running directly away at 19 knots, and zigzagging frequently, it is necessary to get very close—not more than six hundred yards astern of him—before shooting, in order to give the fish a chance to reach him before he is off on another zig. *Tang* manages to get in to 800 yards before the Jap realizes that his little task force has grown. He also notices that the newcomer has the annoying habit of wanting to climb right up on the cruiser's fantail, which would annoy any cruiser captain.

That, of course, is as far as *Tang* gets, for a searchlight suddenly outlines her in pitiless detail, and she barely manages to get under as the first salvo of eight-inch shells screams overhead.

Two days later another convoy is picked up on the radar, a few minutes after midnight. Its disposition is quickly made out to be roughly in the form of a cross, a single column of three tankers flanked by two freighters or transports, the whole group heavily guarded by antisubmarine vessels.

Tankers are the biggest prizes, outside of actual warships, and *Tang* is delighted at the prospect of getting three of them. The night is dark, and the submarine is able to track from dead ahead until, seizing a favorable opportunity, she stops, allowing the enemy ships to overtake her. As they do so, *Tang* turns and sets herself up for the three tankers with all torpedoes ready, six forward and four aft.

On they come, oblivious. The relatively tiny submarine is lying in their path in such a position that the column of three ships will pass across her bow, while the single flanking vessel will cross her stern. Then, when the range to the nearest Jap ship is about three hundred yards, *Tang* commences firing.

Two torpedoes into the first one, one into the second, two into the third. One saved in reserve forward for an emergency. The range is so close that the first two fish hit the leading tanker before the last two are fired, and he goes up in a roaring *whoosh* of flame, lighting up the whole scene as though it were broad daylight. It is too late, of course, for any of the doomed ships to maneuver to save themselves, for the torpedoes are in the water within the space of seconds, and the range is so short that all maneuvers would be useless anyway. As *Tang* watches the destruction she has wrought, all three tankers burst into furious blaze—an unprecedented, unparalleled holocaust!

But in the meantime the freighter is passing astern, and Dick O'Kane must get set to let him have one or two fish. It takes only a few seconds until finally the word, "Set below!" is received on the bridge, but much has happened in the interim. The freighter alters course, having sighted the submarine's low-lying form in the glare of the explosions and flames of the tankers. He obviously intends to ram. Also, the large freighter-transport on the far flank of the convoy has changed course and is heading straight for the submarine with the probable intention of ramming. The situation is desperate. No time to dive, for she would only be hit an even deadlier blow while on the way down. No time to fire torpedoes—they would only miss anyway. One thing to do—avoid on the surface, and trust to your superior maneuverability to get yourself out of this mess.

"Stand by to ram! Collision quarters! *All ahead emergency!* Right full rudder!" The commands crack from O'Kane's lips. *Tang* gathers way, curves to the right, across the bow of the oncoming transport. The latter alters his course to his left, in order to ram the submarine amidships. At precisely the right instant Dick O'Kane shouts the crucial command—*"Left full rudder!"* and swings his stern out from in front of the onrushing enemy with feet to spare. As he does so, there is the sharp rat-a-tat of machine-gun fire from the huge vessel towering above her, and *Tang's* skipper sends everyone below to avoid danger of injury, remaining on the bridge alone in order to handle the ship.

Again the situation changes with catastrophic suddenness. The transport has had to continue his swing, in order to avoid the freighter which had also attempted to ram. A good chance for a shot! Four torpedoes previously made ready aft for the freighter are still ready. "New setup!" The TBT goes into action once more, and the new fire control information is set into the TDC. "Stand by aft!"

Tang's fire control party sets up the new targets in jig time. "Set below!" comes up to the skipper.

"Fire!" The order comes down instantly. Four torpedoes, spaced ten seconds apart, lurch out of the stern torpedo tubes and head for the careening transport. Suddenly, it becomes obvious that he has not been able to avoid the freighter, and with a rending, groaning crash of tortured and distorted steel the two huge hulks rip into each other—at precisely the instant the four torpedoes fired a moment before begin to hit!

A quarter of a mile away the double-barreled crash is tremendous. And the results are equally spectacular. A fantastic surrealistic V, broad and shallow, composed of two smoking, steaming ships, pitching back and forth in the roiled water of their own devastation, men leaping over the sides, bits of debris falling in the water from the explosions, and a huge pall of smoke from the three burning oil tankers covering it all, wafted like a blanket by the stiff north wind.

As *Tang* races away from the area, it is noticed with astonishment that the total elapsed time of the engagement, in which a whole convoy consisting of five ships has been wiped off the face of the earth, is only ten minutes.

As far as *Tang* is concerned, the fateful 24th of October begins quite normally, and it is not until after dark that the last big convoy is encountered. When contact is made, however, the radar goes wild with pips, and there is no doubt that this is really a big outfit. Dick O'Kane orders the customary tracking procedure prior to the attack and commences the approach to a firing position. *Tang* has eleven torpedoes left on board, and this looks like the perfect chance to get rid of all of them.

But the escort vessels apparently have become suspicious—perhaps news was sent to them of the fate which had overtaken another convoy in this same area yesterday—and commence the unusual tactic of running down the length of the group of ships on opposite course, firing bursts of gunfire. A moment later one of them starts signaling to the massed body of ships with a large search-light—which simply makes it easier for *Tang* to pick out the targets. The near column of three huge ships shows up plainly. The leading two are transports, loaded with irregularly shaped deck gear—evidently landing equipment; the third is a large tanker, also heavily laden.

Tang's crew are at battle stations surface torpedo, of course, and again she employs the familiar tactic of ghosting in, bows pointed at the nearest enemy ship to present the minimum silhouette, at slow speed until the best possible firing position is reached. Surprisingly, in spite of the evident alerted condition of the convoy, there is not the slightest attempt at evasion or zigzag by any of the ships. Maybe they think that the protection of the escort ships is sufficient. If so, they are soon disabused of this idea, for two torpedoes, fired at close range, hit into each of the three ships. Even as the explosions start to come in, *Tang* is swinging around to present her stern tubes at another tanker and cargo carrier moving up astern of the chaps just torpedoed. Steadying on course, the new setup is fed into the fire-control instruments, and the never-failing "Set below!" is sent up to the bridge.

In the meantime, pandemonium has been breaking loose. The abrupt transposition of three of the largest vessels of the convoy into three broken, gutted, sinking hulks has thrown the escorts into a tizzy for fair. They mill around, shooting in all directions, flashing their lights indiscriminately, and, in general, doing their best to add to the confusion already generated. The ships comprising the convoy are so closely packed that maneuvers on their part are virtually impossible, but they do what they can, shoot off their guns wildly also, and make large puffs of black smoke as they try to speed up.

Even as Dick O'Kane on the bridge starts to draw a bead for the stern tube shot, there are splashes all about; someone has spotted the submarine's strange low hull, and has rightly diagnosed it as the cause of all the trouble. Unperturbed, Dick puts in the final shooting bearings, and three torpedoes are fired aft at the two new targets.

As the last fish is fired aft, a whole salvo lands alongside *Tang*, just as the skipper shouts, "All ahead flank!" It is undoubtedly high time that the sub got out of here. The four muttering diesels roar their song of defiance, and four puffs of gray-black smoke pour from the exhaust ports as the submarine's screws bite into the water. O'Kane is intently looking aft at the melee he has brought about, when suddenly a large destroyer looms into sight astern of one of the stricken tankers. This, undoubtedly, is the source of that unpleasantly close salvo. And he surely has a bone in his teeth! So thinks Dick O'Kane, while he watches narrowly, in order to make the decision whether to continue running in hopes of giving this new chap the slip, or dive and take the inevitable beating.

At this moment the torpedoes just fired start hitting. One hits the transport and one hits the tanker, who is evidently laden with aviation gasoline, for he blows up instantly. The destroyer is at the moment coming around the stern of this very ship, and either catches the third torpedo or is set off by the explosion of the nearby tanker, for without warning he is blown sky-high himself. And, consequently free from pursuit, *Tang* races away again to reload her last two torpedoes, completely unscathed.

How many times must Dick O'Kane have wished that he had left well enough alone at this point, but that, of course, was never *Tang*'s style. There are two torpedoes left, and there are still ships afloat; so the two fish are thoroughly checked, and then loaded into the forward torpedo tubes. And how the Fates must have laughed as number twenty-four torpedo slips greasily and treacherously into number four tube!

Tang returns to the scene of the recent action, finds the transport which had been damaged during the last attack low in the water, stopped, but not sinking. Two destroyer escorts are patrolling around her, both to seaward. So Dick orders a wide circle, comes in from the land side slowly and quietly, gets all set, and fires torpedo number twenty-three, which runs straight for the doomed ship, a perfect *coup de grâce*. And then, to make sure of the crippled ship, torpedo number twenty-four is fired.

Instantly, this torpedo is observed to begin a circle to the left!

O'Kane screams down the hatch! *"All ahead emergency!"* Then, a moment later, as the ship commences to gather way, *"Right full rudder!"* There is only one thing to do—get out of the way of the oncoming torpedo. If its rudder has jammed, as appears to be the case, or if the gyro or steering engine has gone haywire, the deadly fish will certainly come back to the point from which it was fired.

Will we make it? The question is almost a prayer to those on the bridge. Down below it is known that something is wrong, but they are used to Dick O'Kane's wild and unorthodox maneuvers. Still, this smacks of a real emergency. Then the word comes down via conning tower telephone:

"Torpedo running circular!"

The slightly phosphorescent wake can be seen, off to port, describing a perfect circle. It curves back toward *Tang*—it looks as if it might hit the bridge—there is nothing anyone can do except hope that it will veer off on another erratic phase. With eyes popping out of their sockets, the men on the bridge stare at the Frankenstein monster they have released coming back to claim them— now it looks as though it will hit aft—still it comes— maybe it will pass astern—here it is—here it is—hold your breath—

WHRANGG! A terrific blow strikes *Tang* in the after torpedo room! Instantly the three after compartments fill, and the ballast tanks in that section of the ship are completely destroyed. The stricken hull of the submarine sinks by the stern immediately, as though it had been held up at the bow and the stern and the stern support had suddenly been removed.

O'Kane gives his last order to the white face of the telephone talker in the conning tower hatch at his feet, staring up at his captain as though somehow he could do something which would prevent this monstrous thing from happening to them. *"Shut the hatch!"* But there is no time to carry out this order, which had been intended to help preserve as much of the watertight integrity of the ship as possible. Even as he utters the words, Dick sees the water of the far western Pacific pour into the swiftly submerging hatch, and he is swept off the bridge of his ship into the Straits of Formosa.

And, as he comes to the surface, sputtering and splashing in the choppy but warm salty water, he sees two things—a flash of fire in the distance, followed by the sound of torpedo number twenty-three striking home in the transport which had been his last target, and the gray bow of *Tang* sticking out of water, still buoyant, though the stern of the ship must be on the bottom. His first thought for his crew, O'Kane notes that the torpedo tubes are all under water and that an attempt to escape via that route—assuming that there must have been some men in the forward part of the ship who survived the fatal explosion—could not succeed, and would only result in flooding the forward torpedo room and preventing all chance of escape.

He looks around in the water and counts heads. There are eight in the water with him, like himself swept off the bridge when that part of the ship went under. Only one thing to do now. His heart like lead within him, Dick O'Kane keeps himself afloat, using the minimum possible effort. The instinct of self-preservation dies hard, even though there may not seem to be much left to live for. Every now and then the captain glances back to the bow of his ship, still exposed above the surface. After about five minutes the head of a man appears in the water alongside, and Lieutenant Larry Savadkin swims over and joins the pitiful party of survivors. He had gone down with the ship, inside the conning tower. Finding a tiny pocket where air had been entrapped, he had pressed his mouth into it, taken what breaths he could, and then moved to the still-open hatch, where he found another air pocket. Still another one was under the bridge overhang, and, stopping there for several moments, he had finally ducked out and swum to the surface.

This story he repeats to O'Kane between gasps in the choppy sea. And as he is telling it, there comes a sudden burbling of air from alongside the protruding bow of *Tang*, and it swiftly sinks from sight.

The captain stares, and his heart leaps within him. That was not accidental! That looked as though one of the undamaged ballast tanks had been deliberately flooded, in order to level off the submarine. True, she would sink to the bottom, but she would be on an even keel, the men trapped inside would have a fighting chance to get out! Wild, hopeless plans race through his brain. Maybe enough of his crew will get out to form a good-sized party. Maybe they will be able to capture some small vessel, and in some way arrive intact at some part of the Chinese coast not under Jap domination. Or maybe there will be some way of contacting a friendly submarine.

But nothing comes of it, though O'Kane watches throughout the remainder of the night. The first thing which should come up is the escape buoy, and that he never sees. Japanese patrol boats make their appearance about this time, and they run about, dropping occasional depth charges. Perhaps these explosions have temporarily dissuaded the rest of *Tang*'s crew from attempting to escape. . . .

Dawn finally arrived, and a Japanese destroyer escort picked up O'Kane and several others, who were immediately subjected to merciless beatings and clubbings—hardly what would have been meted out to Jap submariners had the positions been reversed. Of the ten men left floating about in the water when *Tang* went down, including the one who made his escape from the conning tower, only four were ultimately recovered from Japanese prison camps.

And what of the men who remained alive inside the submarine, who leveled her off on the bottom to make it possible for them to escape? Their story is equally tragic.

By quick action they had managed to seal the afterpart of the ship, confine the flooding to the after engine room, maneuvering room, and after torpedo room. The men in the control room, directly beneath the conning tower, had been able to close the hatch between those two compartments, thus localizing the flooding through the open upper conning tower hatch to that compartment alone, but not before considerable water had found its way into the control room; and since the lower conning tower hatch had been sprung by the terrific force of the explosion, it leaked badly and could not be made tight. Then they opened the vent valve to number-two main ballast tank, using the hand operating gear, since hydraulic power had also been lost, and by this means lowered the bow of the ship to the bottom. They were thus in an excellent position for escape. The ship was in 180 feet of water, not too far from the coast of China. They had by no means despaired.

The next operation was to burn all the confidential and secret papers, which was accomplished at the expense of filling the control room and forward battery compartment with smoke. Much of this smoke also entered the forward torpedo room, an unfortunate circumstance. At about this time depth charging commenced, and all escape operations came to a standstill for several hours until it ceased. In the meantime, all survivors gathered in the forward torpedo room, about thirty in all, and they were forced to seal off the door to the battery compartment and the rest of the ship because of progressive flooding from the control room and an electrical fire which had started in the forward battery compartment. This fire increased in intensity, and finally prevented successful escape of many men who otherwise could have got out.

In all, four parties left the ship, using the Momsen lung, via the escape hatch built into the forward torpedo room. Owing to the great pressure due to the depth, this process was laborious, and the men, already debilitated from the effects of the foul air and smoke fumes they had been breathing, suffered exceedingly. Toward the end, the heat from the fire in the forward battery compartment had begun to blister the paint on the after bulkhead of the torpedo room, and puffs of acrid smoke were coming past the door, where the rubber gasket itself was burning. Steadily increasing pressure in the battery compartment, due to slow flooding, also helped to destroy this gasket. Finally, the inevitable happened—the gasket blew out, or was burned out, and all men remaining in the forward torpedo room were asphyxiated.

Thirteen men made an underwater escape from *Tang*'s forward torpedo room several hours after she went down, but only five were picked up by the Japs the next morning. Five of them had never reached the surface, and three, evidently suffering some form of the bends, had been unable to remain afloat.

Of the crew of eighty-eight men and officers, only nine in all came back.

We of the Submarine Force grieved silently, as men are wont to do, at the news that *Tang* was no more. With submarines, this news is not the sudden receipt of specific information; it is the gradual realization that it is a day or two since a certain ship should have reported in from patrol. It is the intensified waiting, hoping against hope that some inconsequential matter, such as a broken-down radio transmitter, might prove to be the cause of the silence. You hear the chatter of messages from boats on patrol, going out, or coming back, reporting contacts, requesting rendezvous, or reporting results to date, but never do you hear the faint, clipped call from the vessel you listen for—never the *right* message comes in over the burdened ether waves. Finally, since it is possible that some casualty may have prevented transmission, although reception of radio signals might still be possible, a "blind" rendezvous is arranged for the nonreporting ship. A message is sent repeatedly, giving the place and setting a period for arrival of the submarine which is within the realm of possibility if the lost boat is still alive. Then an escort vessel is sent out, to wait—and wait—and finally to return, empty-handed. And then you *know* what has happened, and you take the missing boat's name off the operations board, trying to pretend that the lump in your throat doesn't exist, that your action in so doing cannot be considered to have any relationship to what has happened out there.

And, as it was with all the others, so was it with *Tang*. We knew only that she was gone, leaving to the rest of us a legacy of consistent aggressiveness, success, and daring. But after a few months some rather odd stories began to be bruited about. *Tang* had single-handedly taken on a huge convoy, with many escorting destroyers, in shallow water. *Tang* had shot the hell out of the enemy, but had been caught in water so shallow that, upon diving, she struck bottom before the top of the periscope shears went under—and thus was easy meat for an enraged enemy. *Tang* had deliberately entered an enemy harbor at night on the surface, expended all her torpedoes on the anchored Jap ships, and been caught by shore batteries on her way out. *Tang* had been so damaged by a furious depth charging she had undergone in shallow water that she was unable to dive, and had been forced to scuttle herself upon the arrival of enemy forces. And so on.

But all stories seemed to agree on three particulars—great damage to the enemy, shallow water, and *Dick O'Kane in a Jap prison camp!* Knowing the cool daring of which O'Kane and *Tang* were capable, the absolute fearlessness of their tactics, and the unprecedented, original, and completely logical thinking they had time after time demonstrated—a quality partly inherited, no doubt, from Mush Morton and *Wahoo*—it was impossible to conceive of a set of circumstances which would fit all the reported details. But we knew that *Tang*'s last mission had been fraught with more than usual secrecy—and so we wondered, until Dick O'Kane himself came back from the living dead, his starved and bruised body a testimonial to the brutality of his captors, to give us the story of those last glorious moments of *Tang*'s short but action-packed life.

13

TRIGGER

WHILE *TANG WAS GOING* into commission at Mare Island, *Trigger* completed her refit following Dusty Dornin's second patrol, and on Christmas Day, 1943, was scheduled to leave for the area of Truk. "Christmas Day," we moaned. "Surely the war is not going to be lost or won by our departure on that day." It took a strong protest to ComSubPac himself, but finally he agreed that Trigger had earned her first Christmas in port.

We got under way the following day, and in little more than a week took station on a convoy route between Guam and Truk. Here, for the first time, *Trigger*'s luck at finding targets turned sour.

For nearly a month we plied the traffic lanes. Nothing whatever did we see, except an occasional plane or various brightly colored ocean birds, until two or three days before shortage of fuel would have started us back to Pearl Harbor. And then early one evening the sonar operator thought he heard something in his earphones. He listened intently. There could be no doubt of it. There had been an explosion in the water many miles away. And then another.

Fandel, onetime country schoolteacher, marked the

time, listened a little longer, marked the time once more, and then called for the skipper. "Captain," he reported, "somebody is dropping periodic depth charges. Listen."

Sometimes Jap convoy escorts dropped depth charges periodically as they steamed along. Doubtless the idea was to discourage submarines from attacking. Its success depended on whose area they were in.

Dusty and I heard the fifth and sixth explosions. They seemed to be a little louder to the south.

"All ahead flank!" The soft mutter of one diesel engine pushing us along at slow speed was suddenly augmented by three more. Four plumes of smoke poured from *Trigger's* exhaust ports onto the surface of the ocean, and a white tumbled wake stretched farther aft. On the bridge seven pairs of high-powered binoculars searched the dimming horizon, and above them the radar rotated slowly. For ten miles we let the ship run.

"All stop! Secure the engines!" *Trigger* coasted, silenced, slowing. "Rig out the sound heads!"

The pressure-proof speaker on the bridge blared: "Bridge! Sound reports distant depth charges dead ahead!"

"All ahead flank!" We were getting closer. It was now dark, and as *Trigger* picked up speed once more, we carefully adjusted the radar, peaked its tuning and ring time. We concentrated it dead ahead with occasional sweeps sideways to prevent being taken by surprise. For a long time it showed nothing. Finally, *"Radar contact!"* Ralph Korn, now chief yeoman, with the simplicity of long practice swung into the routine of feeding the essential information from the radar to the tracking parties. When combined with the known inputs of *Trigger's* own course and speed the result was target course and speed—data essential to the correct torpedo fire-control solution.

"Conn! What speed we showing?"

"Twenty and a half, sir! Picking up slowly!"

"Bridge! We're overtaking them on their port flank—range now about twelve. Can you see them?" We peered ahead. Nothing.

Trigger continued to eat up the distance on the enemy's left flank, reaching out ahead to get into attack position. With Dusty working out the fire-control solution and handling things from the conning tower, I held the bridge and strained my eyes to spot targets. With my back against the rotating radar mast, I could tell from its motion when it was on the target. A glance at the antenna, and I knew exactly where to look.

Hours passed. Finally I could make out a faint place on the horizon where the haze was a little darker. "Conn—bridge. Enemy in sight. Stand by for a TBT bearing!"

I jammed my binoculars into the TBT, centered on the smudge, pressed the button. The skipper's rasping voice came back: "That's him. How many can you see?"

I could see three smudges now, and my stomach tightened when the word came back that there were, indeed, three large ships on the radar, plus three much smaller ones that I couldn't see.

An hour and a half later we had pretty well overreached on the convoy, and Dusty's voice came up on the speaker. "Ned—what do you think—can we go in on the surface?"

This was the question I had been trying to make up my mind about for the past half hour. We could see them, but we were still too far away for them to see us. Maybe a quick surprise attack could be executed before they could get organized; dawn was already not too many hours off, and we could make a surface attack much sooner than we could possibly get off a submerged one.

The skipper was of the same mind, and so a few minutes later, having attained a position broad on the bow of the zigzagging convoy's base course, *Trigger* turned her lean snout toward the enemy.

This was always the crucial part of the night surface attack—the run in. You kept your bows on the enemy to give him as little to see of you as possible, and you came in fast to get it over with quickly. Then, just before shooting, you had to slow down to let the fish get away properly. Having put your torpedoes in the water, you spun on your heel and ran, trusting to the confusion generated by exploding warheads to help you get away. If there were escorts present, the problem was complicated by the necessity to come in more or less under their sterns, where they would have to turn all the way around to get at you.

The engines were still wide open, and now we and the Japs were approaching each other at our combined speeds. At a closing rate of 35 knots it didn't take long.

"Range, three five double oh!"

"All tubes ready forward!"

"All ahead one third—stand by forward!" The last from the skipper.

I had been keeping my eyes on the nearest escort, a large mean-looking destroyer. No sign yet of his having seen us, but he surely knew his job, for he was patrolling the convoy's quarter and thus making our shot at the big ships very difficult. To get at the big fellows we would have to shoot right across the tin can's bow—then we would have to let him have it also, because he was too close and would be upon us in a matter of minutes. Radar gave range to the tin can as seven hundred yards—broadside to, dead ahead.

A ticklish decision, quickly made. The first three fish at the nearest big ship and the next three at the tin can. That would not give us much time. . . .

"We're shooting now, Bridge!" That wasn't necessary, for I could hear Dusty shout, "Fire!" *Trigger* lurched three times, as three times a ton and a half was ejected from bow tubes. Three streaks of bubbles in a long, thin fan reached for the last transport. Now for the destroyer. "Fire four! . . . Fire five! . . . Fire six!"

"Right full rudder!" I screamed. Number four barely missed ahead. Number five ran erratically to the left, and number six circled to the right. No hits! The destroyer fired three green flares off his stern, started to turn toward us. From somewhere amidships a gun went off, and there was a sharp ripping sound overhead.

Two things to do: avoid those deadly circling torpedoes, and get out of the immediate vicinity. I put my face against the bridge speaker, pressed the button. "Maneuvering, he's after us! Pour it on!" A rather unorthodox order, but it got results.

In the engine room one man knelt by each engine governor, holding it in by hand as he increased engine speed beyond the limits. In the maneuvering room the already overloaded motors and generators were loaded down even more. A cloud of black smoke poured out of our exhaust pipes as *Trigger*'s stern skidded across the slight chop.

"Rudder amidships!" We steadied with our stern dead on the destroyer. With the smoke riding high into the air astern, we could hardly see him.

"Stand by aft! Bridge, give me bearings on the tin can!"

"Bearing—mark!"

"Fire!" And four torpedoes sped from our stern.

We had to hand it to that tin can skipper for a neat job of sidestepping. Not one touched him though they must have streaked by on both sides.

But at any rate they held him up for a bit, and in the meantime *Trigger* was showing a shade under 22 knots. And then came a most welcome sound—depth charges! Not realizing that we could not possibly have dived, that we must have run off on the surface, the destroyer had ceased gunfire and was depth charging the area. Our respect for his acumen diminished appreciably.

Meanwhile, our first three fish had evidently not hit their target, perhaps due to a zig executed when the flares went off. But as we watched—and ran—a heavy flash of light suddenly showed up alongside one of the other escorts, a cloud of smoke appeared over him, and he disappeared. Not what we had been after, but at least we were not completely empty-handed.

Suddenly I realized that Dusty was standing beside me on the bridge. I pointed out the locations of the enemy convoy, the sunken destroyer, and our friend sowing ash cans astern.

He took it all in in an instant, then leaned against the speaker button. "Plot, give me a course to intercept the main body!"

"One six five, Bridge!" Plot was right on its toes.

"Left full rudder! New course one six five!" Dusty bawled the order down the hatch to the helmsman. *Trigger* heeled to starboard, and off we dashed after our fast-escaping quarry.

It soon developed that the Japs had upped their speed about 2 knots, and that we would be lucky to get close enough for another shot before dawn. Dornin set his jaw in characteristic fury, hurled imprecations into the murky grayness, and drove on insanely after the three plainly visible transports. We had been nearly an hour in chase when the radar, which we had kept periodically checking on the Nip destroyer left behind, reported that he was now under way at high speed in our direction. In a few minutes, however, Plot announced that he was apparently not chasing us, but merely rejoining the main body.

Sure enough, this particular Jap evidently still could not see. He swept past us at moderately long range with never a sign of recognition and took station with his convoy once more.

Trigger continued to pound along, hardly hoping to attain another firing position before daybreak, but Dusty was unwilling to give up while some chance remained. It looked pretty hopeless, because the light in the east was becoming too obvious to be ignored. But suddenly the three large silhouettes, which had been quite foreshortened as we viewed them from astern, broadened sharply. Zig left, in the direction of Truk. Just what we had been hoping for. It was now or never.

"Bridge! Bearing on the nearest one!" That was Dusty down below again, and from the preparatory commands floating up the hatch, he was getting ready to shoot. The biggest and nearest target happened to be the right-hand ship, the last one in the column. I trained the TBT exactly on his fat stack—and put the finger on *Yasukuni Maru*.

We fired at long range, but we hit him fair, and he sank in half an hour. One destroyer remained with him, picking up survivors, else we'd have tried to save a few ourselves. The other two ships turned their sterns toward us and disappeared over the fast-lightening horizon.

We returned to Pearl Harbor rather crestfallen. This was the first time in about two years that *Trigger* had brought back torpedoes from patrol. We had been a little spoiled by success, and this time we experienced some of the frustrations of many of our sisters. Nearing the entrance to Pearl, we decided to slip in with the minimum of bombast, and we flew no cockscomb.

Our idea of not attracting attention while entering did not fare too well. Several ships in the harbor blew their whistles as our weather-beaten ship glided past, and several exchanged calls with us by searchlight. Then as we neared the Navy Yard, and commenced the turnaround "Ten Ten" dock to approach the submarine base, we found a great crowd of people gathered around the berth which had been assigned to us. In some consternation we spotted Admiral Lockwood and his entire staff, many of CincPac Staff including the chief of staff, and other high-ranking officers in the crowd. Amazed, Dusty and I decided there had been some mistake; but there was none. And after the first few minutes of vigorous hand-pumping we found out why.

There were two good reasons why we had rated such a welcoming committee. Our intelligence service had just discovered that Admiral Lockwood's opposite number in the Japanese Submarine Force, ComJapSubPac, had been on board the ship we had sunk and had gone down with it. This type of blow touched everyone's sense of dramatic values.

The second reason was that Admiral King had asked ComSubPac to send his most outstanding submarine commander to be his personal aide in Washington. The demise of ComJapSubPac had made the answer to that question an easy one. Dusty's orders were handed him as our gangway was extended to us from the dock.

But Dusty, a great submariner, was not removed from

action merely as a reward for services rendered. Com-SubPac long ago had decided to relieve his skippers while they still were going great guns, before the terrific physical and emotional strain began to tell. Undoubtedly this policy often resulted in relieving a skipper who had several fine patrols left in him, but this was infinitely better than the reverse—keeping him too long on the firing line. If such a policy had been enforced at the time, the loss of Mush Morton and *Wahoo* might have been averted.

14

ALBACORE and CAVALLA

ONE OF THE MOST successful instances of collaboration between our submarine forces and the surface fleets took place at the First Battle of the Philippine Sea. Several subs were involved, but the two principal actors were *Albacore* and *Cavalla*.

Jim Blanchard and Herman Kossler would probably both tell you today that collaboration was furthest from their minds on the 19th of June 1944. Although each knew of the other's presence in the general vicinity, the fact that together they would deprive the Imperial Japanese Navy of two of its largest first-line aircraft carriers would have seemed the height of the unexpected to both of them. Curiously, *Taiho* and *Shokaku* were virtually sister ships, although the former was the newer by about two years and carried the latest improvements in design; and they were sunk on the same day—almost within sight of each other—by sister submarines. *Cavalla* was about two years newer than *Albacore*, but our standardization of design was such that the two were almost identical.

To *Albacore* and Jim Blanchard, veterans of many submarine war patrols, fell the brand-new, unseasoned *Taiho*.

A few hours later Herman Kossler and his *Cavalla*, both fresh out of the building yard, got the veteran carrier *Shokaku*.

So it was that the First Battle of the Philippine Sea found only three large Japanese carriers opposed to our seven, which perhaps was part of the reason why our airmen knew that battle as the "Marianas Turkey Shoot."

This story really starts on June 14. *Albacore* was on her ninth war patrol, operating in the area between Yap and Guam. For the past two days she had experienced heavy wind and seas, and consequently was behind schedule. Another submarine had reported damaging a ship in a convoy apparently en route for her area, and Jim Blanchard had bent on everything but the galley range in his effort to get into position to intercept. His chances looked pretty poor because of the bad weather, but he hung on grimly, running at full speed on the surface, hoping that the convoy also might have been delayed.

On the afternoon of the 14th, however, a message from ComSubPac directed Jim to discontinue the chase and to proceed to a point in almost the exact opposite direction. Since the submariner always works on the theory that the bird in the hand is worth several still in the bush, and since there still seemed to be hope of catching the elusive convoy, it was with some disappointment that Jim reversed course.

Not quite seven hours later another message was decoded in *Albacore*'s wardroom: she was to proceed to yet another spot for patrol. Again Blanchard ordered the course changed, and off they went to the new station. By this time there was little doubt in the skipper's mind that something was happening—or about to happen.

All day long, on the 15th, *Albacore* patrolled assiduously back and forth, never straying more than a few miles from her station, and remaining constantly on the surface in order to increase her search radius. All day long also Blanchard drilled his crew at battle stations for what he hardly dared hope might come his way. A careful check of all messages received in the radio room was kept, and many, addressed to other submarines, were decoded. Pieced together—and then scrupulously destroyed, for you aren't required to decode any messages except those addressed to you—they spelled out that something big was in the wind, and that *Albacore* was one of several submarines to be placed in what looked like strategic positions.

At 0800 on June 18th a message arrived for *Albacore*, ordering her to shift position about one hundred miles to the southward. This itself was encouraging, for it showed that whatever was expected had not yet happened somewhere else, and that ComSubPac was keeping his fine hand right in the deal. Jim Blanchard sent his submarine south at full speed.

When June 19th arrived, things had so built up in the minds of the crew that most of them *knew* this was to be the day.

The feeling was not at all discouraged by the detection of two aircraft on the radar at 0430. *Albacore* promptly dived.

At 0700, the critical period of dawn with its tricky visibility past, she was again on the surface. And at 0716 a Jap patrol plane was sighted by an alert lookout, and once again the submarine dived.

Now sighting three aircraft within such a short interval usually indicates that something interesting is about to come along, for the Japs don't have enough airplanes to waste in indiscriminant area search.

And so it proves. At 0750 ships are sighted. It is still pretty hazy to the west in the direction of the contact, and for a moment the skipper cannot make out what they are—but only for a moment.

"Battle stations submerged!" Before his eyes Jim Blanchard has the submariner's dream come true—an enemy task force. Through the periscope he can see a huge aircraft carrier of the largest class; at least one cruiser, maybe more; and several other ships, some of them no doubt destroyers. It is given to very few submariners to see this sight and to be on the spot with a well-drilled crew, your torpedoes ready in the tubes, your battery warm with a full charge just completed.

"Left full rudder! All ahead flank!" The helmsman leans into the wheel and at the same time reaches up to the two annunciators and rings them over to the position marked FLANK. Men are still tumbling up from below, racing to their battle stations under the stimulus of the alarm, and Lieutenant Commander Ben Adams, *Albacore*'s exec, takes over the job of periscope jockey.

Blanchard's initial observation has shown the carrier's angle on the bow to be seventy degrees port, range about seven miles. It's going to be an all-out race to get to a firing position, and if the enemy is making any speed at all, reaching him *will* be an impossibility, barring a radical zig toward.

"Up periscope!" Time for another look. Also, better take a careful look around. The situation is developing very fast, and you've got to keep the whole picture in your mind as fast as it develops, for you are the eyes and the brains.

The target should bear on the starboard bow, but the skipper suddenly switches his attention to something on the starboard beam. He quickly completes a 360-degree sweep, motions for the periscope to be lowered, and orders, "Right full rudder!"

His exec looks at him questioningly. As all executive officers and assistant approach officers should do, he has mentally visualized the relative positions of his ship and the enemy. Turning to the right is obviously the wrong maneuver for the situation as he knows it. But he does not have to wonder long.

"Another flattop! This one's coming right down the groove. All we have to do is wait for him!"

Both men know the same thought: What a pity that there is only one submarine here. One carrier is sure to get away. The flattops are too far apart for an attack on both, even assuming that the submarine would be able to reach the first one. There is not even any argument about it: The thing to do is take the one which gives you the better shot, and worry about the other one later. As a matter of fact, the decision has already been made, and *Albacore* is even now turning for an approach on the carrier more recently sighted.

"Give me a course for a seventy track!" Blanchard spent many years in the old "S-boats," which had no TDC, and this is S-boat procedure, usually glossed over by skippers brought up in the fleet boats where you only have to glance at the TDC to have the whole picture right before your eyes.

Ben Adams has a small plastic gadget called an Is-Was hung around his neck. Consisting of a series of concentric compass roses of different diameters, plus a bearing indicator, it enables the assistant approach officer to keep

track of the problem without a TDC to help him. It got its
name from the fact that you can set it up for where the
target is, and see from it where he *was*—and thus determine where he probably will be. At the skipper's orders,
Adams picks up the Is-Was and starts turning the two
upper dials. In a moment he announces, "Zero three zero,
Captain."

"Steady on zero three zero!" *Albacore* is still swinging to
the hard-over right rudder, and the helmsman eases the
rudder slightly. A few seconds after the ship is steady on
the course.

Another periscope observation. The range is now
9,000 yards. Distance to track, 2,300 yards—the enemy
will pass 2,300 yards from *Albacore*'s present position, if
he doesn't change course. Angle on the bow, fifteen starboard.

A minute later the periscope whirs upward again, then
slithers downward. "Left full rudder!" Blanchard barks
the order, then briefly explains it.

"There's a destroyer between us and the carrier. He has
a ten-degree starboard angle on the bow, which means
he'll pass fairly close to us. We'll change to north for a
while to let him go by, and then come around for the big
fellow. No zig yet."

One of the customs of the submarine service is that of
continually cutting in your control party on what is going
on. Doubtless this grew out of everyone's desire for the
dope—and the fact that the person at the periscope is the
only one in position to have any.

So Jim Blanchard needs no prodding, and gives with
more dope as soon as he makes another observation.
"The can has zigged slightly away and now has a forty
starboard angle on the bow. He'll pass well clear. We're

coming around to get set up for the flattop. Give me a course for a ninety track!" The last is a command addressed to Ben Adams.

"Zero five zero, Captain!" Ben has been expecting that, and he has the answer ready. A ninety track means that the submarine course and target course are at exactly right angles to each other—the perfect position.

"Steady on zero five zero, sir!" from the helmsman. Blanchard glances at the TDC. The range has certainly closed fast. There isn't much longer to go.

Suddenly a squawk box—a regular commercial interoffice speaker mounted above and alongside the TDC—announces with a tinny voice: "Conn, this is Plot. Target course one four zero, speed two seven—repeat, speed two seven!"

This is the confirmation the skipper has been waiting for. "Set in speed two seven!" he snaps at Lieutenant Ted Walker, operating the TDC.

The latter swiftly whirls a small crank with his left hand, stops it carefully, and sings out, "Set!"

"Up 'scope!" Then, "Looks good! All clear around! Nobody close aboard! Make ready all tubes!" There isn't time to spare now, and Jim makes no effort to describe what he has just seen. *Albacore* is well inside the formation. The destroyer recently avoided is about one thousand yards dead ahead, evidently oblivious of the submarine's presence. He has been heard to echo range listlessly once or twice; you can't blame his lack of interest, for at 27 knots he'd be lucky to hear anything anyhow. A heavy cruiser is crossing *Albacore*'s stern, and the cruiser and carrier first sighted are about three miles away on her starboard quarter. Two destroyers on the target's own starboard quarter look as though they will be in the best position to give a little trouble, but Jim plans to shoot before they can get up to him. Quite a few planes are in the air, and that adds to the problem, for if the submarine is detected now things will go to hell in a hurry. The carrier needs but to turn hard left to stay nicely out of torpedo range, while those two tin cans with him could keep right on coming. Not to mention another destroyer who, if he puts *his* rudder hard *right*, will pass directly over *Albacore*.

Albacore plans to shoot bow tubes, and has so handled the approach; stern tubes are made ready also simply to be prepared for anything. The carrier might zig across her stern, for example, although not a zig has he made so far—he probably is trusting to his high speed to protect him from attack.

"All tubes ready, Captain. Depth set, speed high. Ready to shoot!" As the report is made, the familiar quietness settles in the conning tower. Here comes the biggest chance *Albacore* has ever had. The value of this particular target is incalculable. The very sequence of messages during the past week has proved that. ComSubPac doesn't know yet that one of his submarines has made contact, but he certainly bent every effort to dispose enough submarines along the anticipated track to insure that someone would. Now that he has brought this particular submarine into action, however, it is up to Jim Blanchard and his *Albacore* to take their turn at shaping destiny.

Jim Blanchard squats on his heels before the lowered periscope. He doesn't need to look at the TDC—those years in S-boats have given him the ability to visualize the setup without any mechanical help.

"Six five feet," he orders. The previous order had been

sixty-four feet; now he goes down as deep as he can, leaving only a few inches of periscope exposure.

"Up periscope!" The strident whirring of the electric hoist motor fills the conning tower.

"I figure we'll be on the firing point in one minute, Captain!" This from the executive officer. "Recommend we let them go any time!"

Jim Blanchard motions impatiently. He, too, has figured that out. He squats before the periscope, facing the shiny oily barrel, then raises his head and looks at the members of his fire-control party. Not a word is spoken; all eyes are on the skipper.

Something in their bearing tells Jim what he wants to know. No question about their readiness. As the periscope handles rise into his hands, he speaks softly: "Final bearing and shoot!"

"Stand by number one!" The fire control talker speaks into his telephone mouthpiece. Then he speaks louder, so that the whole party in the crowded conning tower can hear him—"Standing by ONE!"—signifying that the people in the forward torpedo room have the word and are ready.

The ship's control talker speaks softly into his telephone headset. "We're getting ready to shoot now. Final bearing going in!" This is unofficial but very understandable, and it is not known that any skipper ever objected to it.

In the after port corner of the conning tower, squeezed into a space barely large enough to stand in, the ship's torpedo and gunnery officer is attentively watching the spinning dials of the TDC. It is Ted Walker's responsibility that that instrument is correctly lined up, and this, of course, is the crucial point. Suddenly he starts. "CHECK

FIRE!" he bellows. "Correct solution light has gone out!"

"Stop the periscope!" The tip of the 'scope has not yet broken the surface, and Jim stops it where it is, in hopes that the trouble can be quickly discovered and fixed.

The target is sliding by the firing point at 27 knots. It is already too late for the "Banjo" solution—veteran S-boat sailor that he is, Blanchard has not neglected to have the old angle solver broken out and set up also, together with the TDC. But there is no hope for it, for with the target's high speed there is not the slightest possibility of swinging the ship fast enough to catch up with him.

Only one thing to do, if you don't want to let the target get away. If you put up the periscope and feed continuous dope into the TDC, perhaps you can keep close enough to the correct solution to go ahead and shoot anyway, with a good chance of hitting. If the light is merely burned out, this does no harm; if there is something seriously wrong with your gear, this is the only hope anyway.

But this has the tremendous disadvantage of requiring you to keep the periscope up for a very long period. Two destroyers are tearing down upon you in close quarters; they will surely spot you, and be on you within seconds after you get the torpedoes away. Your only hope of nailing the carrier is to be so close that he doesn't have time to turn away to parallel the torpedo wakes—which he certainly will do as soon as he sees them—which means as soon as he spots the 'scope.

Blanchard has had about ten seconds to figure all this out. He cannot wait any longer. The risks, the odds, all facets of what he is about to do flash through his mind. This is a desperate chance he is about to take, and he is putting his ship and his fine loyal crew into grave danger. The carrier, and all that that ship might mean to other

United States forces—Jim must make the decision alone, without help, and instantly!

"Up periscope!" Since it had been stopped just short of breaking surface, it is up almost instantly. "Continuous bearings!" Jim snarls the words as though by their defiance alone he could straighten out the trouble in the TDC. "Sing 'em out, Ben; I'm going to stay right on him!"

Adams starts chanting the bearings as they are matched on the azimuth circle by the hairline on the periscope barrel. "Three three eight—three three nine—three four one . . ."

"Set!—Set!—Set!" from Walker. He has had to make only slight adjustments to his computer. The TDC is following all right, so the trouble is in the angle-solver sections. Possibly the small red light which indicates that the TDC is operating properly has merely burned out, and nothing is actually wrong at all.

Blanchard hazards a quick look at the two destroyers coming along behind the target. No definite sign that anyone has yet spotted *Albacore*'s periscope, despite the long, continuous exposure from close aboard—but it's hard to tell, because the two DD's are bows on anyway.

The skipper's mind is working like lightning. Apparently there is still a chance of avoiding detection, if he doesn't persist in the attack and gets the periscope down immediately. Whatever is wrong with the TDC is either deep-seated or completely inconsequential. If deep-seated—the torpedoes will probably miss by a wide margin; if it is simply a burned-out bulb, he can go ahead and shoot. But somehow he *knows* the trouble is more than a burned-out lightbulb!

Jim Blanchard seizes upon the one thing left to him by which he can rescue his approach from dismal failure.

The huge Japanese carrier, obviously one of the biggest class—the *Shokaku* or one similar—is now right at the firing point, racing past with all his majestic glory, completely unaware of the ominous periscope in the water so close to his starboard side. So near, and yet so unattainable! So near . . . and Jim decides to take that last desperate chance which may yet bring victory out of seemingly hopeless confusion.

"Stand by forward! Stand by ONE!"

"One standing by!"

"Bearing—*mark!*" The skipper has moved the periscope hairline slightly, now holds it perfectly motionless. His voice is loud, commanding.

"Three four eight!" from the executive officer.

"Set!" from the TDC.

"FIRE ONE!"

"One fired, sir!" This is something new in the way of procedure for firing torpedoes. Ordinarily they are fired from the TDC, as the fire control officer gets the instrument set up for each succeeding fish and as the proper time interval passes. The captain has deliberately taken over firing the torpedoes himself, and, by his specific commands, has completely contravened the training they all have had.

It is normal, too, to put the periscope down as you are shooting torpedoes, at least between fish. But Jim Blanchard is not putting down his periscope. Suddenly he speaks again.

"Stand by TWO!"

"Number two standing by, sir!"

The skipper moves his periscope to the right a perceptible amount, stops it, and says, *"Mark!"*

"Three five five!"

"SET."

"FIRE TWO!" And number-two torpedo ejects and runs out toward the enemy.

"Stand by THREE. . . . "Bearing—mark!" . . . "Fire THREE!"

"Stand by FOUR!" . . . "Bearing—mark!" . . . "Fire FOUR!" . . . "Fire FIVE!" . . . "Fire SIX!"

What Blanchard has done, quite simply, is to watch where each torpedo goes, and then compensate for it in aiming the next one. Since he is firing steam torpedoes, it is possible to tell where they are going by their telltale stream of bubbles and the small amount of smoke they make. In each case it has been obvious to the skipper that the torpedoes were passing astern of the target, and in each case he has had to compensate by aiming more to the right. The final bearing of the sixth torpedo was quite a bit on the starboard bow and considerably ahead of the target.

Now there are six torpedoes in the water, and there is nothing left for *Albacore* to do but get away and hope that one or more may strike home. But first a look at the on-rushing destroyers. Jim Blanchard spins his periscope.

"Take her down! Take her down *fast!*" The skipper roars the orders through the lower conning tower hatch to the diving officer in the control room just below. "All ahead full!"

He is answered by the swoosh of air as negative tank is vented into the control room. *Albacore*'s deck tilts steeply forward, and down she rushes. Just before the periscope goes under, the skipper sees three destroyers heading his way, and the airplanes which had been flying overhead have apparently turned and headed for the spot from which the torpedoes had come.

Much as Jim wishes to, there is simply no time to wait and see whether any of his torpedoes hit. He has taken enough chances with his ship and crew already, and it would not be fair to expose them further. Nothing he can do now will change matters, and the obvious maneuver is the well-known *get the hell out of here!*

Down goes *Albacore*, struggling to reach the friendly depths before the ash cans arrive. Throughout the ship her crew are feverishly rigging for depth-charge attack.

Thirty seconds after the periscope goes under, while the submarine is still speeding to deep submergence, a single explosion is heard. One hit! In spite of all the troubles he has had, *Albacore* has managed to get one fish into the target. That will slow him up some. Then the preliminary gladness is submerged in bitterness. A perfect firing position, with six fish fired, for only one hit! *Damn* that fire control system!

So much for the Japanese carrier, for one minute later *Albacore* has something else to think about. Payday arrives with a flourish. Jim Blanchard has, of course, left his periscope up entirely too long. The nearest enemy tin can could not have been more than five or six hundred yards away when *Albacore* completed firing her torpedoes, and is coming for her with express-train speed.

The frenzied beating of the destroyer's propellers resound through the submarine's hull as he races closer. Somehow, there is nothing to compare with the furious menacing cadence of the propellers of an anti-submarine warfare ship of any kind—especially when that particular ASW vessel would have words with you.

With his stopwatch in hand, Commander Jim Blanchard listens as the roar of the enemy screws grows louder, louder, ever more deadly in timbre, until finally it reaches a screaming crescendo of churning, malevolent, revengeful fury; until the very bulkheads vibrate with it, the THUMTHUMTHUMTHUMTHUM coming in such rapid sequence that *Albacore*'s whole hull resounds to it like a huge tuning fork—and then he starts the watch, holding it negligently in his hand, its leather thong looped around his left wrist. No point in looking at the watch—he keeps his eyes on the depth gauge. The submarine is still on her way down, seeking the protection of a few hundred feet of seawater between herself and the attacking destroyer.

With the watch perhaps Jim can get some kind of line on the depth settings the Jap is using. It takes almost as long for the depth charges to go off, once you're reasonably sure the enemy has dropped some, as it does for your torpedoes once they're fired, with the difference that you know exactly when the torpedoes get in the water. It's getting about *that time* now. The skipper is holding his watch hand more attentively . . .

WHAM! . . . WHAM! . . . WHAM! . . . *WHAM!* . . . *WHAM!* . . . WHAM!

Six beauties, evenly spaced and expertly dropped. The fourth and fifth are real humdingers. *Albacore*'s finely attuned steel hull shivers throughout her length with a hundred discordant frequencies. Lightbulbs dance around on the ends of their short cords, and a few of them shatter. Dust and particles of cork fill the air. One or two men are flung sprawling to the deck.

The destroyer proceeds across on his run and turns for another, slowing his propeller beat not one revolution. Overhead he comes again, dead on as before, and again a string of close ones is released. Then he turns, waits for the uproar in the water to subside in order to regain a firm contact, and once again he sails in. Then another short wait, and yet another deliberate attack. There is no question about it, this lad is a graduate of the number-one Japanese anti-submarine school.

Many German submarines, in similar circumstances, simply surfaced and gave up the fight. But not United States submariners, and not Jim Blanchard. Deeply submerged, running slowly at her maximum designed depth, *Albacore* creeps along, hoping and looking for the opening which will facilitate her breaking contact. And, as so often happens, the break comes rather sooner than might be expected.

By noon *Albacore* was at periscope depth again, well out of sight of the task force. When she returned to port, she reported damage to one large enemy flattop of the *Shokaku* class, little knowing of the final irony.

For HIJMS *Taiho*, less than two years old, the newest in a long line of Japanese aircraft carriers, a sister ship—though considerably improved—of the famous *Shokaku*, had indeed received one torpedo hit. The sixth and last fish fired by the American sub hit under one of the elevators. The damage was in itself slight, and *Taiho* reduced speed from 27 to 21 knots more from force of habit and doctrine than anything else. But the gasoline stowage for refueling aircraft happened also to be under that elevator, and the torpedo explosion started a small fire in the gasoline stowage deck. This did not bother the Japs either, for a great carrier like *Taiho* is well equipped to handle a small fire. Nevertheless the three destroyers were ordered to forget the submarine and concentrate on assisting the carrier.

Fighting the fire was a little difficult, as a matter of fact, because of the heavy gasoline fumes about the lower decks, and the order was given to start all blowers and fans, and to open all ventilation lines and bulkhead doors in an attempt to clear the atmosphere, or at least to reduce the concentration of the vapors. And thus it was that the Japanese skipper qualified for the United States Navy Cross, which he certainly deserved for assisting in the destruction of one first-line Japanese carrier.

For the inevitable occurred a few hours after the torpedo hit. With a sibilant *swish* a spark ignited the whole lower deck, and *Taiho* instantly became a mass of roaring flame.

So it was, eight hours after being hit by *Albacore*'s lone torpedo, and thirty miles from the position of the attack, that *Taiho* finally gave up the ghost and, mortally wounded, meekly bowed her head to the sea. Her hull seams opened by the heat within her, some of her compartments above the water line flooded in the effort to put out the fire; her decks and sides gutted with gaping holes, she sank lower and lower into the water and finally, belching great clouds of smoke and steam, disappeared beneath the surface.

Less than one hundred miles away from the spot where *Taiho* had been tagged, *Cavalla* maintained her patrol station. After many patrols as second or third officer during the earlier years of the war, Herman Kossler had been sent back to the States for a much-deserved rest and to put a brand-new submarine into commission as commanding officer. Now he was back on the firing line for his first patrol in command, with his new ship and a newly organized crew. One advantage he had over boats which made their first war patrol in 1942 or early 1943 was that many of his crew and officers, like himself, were already seasoned veterans. It had been merely a matter of training until they were all accustomed to working together, the inexperienced as well as the experienced.

In order to give a new boat a chance to get really shaken down before letting her in for the tough assignments, it was customary to send her on her first patrol in the less active areas—unless, indeed, her performance during the training period marked her as outstanding from the start. Such a boat was *Cavalla*, and so it was that Herman Kossler found himself patrolling, on June 14, between Guam and Mindanao, the route enemy task forces would probably have to take to get within carrier strike range of our forces then engaged in the campaign for Guam and Saipan.

Cavalla also made pretty heavy weather of it on the 14th, somewhat heavier than *Albacore*, and no doubt passed closer to the storm center. On the 15th, with the storm passed, she entered her assigned area and commenced surface patrolling. Except for USS *Pipefish*, also on the same mission, no contacts were made until an hour before midnight on the 16th.

At this time five ships—two large and three small—are contacted by radar. Immediately Herman mans his tracking party and begins maneuvers to close. The convoy is making high speed, and it is not until 0315 in the morning that Kossler is able to submerge on the convoy track. Through the periscope the enemy is identified as two tankers and three destroyer-type escorts. With the crew at battle stations, Herman starts in. He hopes to make his first attack with stern tubes, figuring that the convoy's 15 knots will leave him with a better chance to whip around for a bow shot in case of a bad zig at the crucial moment.

At 0355 the convoy is getting close to the firing point.

A periscope observation shows one of the escorts, a fast destroyer of the *Asashio* class, closing rapidly, showing a slight port angle on the bow. Thinking fast, Herman orders a slight change of course to the right, to give the Jap a little more clearance in the hope of avoiding detection, and at the same time not spoiling his shot at the larger tanker.

No luck! With the main target only five minutes from Torpedo Junction, Sound reports the destroyer's screws have speeded up. A swift look proves the worst: *Cavalla* has been detected.

Herman can't see much of the destroyer, for all the periscope shows is a huge bow boring right in, close aboard, and pushing a tremendous froth of water to either side. *"Take her down!"* The urgency in the skipper's voice galvanizes the diving officer and his crew into instant action. *Cavalla*'s depth gauge registers only seventy-five feet as the destroyer churns overhead. A narrow escape! No telling why depth charges are not dropped—maybe he had not had time to get them ready. Evidently he was trying to ram, and nearly succeeded.

However, the destroyer's own furious rush plays him false, too, for he is unable to regain the contact, now that the submarine is at deep submergence and evading. He remains in the vicinity for half an hour, listening carefully, while *Cavalla*, in turn, silences every bit of machinery except that absolutely necessary for submerged control.

Then he disappears, leaving Herman Kossler a sadder and wiser man, and a bit angry too. But you can't blame the Jap exactly; he's done a beautiful job of protecting his convoy.

One hour after the near brush with the tin can, *Cavalla*

is on the surface, attempting to retain contact, send a contact report, and pursue in the direction of the convoy's original course until late that afternoon. With the speed the Japs were making, plus a possible increase because of the brush with a submarine, not to mention a possible change of course, the chances of regaining contact are small. Three aircraft contacts during the course of the day are no help either, since in each case Herman is forced to submerge to avoid detection.

Nevertheless, *Cavalla* moves along after the convoy, hoping somehow to sight it again, until 2000 when finally the welcome cry, "Radar contact!" electrifies all hands. A few moments' observations suffice to prove that this is not the same bunch at all. On the contrary, it is a much bigger, much faster outfit.

Cavalla maneuvers into position. It doesn't take long this time: the contact has been made with the submarine nearly dead ahead of the enemy ships. It isn't long, either, before Herman realizes that he is really on the track of something important. He had been put in this area, so his operation order stated, to warn of the approach of enemy task forces and to intercept. Unlike *Albacore*'s orders, *Cavalla*'s very specifically stated that warning of the approach of large enemy task forces was of greater importance than a successful attack on even a major unit. Until now, Herman knew, there had been no information of the approach of such a task force. Our carriers and planes were lambasting the stuffing out of Guam and Saipan, and some kind of retaliation was certain to be expected.

Cavalla's contact tracks at 19 knots, and as the range closes many ships begin to be picked up on the radar, in addition to the several large ones first seen. Obviously this is some kind of task force, and from its course and speed it is heading from the Philippines to Guam. This information is vital to our forces engaged there, but Herman resolves to continue the approach until he is certain of his contact. Perhaps it isn't a carrier task force at all, in which case he'll be free to attack. It must be admitted that by this time Kossler is hoping that the ships prove to be almost anything except carriers.

But at 2030 Herman can make out one large carrier, several cruisers, and many destroyers through his periscope as he closes the range. And remaining submerged, his crew at battle stations, he passes right through the whole formation without firing a shot, counting the number and types of vessels in it! It is not until he is almost clear of the task force that two of the escorts begin to be suspicious of his presence, and for an hour they search the area, forcing *Cavalla* to take evasive action until they tire. And finally, with the skipper in a cold fury, the submarine manages to surface and get the all-important contact report off by radio.

Herm Kossler has good reason for being angry with the two little fellows who kept *Cavalla* down that extra hour. By so doing they have almost surely prevented her from catching up with the task force again. For the second time in twenty-four hours the sub chases at full speed, hoping to regain contact, knowing well that there is precious little chance of it.

All day long, that June 18, as *Cavalla* dashed in pursuit, her skipper was a prey to doubts as to whether he had done the right thing. After all, the submariner's creed is to attack whenever you have the chance. Maybe he should have taken the flattop when the Jap went across in front of his torpedo tubes—how would he ever be able to explain his action to his fellows?

But what Herman didn't know, couldn't have known, was the effect of this message and the change it made in the plans of the high command at that important juncture. Since we had a pretty good idea of the composition of the Jap forces, and since Herman had been so careful to detail the exact composition of the particular group he saw, our planners were enabled to make some rather shrewd estimates of the disposition of the enemy's forces and the remainder of his plans. Within a few hours of the receipt of *Cavalla*'s contact message, orders went out to every submarine in the vicinity to shift patrol stations according to a carefully laid out plot. One of these boats was *Albacore* and another was *Cavalla* herself.

Shortly after midnight on the morning of June 19 Herman broke off the chase and headed for his newly assigned patrol station—assigned, although he did not know it—as a result of his own contact report of some twenty-eight hours previous. By this time he was racked with disappointment, and completely exhausted from having been on his feet for nearly forty-eight hours. Some sleep was possible now, although it was broken three times in the next nine hours by plane contacts which forced *Cavalla* to submerge.

At 1039, as the submarine is preparing to surface after the last dunking, Herman sights four small planes circling in the distance. A few minutes later the sound operator reports some peculiar water noises in the same direction. All thoughts of immediate surfacing are now forgotten, as a careful watch is kept on the planes. They are too small to be patrol planes, so maybe something of interest will come of the contact.

Sure enough! Masts are sighted directly under the planes, and screws of other ships are heard on the sound gear. Once again the musical chimes resound through *Cavalla*'s steel hull, calling her crew to battle stations for the third time in two days. Once again men race through the ship, rubbing the sleep from their eyes, hurriedly throwing on some clothes as they go, wordlessly taking their stations as they wonder what fate has in store for them this time, and hope that *Cavalla* will be able to sink her fangs into something.

"Up 'scope!" Herman spins it around once. "Down 'scope!"

"One carrier, two cruisers, one destroyer! Angle on the bow, starboard two five." The bearing and range have already been set in. There are four ships in sight. The two cruisers are on the carrier's port bow and the destroyer is on his starboard beam about one thousand yards distant. This is bad, because *Cavalla* is on the carrier's starboard bow, and the situation indicates that she'll have to fire from the starboard beam—in other words—from right beneath the destroyer. So Kossler will either have to let his fish go a little sooner than he would like to—which won't prevent the escort from immediately letting go with a most effective counterattack—or try to outmaneuver the destroyer and shoot after he has gone by. The latter is perhaps the safer tactic, but it is also fraught with the unthinkable possibility of losing the target entirely.

Without further ado Kossler makes the decision to press home his attack on the carrier without regard for the destroyer. Perhaps he'll fire a little early, in order to make sure of getting his fish off, but that's the only concession he'll make.

Target speed is tracked at 25 knots. He is making a large bow wave as he plows steadily through the water, pitching slightly to the seas. The planes originally sighted are in the landing circle, and Herman has a close view of Japanese carrier landing tactics during his quick periscope observations. He notices that the forward end of the flight deck is crowded with aircraft, and that there are only one or two planes left in the air, one of which appears to be coming around for his landing approach.

It won't be long now! Kossler motions to Tom Denegre, his executive officer. "You make the next look!" Herman had previously decided to let two other officers also look at important targets, partly for their own indoctrination, but principally for identification purposes.

"Up periscope!" Number two squats before it, goes up with it, makes a quick look, shoots it down again. "*Shokaku* class, Captain! I'm sure of it!"

"I think so, too, Tommy. Just remember what you saw, so we can pick him out when we go through the silhouette identification book!" The skipper answers shortly, then speaks to the torpedo officer, who up to now has been running the TDC. "Take a look, Jug!"

Up goes the periscope once more, just long enough for Jug Casler to photograph the unforgettable scene in his mind. The carrier is one of the largest class with a flight deck extending almost, but not quite, from the bow to the stern. The island is rather smaller than is customary on contemporary American ships and located farther forward. The smokestack is subordinated to the rest of the island structure, and dominating the whole thing is a large "bedspring" type radar rotating slowly on top of the single mast.

"Up 'scope for a setup! Bearing—mark! . . . Range—mark! Down 'scope!"

"Angle on the bow, starboard forty! Make ready all tubes!"

"Set!" from Casler on the TDC. "Perfect setup, Captain."

"All tubes ready forward," from the telephone talker. "All tubes ready aft!"

"Normal order, speed high, set depth fifteen feet!" Herman is echoed by the telephone talker.

"This will be a bow shot!" orders the skipper. "One more observation—up 'scope! Down 'scope!"

Herman has taken the opportunity to snatch a quick look at the destroyer on the carrier's starboard beam, and what he sees heightens the urgency in his voice. "Angle on the bow, starboard five five! The destroyer is heading right for us, about one oh double oh yards away. We've got to shoot right now!"

"Stand by forward!" This is the culmination of the approach.

"Check bearing method!" to the TDC. This simply means that the skipper plans to get one or more check bearings during the firing.

"Up 'scope! . . . Final bearing and shoot! . . . Bearing— *mark!*"

"Three four two," snaps Denegre, as the periscope starts down.

"Set! . . . FIRE!" from Casler, and all hands feel the torpedo leave the tube.

Then numbers two, three, four, and five. The moment number-five torpedo has been fired, Kossler shouts down the hatch, "Take her down!" Then, to Casler, "Let the sixth one go on time!"

All the while *Cavalla* has been firing, Herman has been ticking away in his mind the yards yet separating her from the onrushing Jap destroyer. There has been no time to look at him, but he will surely spot the telltale torpedo wakes in the water and begin an immediate harassing attack.

As *Cavalla* lowers her periscope and starts for deep submergence, the racing beat of the enemy propellers can be heard, rapidly becoming louder, in the sound operator's earphones. With maddening slowness the submarine tilts downward.

"All ahead flank!" Herman is anxious to put as many feet of protective water between him and the surface as possible, and with *Cavalla*'s nose once pointed down, he gives her the gun.

"Rig for depth charge!" This is where the veteran submariners among the crew show their worth, and where the initiative assiduously cultivated among them begins to pay off.

Slowly, all too slowly, the depth gauges creep around. The propeller beat of the enemy destroyer becomes more and more audible.

"WHANG! . . . WHANG! . . . WHANG!" Three rather tinny metal-crushing explosions are heard throughout *Cavalla*'s straining hull. Three hits! Nothing in the world sounds the same as the noise of your torpedoes going off. Nothing in the world equals the thrill of hearing them. A subdued cheer echoes in the submarine's confined hull and a grim smile of satisfaction appears for a moment on the skipper's face.

One hundred fifty feet, by *Cavalla*'s depth gauges. Hang on to your hats, boys!

"Left full rudder!" Herman is hoping to alter course a bit and thus throw the Jap destroyer off, but there is hardly time for the change to take effect before the first four depth charges arrive.

For the next three hours 106 depth charges are dropped on *Cavalla*, and things grow progressively worse for the submarine. This Jap is no novice. Since *Cavalla* is a new boat, and consequently not yet depth charge proved, seams leak water here and there. The propeller shaft packing is apparently not properly set up and, under the double effect of the deep depth and the series of trip-hammer shocks received from the depth charge explosions—luckily none quite within lethal range—seawater pours into the motor room bilges at an alarming rate. Shortly after the depth charging begins there is a loud hissing heard in the galley overhead. No water comes into the ship, but she immediately becomes heavy aft and starts to sink deeper. It is believed that the main induction piping outside the pressure hull must have been flooded, probably through rupture of the line somewhere. An immediate test is made by opening some of the main induction drains, and sure enough, a steady stream of water spurts out under full sea pressure. The combination of this, plus the water taken into the motor room, forces the submarine to increase speed and run with an up angle in order to maintain her depth.

But as was so frequently the case during the war, the Japs finally either got tired, lost contact and could not regain it, ran out of depth charges, or simply gave up—maybe because they had something else to think about.

For with three torpedoes evenly spaced throughout her length, the Japanese carrier *Shokaku*, member of the Pearl Harbor attacking force on December 7, 1941, and veteran of many engagements in the Central and South Pacific, sank with all her planes on board just three hours after having been hit.

Cavalla showed up at Saipan a few days later while the attack on that hapless island was still going on full blast. The Japanese Navy had just been decisively defeated in the First Battle of the Philippine Sea—the Marianas

Turkey Shoot—which to a large extent showed the pattern for the remainder of the battles of the war.

But on the day of the battle, despite the fact that our carrier-based planes shot practically every Jap plane out of the sky, only one Japanese carrier was sunk—the ill-fated *Hitaka* on her maiden voyage. Incidentally, this was the same carrier which had stopped two torpedoes from USS *Trigger* a year earlier at the mouth of Tokyo Bay. Try as they might, however, the American airmen could find but three Jap carriers the day of the battle, although it was known that five had left the Philippines. At first the supposition was that somehow the enemy had out-guessed our people, for the number of planes they put into the air was obviously more than the complement of three carriers.

The explanation was simple, when the pieces were finally put together. Five carriers had started out originally with intentions of making a surprise attack on our fleet, which at the moment was engaged in giving Saipan and Guam the works. Our high strategic command had placed a cordon of submarines across the route which it seemed most logical the enemy would use.

A submarine reconnaissance had reported the passage of the task force through San Bernadino Strait on the 15th, but Herman Kossler's contact on a convoy of fast tankers on the early morning of June 17 was the first proof of the direction of the Jap move. The location of the convoy gave a good indication of the prospective course of the enemy task force, since these could only be fleet tankers (because of their speed and position) en route to a refueling rendezvous. A redisposition in submarine patrol positions was thereupon ordered. While this repositioning was still under way, however, Kossler reported his second contact, on a carrier force this time, and our whole Pacific Fleet command went into immediate action. Although Herman had some idea of the import of his contact, he could have had no conception of the tremendous difference made by the fact that he chose to report the contact instead of attacking it. Had he done so, he might have sunk the carrier; but there would not have been the timely warning to alert our own people, and there was always the chance, of course, that *Cavalla* might have been sunk during or after the attack, and thus not able to make a contact report at all. *Albacore*'s position would then not have been changed, and *Taiho* might well have escaped detection.

Shokaku's planes went down with her, since they had just been taken back on board when *Cavalla*'s torpedoes struck home. *Taiho*'s, however, were in the air when she sank, and having nowhere else to go, they landed on the already-loaded decks of the remaining carriers, seriously overloading them. Loss of the battle, and of many of the engaged units including three of the few remaining carrier-trained air groups, was a foregone conclusion.

Brought home once more to our own people, and presumably to the Jap admirals also, was this tenet: You cannot operate on the sea during war unless you have command of the sea, the air above it, and the depths beneath it.

15
TRIGGER

TRIGGER HAD SHATTERED five convoys with Dusty Dornin at the conn, before he was relieved by order of Admiral King. Dick Garvey, now Lieutenant, USNR—next to me and Wilson, the senior man in point of service aboard—was detached at the same time. Fritz Harlfinger became her fourth master. We decided that because of my good fortune in having excellent night vision, I should function for him exactly as I had for Dusty—that is, on the bridge during night surface attacks, on the periscope when submerged. This was *Wahoo*'s system, which *Trigger* had adopted.

On Fritz's first patrol, off the Haha Jima Retto in the Marianas, the worst beating of *Trigger*'s career—and one of the most severe experienced by any sub in our Navy— took place. About four hours before dawn we picked up a convoy, tracked it a bit, and prepared to "pull the *Trigger*" on it.

Radar indicated many ships. While we were still 20,000 yards ahead of the main body, we detected two radar-equipped escorts patrolling 10,000 to 15,000 yards ahead of the convoy. "What a stupid place to patrol," we thought. "This will be a cinch." So we dived under the escorts and passed safely (we thought) through the outer screen of the convoy. We later realized we had been detected by radar and the whole convoy was alerted.

Returning to periscope depth, we are preparing to surface when more escorts are detected. Down we go again, passing under a second feverishly pinging screen. Five destroyers or more in that one, and they're not merely carrying on a routine search. They're *hunting*, and finally one of them gets a "probable contact." He and one of his friends turn around and follow us, still a little doubtful, but—oh—so—right!

It is only a moderately bright night, so we leave the periscope up for lengthy intervals, confident it cannot be seen. For long periods we stare at those two chaps astern, zigzagging back and forth in their cautious search plan, slowly but surely tracking us down. We feel like the hare in a game of hare and hounds and it's not funny. Inexorably the finger has been put upon us. We're going to catch it no matter what happens—and so far we haven't even seen the enemy convoy.

Gone are ideas of making a night surface attack. We'll be lucky even to get in a submerged shot before the beating lying in wait for us catches up to us. Resignedly we stand by to take it—when, finally, the main body heaves into sight.

My God! We see through the periscope four columns of ships, five or more ships in each column. Tankers, freighters, transports, and auxiliaries, all steaming toward Saipan. And closely spaced around the mass of merchant vessels is yet a third ring of at least ten, probably more, escorts.

No time to surface and send a message—even if we could, with those hounds on our tail. No time even to prepare a message. No time to do anything except shoot.

On its present course the convoy will pass about two thousand yards ahead of us. The port flank group of escort vessels will pass almost exactly over us, one after another. We may get a shot, if conditions don't change.

We'll get some fish in the water, anyhow. *Make ready all tubes!* A big tanker moves up into position, will soon line himself up broadside for a shot from our bow tubes. Behind him is a solid phalanx of ships. If the torpedoes run straight, or run at all, we can't miss. We plan to fire all six bow tubes, swing and fire all four stern tubes, and then take her down fast. Too bad, but we won't be able to sit around to verify sinkings. We'll be fortunate if we distinguish our torpedo hits from the unholy barrage of depth charges sure to follow.

Stealthily, silently, *Trigger* creeps into firing position. One minute to go, just about. Fritz takes the periscope for a moment, swings it aft for a quick look, dismay on his sweat-studded face.

"He's signaling to the convoy," he mutters. "They must have us pretty well spotted by now. He's sending 'Baker,' the letter 'Baker' over and over—That's International Code for 'I am about to discharge explosives.' "

Someone who recently read *Horatio Hornblower* murmurs, "For what we are about to receive, oh, Lord, we give thanks." But it's not funny.

Our tanker should be about in the spot now. *Stand by forward!* I turn *Trigger*'s periscope back to give the firing bearings. We're going to catch it, but we're going to dish it out too.

But the periscope can see nothing. Helplessly I turn it back and forth in high power. "Something peculiar here. Can't see anything. Mighty funny-shaped cloud there—

looks like a ship . . ." I flip the periscope into low power, which gives greater field with less magnification.

"Wow! It's a destroyer! He's trying to ram! He's just barely missed us—within twenty-five yards! He's firing a machine gun through his bridge windows! They're dropping depth charges!"

Thought: How long does it take a depth charge to sink to fifty feet?

"He's by, now. There's the tanker! Bearing—mark!"

"All ahead full! Take her down!"

"Fire ONE!"

"Rig for depth charge and silent running!"

"Fire TWO!"

"Fire THREE!"

"Fire FOUR! Secure the tubes!"

The air pressure inside *Trigger* suddenly increases as negative tank is vented, and down she goes. Four torpedoes are all we fire, for we don't want depth charges going off and possibly exploding a torpedo warhead lying unprotected in a tube with the outer door open.

But no depth charges go off, despite the whole gang of Japs seen frantically working at the destroyer's depth charge racks. We suspect he was caught a little by surprise, too, and either his release gear jammed, or he still had his depth charges secured for sea. At any rate, the first explosions we hear are the beautiful, painful, wonderful sounds of four solid torpedo hits: two, according to the time interval, probably in our tanker, and two in one or two ships in the next column over.

Then, for a moment we hear only the thrashing of many screws, in particular the set belonging to the little man who sent "Baker" by light. We are at 300 feet, but he comes in as if he could practically see us, and drops twenty-five absolute beauties on us. How *Trigger* manages to hold together we'll never know. Her heavy steel sides buckle in and out, her cork insulation breaks off in great chunks and flies about. Lockers are shaken open and the contents spewed all over everything. Ventilation lines and other piping familiarly start to vibrate themselves almost out of sight. Light sheet-metal seams and fastenings pop loose. With each succeeding shock, gauges all over the ship jiggle violently across their dials, and several needles knock themselves off against their pegs. In spite of careful and thoughtful shock mounting, instruments are shattered and electric circuits thrown out of order.

During the height of the depth charge barrage the forward auxiliary distribution board circuit breaker emits a shower of sparks and a sudden crackling "phf-f-f-ft." The electrician's mate standing by hastily opens the "depth-charge 'look-in' switch"—and throws the circuit breaker out. All lights in the forward part of the ship go out, but the emergency lights, turned on at "Rig for Depth Charge," and various hand lanterns strategically located, furnish sufficient illumination for essential operations. Electrician's mates in the forward repair party quickly and silently turn to, working to locate and eliminate the trouble in the near-darkness amid the shattering noises of the depth charges, the convulsive whipping of *Trigger*'s hull, and the bouncing of the machinery. In a matter of minutes it is spotted, the offending water-soaked gear disconnected, and the forward board thrown back in. The lights come on again, and we feel a little better.

Finally the barrage is over and we listen while five more escorts detach themselves from the convoy and come back to look for us, signaled, no doubt, by the chap who had so vigorously counterattacked us. No more depth charges for a while, and we think that perhaps we're going to get away with just a little beating. Hopes begin to rise, but no such luck!

The six Japs form a ring around us, and keep contact, moving with us so as always to keep us in the center. No matter which way we go, which way we turn, they keep up with us. Every half hour or so one breaks off and makes a run, dropping only a few charges each time—thum, thum, thum, THUM, THUM, THUM—WHAM, WHAM! WHAM! Now and then they vary their routine, and make a "dry run," as if to say, "We know you're there, old boy. Might as well surface and get it over with." But *Trigger* sticks it out, long past dawn, past noon, until late afternoon.

We had dived at a little after midnight. Seventeen hours later we are still creeping along under continual harassment by our pursuers. All bilges are full of water to the danger limits. We have been bailing from the motor room to the after torpedo room for twelve hours, keeping the water out of the motors and reduction gears. The temperature has risen to a fantastic 135 degrees throughout the ship. Two or three men are near collapse from a combination of nervous strain, lack of sufficient oxygen, and loss of salt from the system—though we all eat handfuls of salt tablets. We sweat profusely, and our clothes are drenched, our socks soggy, and our shoes soaked. In an attempt to lessen the nuisance of constantly wiping the sweat out of their eyes or off their bodies, many men knot rags around their foreheads or drape them over their shoulders and around their necks. The atmosphere is laden with moisture, which condenses everywhere. Bulkheads and vertical surfaces are simply beaded with water, perpetually running in sudden little rivulets to the deck. Our green linoleum decks are themselves a quarter of an inch deep in water already, and the constant moving about by men in greasy, soggy shoes has churned it up into a disgusting, slimy, muddy ooze through which we shuffle, oblivious to anything but the awful nearness of those menacing propellers overhead, the labor of breathing the foul air, and the terrific concussions of the unrelenting depth charges.

Three hundred feet below the surface, where the water is black and always cold, and the sea pressure compresses the hull with a force of 150 pounds per square inch, sustaining a total "squeeze" of about three hundred million pounds, *Trigger* fights for her life. Her sleek black hull, now tortured and strained, is heavier than the water it displaces by many thousands of pounds. This condition is due to loss of buoyancy caused by the compression of her hull and to the fact that her seams have been leaking steadily under the pounding she's been taking—and the pumps cannot be run, for the noise would immediately betray her exact position. With bow and stern planes at full rise and herself at a ten-degree up angle, *Trigger* struggles to keep from sinking any deeper. Gradually, as the water inside increases and she becomes heavier, she is forced to assume more and more of an up angle, like a heavily laden airplane climbing under full throttle—only her problem is to maintain the same depth with minimum power.

That the water at 300 feet is colder than at the surface is a help, because it is denser, giving *Trigger* more buoyancy—but we've used up this "velvet" long ago. This difference in surface and deep-water temperatures should also hinder the Japs' sound-detection apparatus, but so far as we can discern, it hasn't bothered them much.

No matter which way we go, the deadly circle moves with us. We try several times to go through the gap in the circle left by the destroyer making the current attack, but that move apparently has been foreseen, for we are invariably blocked by not one but two sets of screws—those of the two vessels adjacent to the one making the run.

We wonder why the six escorts do not make a single coordinated attack on us. They have us so well boxed in that such an attack really would be a lulu! The thought grows that possibly they expect us to surface and surrender. If they keep up these tactics, and don't sink us with a lucky depth charge, eventually we will run out of oxygen or battery power and be forced to surface.

But we lay our plans for that contingency. *Trigger* will never surrender. We'll come up in the darkest hour of the night, at full speed, all hands at gun stations, and twenty torpedoes ready. It will be mighty dangerous for anything short of a full-fledged destroyer to get in our way.

The decision is made to surface at about 2100, after sunset and evening twilight are over, and before moonrise. Our battery and oxygen would probably last us another twenty-four hours, but then we'd *have* to come up. This way, at least, we still can dive and hide, and if we can only get up for two hours or so we'll be almost completely recovered, battery more than two-thirds recharged, and ready for anything.

Such are the plans and arguments that pass through our minds that long and horrible day. Late that afternoon, however, fortune once more smiles our way. We realize that we have approached the southern edge of the circle, that the Japs have apparently temporarily lost contact, perhaps grown a bit careless, and that no depth charge runs have been made for quite some time.

We've tried it before, but here goes again. We head for the biggest gap in the circle, and slowly increase speed as much as we dare—which isn't much. We listen with bated breath, hardly daring to breathe, plotting in those malevolent screws, trying to identify the bird who is supposed to cover the sector we've chosen for our escape route.

Here he comes! One set of screw noises slowly gets louder and begins to draw ahead. We shudder as he gains bearing on us. Surely he'll pick us up, because he'll be practically right on top of us! But—another smile from the blindfolded gal—all at once he stops drawing ahead. Now, as we cluster around the sound gear, we watch the telltale bearing pointer move aft, ever aft, till finally he passes across our stern! A guarded cheer breaks from the desperate men in the conning tower. We've broken through!

There is nothing to compare with the fresh, cool sweetness of the pure night air. It overpowers you with its vitality, reaches deep down inside you and sweeps away every remaining vestige of tiredness, fear, or unhappiness. It is frank, pure, undiluted Joy.

Three weeks later, after bumming some urgently needed repair parts from *Tang* at a midnight rendezvous, *Trigger* sank four freighters and one escort out of a convoy of five freighters and five escorts. With one torpedo left, she chased the remaining freighter and four escorts, snapping at their heels, till finally, for fear of grounding herself, she desisted. But she had the pleasure of knowing that all five ships had run hard aground, as verified by another submarine.

Harlfinger's first patrol was my last in *Trigger*, for when we returned to port my orders were waiting for me, and I was relieved by my Naval Academy classmate, Johnnie Shepherd. *Trigger* was adjudged so badly damaged that she required a six-week repair period in a navy yard in the States, instead of the customary two-week refit.

When she headed west again, after a thorough over-haul, the old girl waved a cockscomb of thirty-six minia-ture Jap flags, a Presidential Unit Citation pennant, and a homemade blue flag with a large white numeral on it, emblazoning her claim to be number one submarine of the fleet, while at the top of her fully extended periscope fluttered a rather weather-beaten brassiere.

16

BATFISH

USS *BATFISH* GOT UNDER WAY from Pearl Harbor on December 30, 1944, on what was to be her sixth war patrol. It was also to be one of the epoch-making patrols of the war, one whose influence may be discerned even at this late date. Her skipper was Commander J. K. Fyfe, a Naval Academy graduate of the class of 1936, who had already built up an outstanding record of successful submarine action. From the time when the PC boat escorting her out of Pearl Harbor was dismissed until she arrived at Guam, Jake Fyfe kept his ship at flank speed. He, in common with most submariners, saw no reason for delay in getting into the war zone, except the necessity of conserving fuel. The capture of Guam removed that necessity, insofar as the first leg of the trip was concerned. After leaving Guam or Saipan it usually paid to be a bit conservative, in case you ran into a long chase, or were given a prolonged special mission.

On January 9, 1945, *Batfish* arrived at Guam, and on the next day she departed en route to an area north of the Philippines. On January 12 she sighted what was probably her first enemy contact on this particular patrol, presaging the turn which the whole patrol would subsequently take. A periscope suddenly popped out of the water some distance ahead. Since you don't stick around to argue with an enemy submarine which has the drop on you, and since, besides, Jake was in a hurry to get to his area where he was scheduled for immediate lifeguard services, he simply bet on everything she would take and got out of there. Sightings of Japanese periscopes by our boats were fairly numerous during the war. The Japs never learned how *doubly* cautious you must be when stalking one of your own kind; we never learned a lesson better.

Between January 13 and February 9 *Batfish* had rather a dull time. She wasted two days looking for several aviators who were reported ditched near her track; investigated twenty-eight junks to see what kind of cargo they were carrying; dived at occasional aircraft alarms. Then, on February 9, while she was patrolling in Babuyan Channel, south of Gamiguin Island, the radar operator sounds a warning.

Something in his radar arouses his attention—he looks closely—there it is again—and again. It is not a pip which he sees; if it were, he would not wait to sing out "Radar contact" and thereby immediately mobilize the ship for action. This is something more difficult to evaluate. A faint shimmering of the 'scopes—a momentary unsteadiness in the green and amber cathode ray tubes—which comes and goes. Almost unconsciously he times them, and notices the bearing upon which the radar head is trained each time the faint wobble in the normal "grass" presentation is noticed. A few moments of this, and—*"Captain to the conn!"* No time to wait on ceremony. This particular lad wants his skipper, and he wants him badly.

A split second later the word reaches Jake Fyfe in his

cabin, where he had lain down fully clothed for a few minutes of shut-eye. In a moment the skipper is in the conning tower.

The radar operator points to his 'scope. "There it is, sir! There it is again! I just noticed it a minute ago!" The operator is doing himself an injustice; from the time he first noticed there was something out of the ordinary to the moment Fyfe himself was beside him could not have been more than thirty seconds.

The captain stares at the instrument, weighing the significance of what he sees. This is something new, something portentous—there is a small stirring in the back of his mind—there seems to be a half-remembered idea there, if he can only dig it up—then, like a flash, he has it! If he is right, it means they are in grave danger, with a chance to come out of it and maybe add another scalp to their belts; if he is wrong, what he is about to do may make a bad situation infinitely worse. But Jake knows what he is doing. He is not playing some far-fetched hunch.

"Secure the radar!" he orders. The operator reaches to the cutoff switch and flips it, looking questioningly at his skipper.

"What do you think it is?" Fyfe asks the lad.

"It looked like another radar to me, Captain." The reply is given without hesitation.

"What else?"

The boy is at a loss for an answer, and Jake Fyfe answers his own question:

"Japanese submarine!"

Submarine *vs.* submarine! The hunter hunted! The biggest fear of our submarine sailors during World War II was that an enemy submarine might get the drop on them while they were making a passage on the surface. It would be quite simple, really. All you have to do is to detect the other fellow first, either by sight or by radar, submerge on his track, and let go the fish as he passes. *All you have to do is to detect him first!*

Our submarines ran around the coast of Japan as though they were in their own backyards. They usually condescended to patrol submerged only when within sight of the enemy shoreline in order not to be spotted by shore watchers or aircraft patrols, for you can't sink ships which stay in port because they know you are waiting outside. But when out of sight of land, and with no planes about, United States submarines usually remained on the surface. Thus they increased their search radius and the speed with which they could move to new positions. And it should not be forgotten that the fifty-odd boats doing lifeguard duty at the end of the war were required to stay on the surface whether in sight of land or not! Small wonder that our submarine lookouts were the best in the Navy.

United States submariners were, as a class, far too well acquainted with the devastating surprise which can be dealt with a pair of well-aimed torpedoes to take any preventable risk of being on the receiving end themselves. Submarines are rugged ships, but they have so little reserve buoyancy that a torpedo hit is certain to permit enough water to flood in to overbalance what remaining buoyancy there is. Even though the submarine might be otherwise intact, she would instantly sink to the bottom of the sea with most of her crew trapped inside. *Tang* was a prime example. Ordinarily there are no survivors from sunken submarines, with the exception of the Germans, who had a habit of surfacing and abandoning ship when under attack.

The submarine, which hunts by stealth, is therefore itself peculiarly susceptible to attack by stealth. But don't make the mistake of underestimating the enemy submarine crew. The fact that they are operating a submarine at all indicates that they are picked men, who know as much about the game, in all probability, as you do. The odds are definitely even, and it is a question of dog eat dog. The only advantage lies in superior ability and equipment.

Not counting midgets, the first Japanese submarine sunk by our forces was the *I-173*, which fell victim to the *Gudgeon* on January 27, 1942. The last such was sunk by the *Spikefish* on August 13, 1945. Between these dates twenty-three additional Japanese subs were destroyed by our own undersea warriors. And we regret to chronicle that some five of our own subs, it is thought, went down under the periscope sights of Japanese submarines. Unfortunately the Jap records are so poor that the precise manner in which all of our lost submarine vessels met their doom will never be discovered. The fact remains that our submarines were convinced that the Japs were sending the two-man midgets out at night, looking for them. And almost every patrol report turned in by our people toward the end of the war records that one or more torpedoes had been fired at them.

The most outstanding record of enemy subs sunk was the one hung up by *Batfish*, beginning that fateful February 9.

"Secure the radar!" Jake Fyfe turned to a shocked conning tower crew, and ordered crisply, "Battle stations torpedo!"

The helmsman instinctively had already extended his

hand in the direction of the general alarm. Now he grasped it, pulled it out, and then down. The low-pitched chime of the alarm resounded through the ship, penetrating every corner, waking men who had turned in dead tired, vowing to sleep for a year—meaning only until their next watch—bringing them upright, fully alert, instinctively racing to their battle stations, all in the space of an instant.

What is it? What is it?

Don't know. Something on the radar.

Skipper says a Jap sub out there.

How does he know that?

The process of deduction by which Fyfe arrived at the conclusion that the source of the radar peculiarities was an enemy submarine was not at all illogical. The wavering of his radar scope was probably due to the presence of another radar. It was known that the Japs had radar, though of an inferior type to ours. If this radar came from a vessel as large as a destroyer, he should have been detected on *Batfish's* radar before the emanations from his low-powered radar had been noticed. This, of course, was the usual case. Since the radar waves had been the first to be picked up, it followed that the ship producing them must be small and low on the water. Yet it must be a valuable ship, sufficiently important to rate one of the relatively few radar sets the Nips possessed. *Hence, a submarine.*

The reason why Fyfe ordered his own radar temporarily secured was simply to deny the Jap the same information which he himself had just received, while he and his executive officer, Lieutenant C. K. Sprinkle, USNR, broke out the charts and did some very rapid figuring.

The enemy radar emanations have been from 220,

approximately southwest. Babuyan Channel runs more or less north and south. Therefore the target must be on a northerly course, approaching from the south.

To check this deduction *Batfish*'s radar is cautiously turned on for only a moment. Sure enough, the bearing of the other radar has changed slightly. It is now 225.

"All ahead full! Right full rudder!" *Batfish* leaps ahead and steadies on a course calculated to get to the north of the approaching enemy vessel. She runs for a short time, every now and then checking the situation with her radar. All clear—no other ships around. Just the Jap, and his signals are becoming stronger, while his bearing is now drawing to the southward. This is as it should be.

But Fyfe does not, of course, propose to make his approach and attack on bearings alone. He wants to close the range, but on his own terms, with his bow on the enemy, his torpedoes ready—in short, with the drop on him.

Finally, Jake Fyfe and Sprinkle figure their position is about right. *Batfish* turns toward the enemy and ghosts in, keeping the darkest section of the midnight horizon behind her, and sweeping frequently, but at odd intervals, with her radar.

"Radar contact!" The word from Radar this time startles nobody—they have all been expecting it for several minutes. The tracking party now goes to work in earnest, with some concrete information instead of the rather sporadic and un-precise dope they have had up to now.

Target is on course 310, speed 12. The dials whirl on the TDC in the conning tower, where Sprinkle is in charge.

The range continues to decrease, the radar operator and the TDC operator tirelessly feeding in the essential information on the fire-control instruments. The plotting party also has its part in this, for all solutions must check before torpedoes may be fired.

On the bridge, the captain strains his eyes, and so do the lookouts up there with him. Suppose the Jap has somehow learned of the presence of the American submarine! It is possible. In this case, if he deduces what is going on, he might very logically turn the situation to his own advantage by firing his torpedoes first. After all, when you make an approach on another ship, there is a period during which you are in a much better position for him to shoot torpedoes at you than you at him—at a somewhat longer range, of course. Or, more probably, he might simply dive, thus spoiling the shot *Batfish* has worked for so long, not to mention making it immediately imperative for her to get the hell out of there!

Closer and closer comes the unsuspecting enemy sub. It is so dark that as yet he cannot be seen by the tense bridge party. As the situation develops, it is apparent that he will pass through the firing position at just under 2,000 yards' range. This is a little long for optimum torpedo fire, but Fyfe wants to take no chances of being detected. On he comes—only a little more now—then from the conning tower, "On the firing bearing, Captain!" This from the exec.

"Let them go when ready, Sprink. Shoot on radar bearings. I still can't see him from up here." From the skipper.

Silently, four torpedoes are loosed into the water. Four new wakeless electric fish start their run toward the target. They have 1,800 yards to go; it will take a while. The watch hands crawl slowly and maddeningly around their faces. The wait grows longer, more anxious. *Something should have happened by now! Those fish should surely have arrived! We could not have been so far off that our spread missed also!*

But miss they do, all four torpedoes. Finally there is no escaping that conclusion. The whole careful and well-executed approach—wasted! All hands are bitterly disappointed. What can have gone wrong?

The question is answered by Plot, dramatically. "Target has speeded up! Speed now fourteen knots!" Too bad this was not detected a minute or two earlier. At least it explains the trouble, and allays the suspicious doubts which had already inevitably crept into the minds of both skipper and exec.

But the target continues serenely on his way, giving no sign of being aware of having been fired upon. Maybe *Batfish* will be able to try again.

No sooner thought than tried. The four murmuring diesels of the hunter lift their voices, and the submarine slips away through the water, seeking another position from which to launch her deadly missiles. But by this time, of course, the target has passed beyond *Batfish*, and in order to regain firing position it will be necessary to execute an end around.

Jake Fyfe has elected to remain on the surface for the whole attack, crediting to his superior radar the fact that he had been alerted before the Jap; and trusting to his belief that he could keep the enemy from detecting him. His plan is to get up ahead of the other submarine, and to head in toward him while the unsuspecting Nip is pounding along in nearly the opposite direction. Thus the range would close rapidly, and the amount of warning the other submarine could expect before torpedo junction would be very little. It was surprising that the Jap sub gave no indication of being aware he had been shot at. Whereas Fyfe had expected only one chance at him, he now finds another. "Obviously the fellow isn't as good as I gave him credit for!" And concurrent with this came the resolution to get in closer the next time, play his luck a little harder. If he could only sight the enemy, and fire on optical bearings instead of radar bearings, he would have a much neater solution to his fire-control problem—and thus greater certainty of hitting.

And besides, although Jake was morally certain the ship he was stalking was another submarine—and therefore Japanese, for he knew positively there were no friendly submarines in that area—he naturally wanted very badly to see him, just by way of confirming things. He had thought that visibility was good enough to see 2,000 yards—a mile—and therefore had settled on about 1,800 yards for firing range. Events had proved him too optimistic, and he had not been able to see him at that range. This time he *would* get a look!

All the while, *Batfish* is racing through the black night at full speed. She has pulled off abeam of her quarry, just within maximum radar range in order to be outside range of the less-efficient radar carried by the enemy, and she is rapidly overhauling him. Jake is still very careful with his own radar, searching all around and getting a radar range and bearing on the enemy as frequently as he dares, but he is not going to take a chance on being detected. All this time, of course, the radar emanations from the Jap have been coming in regularly, and their unchanged characteristics add proof that he is still sound asleep.

The skipper stands on the bridge of his ship during the whole of the new approach, for the situation could change so radically and so quickly that he must remain where he can take immediate action. So he must trust the coordination of everything belowdecks to Sprinkle.

Batfish has worked up somewhat ahead of the enemy's beam. Fyfe is trying to visualize the chart of the channel, for if he remembers rightly, some kind of a change is going to have to be made at the rate they are covering ground. The sea is fairly smooth, as it so often is in these southern waters, and hardly any solid water comes over *Batfish*'s main deck, although considerable spray is whipped across it by the wind of her passing. It is an absolutely pitch-black night. No distinction can be seen between sky and water—the horizon simply doesn't exist. All about is warm, dank, murky grayness, broken only by the white water boiling along your side. It is as though *Batfish* were standing still, dipping and rising slightly, and occasionally shaking herself free from the angry sea which froths and splashes beneath her.

In a moment Clark Sprinkle's voice is heard on the interior communication system: "Plot says target is changing course. They'll let us know for sure in a minute."

The skipper presses a large heavy button on the bulkhead beside him and leans forward to speak into the bridge speaker: "Fine! As soon as you're sure, we'll change too."

About a minute later a speaker mounted to the overhead of the conning tower squawks: "This is Plot. Target has changed course to the right. New course, zero one five."

"I've got the same, Sprink," says the TDC operator. "New course about zero two zero, though."

Sprinkle pulls a portable microphone toward him, presses the button. "Bridge, Plot and TDC have the target on new course between zero one five and zero two zero. Suggest we come to zero two zero."

"Right full rudder! Come right to new course zero two zero!" The order to the helm is sufficient acknowledgment.

"Rudder is right full, sir! Coming to zero two zero!" the helmsman shouts up the hatch.

Batfish heels to port as she whips around. Her white wake astern shows nearly a sharp right-angle turn as her stern slides across the seas.

Several more minutes pass. Fyfe is on the point of asking for more information, when again the bridge speaker blares its muffled version of Sprinkle's voice: "Captain, we've got him on zero two zero, making fourteen knots. Range is seven oh double oh, and distance to the track is two five double oh. This looks pretty good to me. Recommend we come left and let him have it!"

"Okay, Sprink. Give me a course to come to." The captain's voice has assumed a grim finality, a flat quality of emotionless decision. This is always a big hurdle; until now you really have the option of fighting or not fighting—of risking your neck or not—that is, if you can remain undetected. But when you start in, you are committed. You go in with the bow of your ship pointed directly at the enemy; you get well inside his visibility range, and radar range, too, for that matter; and you depend upon the quickness with which the attack develops to give you the opportunity to get it off. Keeping your bow on him gives him less to look at, a very important factor in the night surface attack; but if you change your mind and try to pull out of there you've got to change course, give him your broadside—and set yourself up for a beautiful counterattack on his part. Destroyers are supposed to be able to get a half-salvo in the air within seconds after having been alerted; submarines always carry one or two torpedoes at the ready, which can be fired instantly from the bridge. Small wonder that starting in is a crucial decision!

"Left full rudder!" Fyfe's command whips down the conning tower hatch to the helmsman.

"Rudder is left full, sir!"

"All ahead two-thirds!" Fyfe has waited a moment before slowing, in order to make the turn faster.

"Answered all ahead two-thirds!" Maneuvering room has matched annunciators with the conning tower, thus indicating that they have the word.

Sprinkle has been following things closely from the conning tower—checking bearings, ranges, courses, and speeds. He performs a rapid mathematical computation, drawing arrows this way and that, and measuring angles. Then he speaks into his little mike: "Captain, if we steady up on two four oh we'll have him ten degrees on our port bow, going across. His angle on the bow is now starboard forty."

"Steady on new course two four oh!" The ship has about thirty degrees more to swing, and the helmsman eases the rudder upon receipt of the command from the bridge.

"Steady on two four oh, sir!"

The exec speaks again. "Captain, he is on course zero two oh, making fourteen knots. Angle on the bow is starboard forty-five, and he now bears five degrees on our port bow. The distance to the track is two three double oh. Range, five oh double oh."

No answer from the bridge, but that doesn't bother Sprinkle. He knows he will hear quickly if the skipper isn't satisfied with the way things are going or the reports he is getting.

A few more tense moments pass. Again the speaker near the skipper's left elbow reproduces Sprinkle's familiar voice. "He's crossing our bow now. Range, four oh double oh."

"Come right to two five oh." Fyfe, who is working the same problem in his head that Sprinkle is solving mechanically in the conning tower, has the situation firmly fixed in his mind. He wants to keep coming around to head for the enemy, and has anticipated by seconds only the latter's recommendation.

"What is the distance to the track?"

"Two oh double oh, Captain."

"All ahead one-third." *Batfish* is closing the target's projected track too quickly, and the firing range will be too short, or the target might detect her before firing. Fyfe's brain is now in high gear, and he can feel every part of the problem falling into place. In fact, it is almost as if he could reach out and control the movements of the Japanese skipper also, and his mind wills the enemy to keep on coming, to keep on the course and speed as set up; to come unerringly and steadily on to his doom.

And on and on he comes, totally unaware of the trap set for him, totally unaware that he is springing the trap on himself, that any change whatsoever which he might make would be to his advantage, that the most serious mistake you can make, when it's submarine against submarine, is to relax—*ever.* Of course, to give him his due, the Jap doesn't know he is being shadowed. But he knows very well that he is proceeding through a submarine-infested area—and in this little game no excuses are accepted.

At 1,500 yards the keen eyes on *Batfish's* bridge distinguish a blur in the gray murk, and at 1,000 yards the sinister outline of a Japanese I-class submarine is made out—the first time during the whole evening that the enemy has actually been sighted. He wallows heavily in the slight chop of the sea—low, dark, and ungainly.

At 1,000 yards the Jap is broadside to *Batfish*: Fyfe's plan has borne fruit, for his own bow is exactly toward the enemy, and he has all the advantage of sighting. Furthermore, the darkest portion of the overcast is behind him.

Sprinkle is beside himself with eagerness. For about thirty seconds he has been imploring his skipper to shoot. He has a perfect solution and doesn't want to let it get away from him. "We've got them cold! Ready to shoot any time, Captain!" He repeats the same formula over and over, a veteran of too many patrols to say what he really means, which would be more on the order of, *"Let's go, Captain! What are we waiting for?"*

But Fyfe refuses to be hurried. He's worked too long for this moment, and he has already missed once, possibly because of a little haste in firing. Carefully he takes a bridge bearing and has it matched into the TDC, swings the TBT and takes another, to make sure there is no transmission lag which might cause an error. Then, for the first time using the word, he says, in a curious flat voice, "Fire torpedoes!"

"Fire one!" Sprinkle's voice is a split second behind that of his skipper's.

Almost immediately the telephone talker standing under the conning tower hatch shouts loudly, so that his message is heard in the conning tower as well as on the bridge:

"Number one did not eject! Running hot in the tube!"

Something has gone wrong. The torpedo should have been pushed out of the torpedo tube by the high-pressure air ejection system. Instead, it has stuck in the tube, and the torpedomen forward can hear it running in the tube. This is critical, for it will be armed within a matter of seconds, and then almost anything could set it off. Besides, the motor is overspeeding in the tube, and it could conceivably break up under the strain and vibration—which might itself produce sufficient shock to cause an explosion.

But there isn't time to think much about possibilities. The skipper's reaction is instant. "Tubes forward, try again, by hand. Use full ejection pressure!" Full pressure is used only when firing at deep submergence, but this is an emergency.

The next command is for Clark Sprinkle in the conning tower. "Check fire!" Fyfe is not going to let the Jap get away while he waits for the casualty to be straightened out, but neither does he want the faulty torpedo to be ejected at the same time as a good one, and possibly interfere with it. If it does not eject on the second try, he will shoot the remaining tubes, and then return to the balky one.

"Number one tube fired by hand. Tube is clear!" The very welcome report is received after a few anxious seconds with a profound sense of relief. Only half-a-dozen seconds have been lost, altogether, and the situation is still good for the remaining fish.

"Resume fire, Clark!" But the exec has not needed that command. Number two torpedo is already on its way, followed a few seconds later by number three. Torpedoes number four, five, and six are held in reserve in case the first salvo misses.

Because these are wakeless electric torpedoes, Jake Fyfe, on the bridge, does not have the pencil-like wakes of steam and air to mark where they have gone. There is a slight disturbance of the surface of the water to show the direction they took, but that is all. Seven pairs of binoculars are glued to the Jap's low, lumbering silhouette and his odd-shaped bridge.

Down in the conning tower, the radar operator and the exec are staring at their screen, where the blip which is the target is showing up strongly and steadily, showing radar emanations still at the same uninterrupted interval. Suddenly, however, the radar waves become steady, as though the enemy operator had steadied his radar on a just-noticed blip, possibly to investigate it.

"I think he's detected us, sir!" whispers Radar. "See— it's steadied on us!"

Sprinkle has also seen. Eyes fixed on the cathode tube face he reaches for the portable mike to tell the skipper about this new development, when he drops it again. Before his eyes the blip has suddenly, astoundingly, grown much larger. It is now nearly twice the size it had been an instant before. Small flashes of light can be seen on the screen, going away from the outsized pip and disappearing. Then, swiftly, the pip reduces in size and disappears entirely. Nothing is left on the scope whatsoever.

At this moment a jubilant shout from the bridge can be heard. "We got him! We got him! He blew up and sank!" Sprinkle mops his brow.

The watchers on *Batfish*'s bridge had hardly expected anything quite so dramatic as what they saw. One torpedo had evidently reached the target, and must have hit into a magazine or possibly into a tank carrying gasoline. The Nip sub had simply exploded, with a brilliant red-and-yellow flame which shot high into the night sky, furiously outlined against the somber, sober grayness. And as quickly as the flame reached its zenith, it disappeared, as 2,500 tons of broken twisted Japanese steel plunged like a rock to the bottom of the ocean.

There was nothing left for torpedo number three— following a few seconds behind number two—to hit, and it passed over the spot where the enemy ship had been.

Batfish immediately proceeded to the spot where the sub had sunk, hoping to pick up a survivor or two, but the effort was needless. Undoubtedly all hands had been either killed instantly by the terrific explosion, or had been carried down in the ship. There had been absolutely no chance for anyone not already topside to get out. All Jake Fyfe could find was a large oil slick extending more than two miles in all directions from the spot where the enemy had last been seen.

Strangely—delighted and happy though he was over his success in destroying the enemy sub—the American skipper felt a few twinges of a peculiar emotion. This was very much like shooting your own kind, despite the proven viciousness and brutality exhibited by some of the enemy—and but for the superiority of his crew and equipment, the victim might have been *Batfish* instead of HIJMS-*I-41*.

The final attack on the Jap sub had been made at exactly two minutes after midnight on the morning of February 10. Then, an hour or so after sunset on the 11th, at 1915—

"Captain to the conn!" The skipper is up there in an instant.

The radar operator points to his radar 'scope. "There's another Jap sub, Captain!"

Sure enough, there, if you watch closely, is the same tiny disturbance which alerted *Batfish* two nights ago. This time there is less doubt as to what action to take. The same tactics which were heralded with such signal success on the first occasion are immediately placed into effect. The crew is called to battle stations, the tracking parties manned, and all is made ready for a warm reception. The radar party is cautioned—unnecessary precaution—to keep that piece of gear turned off except when a range and bearing are actually required.

If anything, it is even darker than it was the first night. Having found how ineffective the Jap radar really is—or was it simply that the Jap watch standers were asleep?—Fyfe determines to make the same kind of attack as before.

The situation develops exactly as it did before, except that this submarine is heading southeast instead of northeast. At 1,800 yards he is sighted from the bridge of the American submarine. He is making only 7 knots, somewhat slower than the other, and it takes him a little longer to reach the firing bearing. Finally everything is just about set. Sprinkle has made the "ready to shoot" report, and Fyfe will let them go in a moment, as soon as the track improves a bit and the range decreases to the optimum. About one minute to go—it won't be long now, chappy.

"Hello, he's dived! He dived right on the fire bearing!" Where there had been an enemy submarine, there was now only the rolling undulation of the sea. Nothing to do now but get out of there. *Batfish* must have waited too long and been detected. The Jap was keeping a slightly better watch than Fyfe had given him credit for, and now *Batfish* is being hunted. Just as quickly as that the whole situation has changed. With an enemy submarine known to be submerged within half a mile of you, there is only one of two things to do. Dive yourself, or beat it.

If you dive, you more or less give up the problem, and concentrate on hiding, which many skippers probably would have done. If you run away on the surface, however, there is a slight chance that he'll come back up, and you'll have another shot at him. Jake Fyfe is a stubborn man, and he doesn't give up easily: he discards the idea of diving. "Left full rudder!" he orders instead. His first object is to get away; and his second is to stay in action. Maybe the Jap will assume that he has continued running—which is precisely what Jake hopes he will do.

"All ahead flank!"

The Jap was on a southeasterly course before he dived. Knowing that his periscope must be up and watching his every move, Fyfe orders a northerly course, and *Batfish* roars away from the spot, steadying on a course slightly west of north. Three miles Fyfe lets her run, until he is reasonably sure to be beyond sonar as well as visual range. Then he alters course to the left, and within a short time arrives at a position *southwest* of the position at which the Jap sub dived.

In the conning tower, at the plotting station, and on the bridge there is some rapid and careful figuring going on. "Give the son of a bitch four knots," mutters Sprinkle to himself. "That puts him on this circle. Give him six knots, and he's here. Give him eight knots—oh, t' hell with 8 knots!" Clark Sprinkle's exasperation is almost comical as he grips his pencil in sweaty stubby fingers and tries to decide what he'd do if he were a Jap.

The point is that *Batfish* wants to arrive at some point where she will be assured of getting a moderately long-range radar contact the instant the Nip surfaces, in a position to be able to do something about it. *But don't let her spot us through the periscope, or wind up near enough for her to torpedo us while still submerged.* This is where the stuff you learned in school really pays off, brother.

Naturally, *Batfish* cannot afford to remain overly long in the vicinity. Every extra minute she spends there increases by that much the diameter of the circle upon which the enemy may be; and even at that very moment he may be making a periscope approach—while she hangs around and makes it easy for him. But Fyfe has no intentions of making it any easier than he can help. Once he has put his ship in what he has calculated to be a logical spot to await developments, he slows down to one third speed—about 4 knots. Then he orders the sound heads rigged out. With his stern toward the direction from which the enemy submarine would have to come, were he making an attack, and making 4 knots away from there, *Batfish* is forcing the Jap to make high submerged speed in order to catch her; she is banking on detecting him by sound before he can get close enough to shoot, or on detecting the torpedo itself if a long-range shot is fired.

Twenty minutes pass. Fyfe cannot guess how long the Nip sub will stay down, but his game is to outwit him. If his initial gambit of running away to the northward has fooled him, he'll probably show within an hour after diving. The soundmen listen with silent intensity, their headphones glued to their heads. The radar operator scrutinizes his 'scope with equal urgency. It would not do to miss any indication.

Suddenly, both sound operators look up at the same time. The senior one speaks for both. "Mr. Sprinkle! There's a noise, bearing zero one five!"

Clark is there in an instant. "What's it like?" He flips on the loudspeaker switch.

Clearly, a rushing sound can be heard, a sort of powerful swishing sound. It changes somewhat in intensity and tone, then suddenly stops. Like a flash the exec grabs the portable mike. "Captain," he bellows to the bridge. "He's blown his tanks, bearing zero one five. He'll be up directly!"

The blast from the bridge speaker nearly blows everyone off the bridge, for Sprinkle has a powerful voice. All binoculars are immediately turned to the bearing given. But the black night conceals its secrets well. Nothing can be seen.

The bridge speaker blares again. "Radar contact, zero one eight. That's him all right!"

Apparently convinced that all is clear, the Japanese submarine has surfaced, and is evidently going to continue on his way. *Batfish* is to get another chance. Whether the target saw them, or thought he saw them; heard them or thought he did; detected them on radar, or simply made a routine night dive, will never be known. One thing Jake is definite on, however: He will get no chance to detect *Batfish* this time.

Once again *Batfish* goes through all the intricate details of the night surface approach—with one big difference. The skipper is not going to go in on the surface. The Jap detected him the last time. He's got more strings to his bow than that.

The Jap has speeded up and changed course slightly. *Batfish* again seeks a position in front of him, and when the range and distance to the track are to Fyfe's liking, *Batfish* dives—but not entirely. Since the radar antennae are normally on top of the highest fixed structure of the ship, it follows that they are the last things to go under when a submarine dives. All Fyfe had done was dive his ship so that these vital antennae were still out of water, although nearly all the rest of the submarine is beneath the surface. This is a good trick; that *Batfish* had been able to do it so neatly is a tribute to the state of training and competence of her crew. With her radar antennae dry and out of water, they still function as well as when she was fully surfaced, and the dope continues to feed into the fire-control gear, even though not a thing can be seen through the periscope.

And of course the Jap, probably alerted and nervous—maybe he has heard of the failure of one of his brother subs to get through this same area two nights ago—has no target to see or detect by radar, unless you consider a few little odd-shaped pieces of pipe a target.

So on he comes, making 12 knots now, fairly confident that he has managed to avoid the sub which had stalked him a couple of hours ago. He doesn't even notice or pay any attention to the curious structure in the water a few hundred yards off his starboard beam—for Jake Fyfe has resolved to get as close as possible—and four deadly fish streak his way out of the dark night.

Mercifully, most of the Nip crew probably never knew what hit them. The first torpedo detonated amidships with a thunderous explosion, virtually blowing the ill-fated ship apart. As the two halves each upended and commenced to sink swiftly amid horrible gurgles of water and foaming of released air and fuel oil, the second and third torpedoes also struck home. Their explosions were slightly muffled, however, as though they might have struck some stray piece of metal and gone off mostly in water; but they served to increase the probability that none of the enemy crew had survived the initial attack.

Three minutes later Fyfe logged two more blasts from deep beneath his ship, evidently some kind of internal explosions in the broken hulk of the sinking submarine. Eight minutes later one terrifically loud explosion rocked *Batfish*. First thought to be an aircraft bomb, the explosion was finally put down to part of the swan song of the Nipponese sub. All during this period, and for some time later, Sound heard the usual noises of a sinking submarine—mainly small internal explosions and escaping air.

This time Jake Fyfe was prevented from trying to rescue any of the possible survivors of the catastrophe by the presence of a plane, which was detected just as *Batfish* was getting ready to surface. It is highly doubtful, however, that there could have been any survivors, in view of the triple-barreled blow the submarine had received.

Shortly after midnight, some twenty-four hours later, one of the more irrepressible members of *Batfish*'s crew was heard to mutter, "What, again? Ho hum; here we lose another night's sleep playing tag with these slant-eyed submarines!"—as Captain Jake Fyfe rushed past en route to the conning tower.

For the third time in four days the radar operator has called his skipper—unfortunately the patrol reports of our submarines do not usually list the names of the crew, nor their stations—it would be interesting to know whether the same man spotted the enemy each time. From the times of the three contacts, however, 2210, 1915, and 0155, it would appear that one contact was made by each of the three watch sections, and that therefore the three men standing the radar watches each can lay claim to one Nip sub.

Naturally, the particular peculiarity in the appearance of the radar 'scope which had first served to alert *Batfish* had been carefully explained to all radar watchers, and they all knew what to look for. In this case, as in the last, the operator simply pointed to his 'scope and stated flatly, "There's another one of those Jap subs, Captain!"

One look at the screen, and Jake Fyfe raps out the command to sound the general alarm.

This time Fyfe himself gets on the ship's interior announcing system. "It looks like another Nip submarine, boys," he says. "We ought to be written right into their operation orders by this time. Let's see if we can't help him along the same road as the other two!"

Fyfe and his tracking party are pretty fine hands by this time, and it only takes a short while before the Jap is picked up for sure on the radar, and his course and speed are known. The United States submariners are fairly certain he will either be on the northerly course of the first sub, or the southeasterly one of the second. It proves to be the latter—course one two zero, speed 7. *Batfish* heads to intercept, playing it cagily, as always, but a little more self-confident this time. Somehow these Japs don't seem to have as good equipment as our own—we can thank the home front for that—and they surely are not using what they have to the best advantage—for which we can thank *them.* And we will—in our own unique fashion.

But with the range still quite long, and before *Batfish* is able to get into attack position, the Japanese sub dives. Just why he does, no one knows. Possibly he detected an aircraft, or thought he did—although *Batfish* sees no planes on her radar—or perhaps he got a momentary contact on *Batfish* through some unexplained vagary of his radar equipment. The most probable explanation is that he has heard of the failure of two other boats to get through this particular stretch, and is attempting to make pursuit more difficult by diving occasionally.

But Jake Fyfe has the answer for this one cold. Last night qualified him in its implementation. He heads, despite this new development, to the spot originally selected for attack position. Then, instead of diving, he proceeds down the track at 4 knots, sound gear rigged out, radar sweeping steadily and deliberately, lookouts alerted and tensely watching.

Half an hour after the Jap dived, *Batfish*'s radar once again picks up the faint, shimmering emanations of the Nip radar. He's back up again, though this time no blowing of tanks has been heard. Fyfe, Sprinkle, and the tracking party start the same old approach game.

The first thing to do is to get actual radar contact; this wobble in the 'scope is no good for tracking, even though it does give a vague indication of the enemy's bearing. So *Batfish* heads for the source of what her radar operators now term the "wobbly," expecting to get contact momentarily. Several thousand yards are covered in this manner, with no result, except that the wobbly is getting stronger. Fyfe and his exec become worried over this development. They know the Jap is surfaced—or can he have thought of the same dodge they themselves used only last night? Suppose the Jap is even then in the process of making the same type of approach on *Batfish!* An unpleasant thought to entertain. The lookouts redouble their vigilance, especially directing their search at the water surface within half a mile around them. At the skipper's order everything else in the ship is subordinated to the sound watch. Fans and blowers are secured. Unnecessary gear throughout the ship is turned off. Most important, the diesel engines are secured and propulsion shifted to the battery. Silently, eerily, *Batfish* glides through the water, peering and listening for the telltale swoosh of a torpedo coming at her. If the Jap is very smart indeed, he will silence also, and will get so close before shooting that *Batfish* will not have a chance of avoiding the torpedoes, even though she might actually hear them on the way.

The lapping of the water alongside is excruciatingly loud in the unnatural stillness. The very air seems stifling and oppressive on the bridge, as it most certainly is down below, with all blowers turned off. Your breath seems to stop, and your heart beats with a muffled thump. The tiny blower motor in the radar gear whines insistently in the conning tower; impossible to shut it down because it keeps the radar tubes from overheating. Sprinkle makes a mental note to have it pulled out and overhauled at the first opportunity.

Down below everyone talks in whispers, not that whispering could do any good, but in tacit recognition of the deadly desperateness of the situation. The Jap sub, submerged, possibly making an approach, and *themselves still on the surface!*

The basic problem, of course, is to compute how far the Jap sub can travel toward them, assuming his most probable course and speed for the time since he dived, and then to stay at least that distance, plus a little to be on the safe side, away from the spot where he submerged. Fyfe, straining for that elusive radar contact which his reasoned deductions say should come soon, allows *Batfish* to go as far as he dares before reversing course again. Just as he gives the order, someone in one of the engine rooms drops a wrench on the steel deck. The sharp noise is carried up the silent main induction pipe and hits the tensely waiting and watching bridge with a shock. All hands are visibly startled, and one lookout almost drops his binoculars. The skipper half opens his mouth, then shuts it again. It wouldn't do to show exasperation at this point.

And then, finally, with *Batfish* still swinging to her hard over rudder, it comes at last. "Radar contact, bearing three three six!" Fyfe's judgment and nerve have been vindicated again. The Jap was probably just being cagey himself, and had no knowledge of the presence of the United States submarine.

It happens that there are only two torpedoes left forward in *Batfish,* which really does not matter much since she is due shortly to depart station en route to Pearl Harbor. But it must be admitted that no one expected to run into three nearly identical situations like this—and until the third submarine was detected Fyfe had held no qualms whatever at being nearly dry forward. Now, however, a problem presents itself.

It is necessary to maneuver *Batfish* so that the Jap goes across her stern instead of her bow. Not too easy to do, since you have to be going away instead of toward the target. Fyfe plays his target slowly and carefully, somewhat like an expert fisherman campaigning against a crafty big one. The cast has been made, the fly has landed, the big fellow is nosing toward it, ready to head back for the deep water at the slightest suspicious sign.

This particular submarine has shown considerably more wariness than either of the other two. His peculiar actions on surfacing have proved him to be astute and careful, and Jake Fyfe is not the man to underrate his opponent. His recent scare is rather fresh in mind, and the ice is still mighty thin, measured as it is only in the superiority of United States equipment and alertness.

So *Batfish* tracks the target, gets his course and speed entirely by radar without ever having seen him, and finally submerges dead ahead of him, several miles away. Once again Fyfe uses the stunt of leaving his radar antennae out of water, so that the all-important information on the target's movements will continue to be available to his fire control party and the intricate instruments they operate. Only this time he keeps his stern toward the target and moves slowly away from him, turning as he does so, with the result that the doomed Jap passes directly across his stern at the desired range, and three torpedoes are on their way to meet him. This is really a deliberate shot.

It also is slightly longer in range than the two previous attacks, and there is a longer wait in *Batfish*'s conning tower after the fish are finally sent on their way.

The skipper is watching through the periscope. He can now clearly see the long, low shape of the enemy, his odd-shaped bridge, and his peculiar undulating deckline. He is not a bad-looking ship, Fyfe must admit to himself, and most of these big Jap boats are pretty fast—at least as fast as our own. Not much is known about how they handle under water, however, and, like all United States submariners, Fyfe will reserve his judgment on that score. Our experience with big boats is that you pay for size with submerged maneuverability, and that the well-established theory about efficiency varying with the size of the vessel does not apply to submarines. The Nip is painted black, which makes him just a little easier to see against the gray night, and on the side of his bridge can quite plainly be seen a white rectangle with a dark disk in the center.

On he comes, ominous and a bit pathetic, entirely unaware of the three messengers of doom speeding his way. Fyfe, in the meantime, is a bit anxious. Without taking his eyes from the periscope, he calls out, "How long since the first one?"

Clark Sprinkle answers obliquely, "About fifteen seconds to go, Captain."

"Fifteen seconds! Damn!"

But the torpedoes run true and as intended, and Fyfe's impatience finally is brought to an end. "A hit!" he shouts, "a beautiful hit!" And so it is: a single hit which produces a brilliant orange explosion right in the center of the stricken ship.

Simultaneously, a wide diffusion of pips is noted on the radar screen, indicating that the target has blown apart. Then all the pips die away. The whole catastrophe has been silent; no sound whatsoever has reached the eager listeners in *Batfish*. A moment later, however, the noise of the explosion with its terrifying aftermath crackles over the sound gear into the headsets of the operators, and, indeed, comes right through the pressure hull, so that no man in the crew need have it described to him.

The loud WHAM of the warhead going off is followed instantly, and almost as though it were a single explosion, by a much louder and more prolonged WHRROOOM. This undoubtedly must be the enemy's magazines going up— and there exists a strong probability that he is carrying an extra-heavy load, possibly intended for the beleaguered Japs in the Philippines.

One of the three stopwatches is stopped with the first hit, and there is no doubt that this was the first torpedo, running the calculated range at exactly the calculated speed. But there are no further hits, despite the care with which the other fish had been launched on their way. This occasions no disappointment, however, since there is simply nothing left for the last two fish to hit.

As for *Batfish*, Jake Fyfe had her fully on the surface again within three minutes after the torpedo hit. Though he strongly doubted that there could possibly be any survivors of the terrific explosion he had witnessed, he was determined, as before, to give them a chance for their lives. It was nearly dawn, and no good came from use of the searchlight, which Fyfe had ordered turned on and played upon the water, so the decision was made to wait until daylight, in hopes that Jap planes patrolling the area would somehow not be immediately in evidence.

Parenthetically, one cannot help comparing *Batfish*'s repeated magnanimous attempts to succor the victims of her attacks with the treatment meted out in similar circumstances by the Japanese. There is one instance on record in which most of the crew of an American submarine were picked up by a Japanese destroyer; one man was injured, and was promptly thrown overboard. Another had swallowed so much salt water that he was retching heavily, and would also have gone overboard had he not fought clear of his saviors and joined the remainder of the group of survivors. In the case of *Tang*, the pitifully small number of survivors were mercilessly beaten and clubbed about the head and body. By contrast, *Batfish* deliberately exposed herself by turning on a searchlight to assist in locating survivors of her night's handiwork, and then voluntarily remained on the surface in these enemy waters until long after daybreak, in hopes of possibly finding one or two. Since her position was well within enemy aircraft patrols, the unofficial rules by which most United States submarines guided their actions required that she be submerged during daylight.

Several of our submarines were enabled to rescue enemy survivors in some manner or other, after either they or someone else had torpedoed them. In more than one instance American sailors or officers had to go overboard after survivors and force them to accept their hospitality. In no case was such a prisoner badly treated after rescue; most of them gained weight during their sojourn on board, and were so well treated that instructions had finally to be issued to treat them with greater severity in order not to "spoil" them.

With the dawn *Batfish* sighted much oil, bits of wood and paper, debris of various kinds, all newly in the water and quite evidently from the sunken submarine. No Japanese were seen, however—dead or alive. It appeared that once again there was to be nothing tangible to reward Jake Fyfe for his brilliant achievement, but finally a small wooden box recovered from the water was found to contain the Jap navigator's workbook and navigational instruments. Evidently he had just brought it topside, perhaps preparatory to taking a sight or two despite the not-too-favorable weather, but had not yet opened it.

Because the Japanese use Arabic numerals for navigational purposes, there was no difficulty in reading the workbook. Apparently the Jap departed Nagoya for Formosa, and had left there for Luzon—where he never arrived.

Batfish left her area for Guam three days later, and on February 21 she moored alongside the submarine tender *Apollo* in Apra Harbor, Guam.

To say that Jake Fyfe was received with open arms by the submarine brethren is putting it mildly. Though no public announcement of his magnificent feat could be made, owing to the well-laid policy of cloaking our submarine activities in anonymity, it instantly became known and broadcast throughout the Submarine Force. Here was another patrol nearly on a par with Sam Dealey's famous five-destroyers cruise. Here was additional proof that the spirit of the submarine force, so beautifully exemplified by Dealey and O'Kane and Morton, was still going strong, and that those who came after had not lost the touch of their predecessors.

There was, however, an even more important and far-reaching effect. To a nation like the United States, with its far-flung merchant marine, the submarine is perhaps the greatest menace to successful prosecution of war. That is to say, if and when we should get into another war our backs will immediately be up against the wall if the powers arrayed against us have a powerful submarine force. Witness what the Germans did to Great Britain in two world wars, and to us in World War II. In both instances the Allies won, but only by the narrowest of margins.

However, born of the imminence of defeat, a new type of submarine was developed in the closing days of World War II by the Germans. True, they did not invent anything extraordinary, but they put together several known but unused ideas to develop the high-speed snorkel submarine, and it may safely be said that this vessel has revolutionized previous concepts of anti-submarine warfare. It is virtually immune to the countermeasures we used so successfully against German and Japanese submersibles, and its efficiency in attack is trebled.

Fortunately, our military leaders have not neglected the challenge laid down by the fast submarine. A tremendous amount of thought has gone into the problem of how to get enemy subs before they can wreak their threatened damage upon our commerce—our lifeblood, so to speak. And every time the discussion in the halls of the Navy Department or the Pentagon—or even in the White House—has waxed long and earnestly, someone is sure to come up with a reference to Jake Fyfe and the fact that *Batfish* sank three enemy submarines within the space of four days with no damage and very little danger to herself. *Why not set a submarine to kill a submarine?*

The idea has grown until now, seven years after Fyfe's exploit, something is being done about it. It is obvious that the submarine will enjoy, in relation to another submersible, those same advantages which all subs always have had. That is, surprise, the ability of concealment, and so on. With one difference: since the hunt is to take place in the natural environment of the submarine, *either one may become the hunter and either the hunted.* Prior detection will assume much greater importance than ever before—if that is possible. There is no question but that it will still be a nerve-racking occupation.

17 ————

TIRANTE

From: The Commander, Submarine Force,
          Pacific Fleet
To: Lieutenant Edward L. Beach, Jr., U.S.
          Navy
Via: The Commanding Officer, U.S.S.
          TRIGGER (SS 237)
Subject: Change of duty

1. In accordance with a dispatch from the Bureau
   of Naval Personnel dated 16 May 1944, which cannot be quoted herein, when directed by the
   Commanding Officer, U.S.S. TRIGGER, you will
   consider yourself detached from duty on board the
   U.S.S. TRIGGER, and from such other duties as
   may have been assigned you; will report to the
   Commandant Fourteenth Naval District for first
   available government transportation, including
   air, to a port on the West Coast of the United
   States. Upon arrival, proceed and report to the
   Commandant, Navy Yard, Portsmouth, New Hampshire, for temporary duty in connection with the
   fitting out of the U.S.S. TIRANTE (SS 420), and for
   duty on board that vessel when commissioned . . .

• • •

There was a lot more to my orders, including the fact that the Secretary of the Navy had determined this employment on shore duty was "required by the public interests," and in early June 1944, wearing brand-new lieutenant commander's stripes, and accompanied by my bride of one month, I arrived in Portsmouth.

Memories of the *Trigger* were strong. Only a few weeks earlier, as I was packing shortly before midnight to catch an early-morning plane for San Francisco, one by one members of her crew had come forward to say good-bye. And as I had walked alone down the dock, I looked back at her, lying low and gray in the dim moonlight, splotched with rust and peeled-off paint, and knew she was no longer mine.

Now I had a new ship, as yet uncompleted, and a new skipper, and there was everything to do all over again. *Tirante* was to have the latest devices, the strongest hull American engineering skill could devise, the most powerful engines, and an enlarged torpedo-carrying capacity. She would be an improved instrument for the art of underwater warfare, and should be able to outdo anything old *Trigger* had done. Yet I wondered whether she would possess that same flair, that same capacity for finding action and bringing it to a successful conclusion.

There was only one answer to this, and many were the discussions with the new skipper—himself in his first command—as to how to imbue our new ship with the fighting spirit and derring-do we wanted. I came to admire George Street more and more as time went on, for he seemed to combine the qualities of thorough preparation with a certain amount of respect for the ideas of others, and, when convinced, an intelligently directed follow-through.

It took about eight months from the time *Tirante*'s keel was laid until we broke her commission pennant on November 6, 1944—about three months from the time her crew arrived—and nearly another month passed before we had her at sea.

Our first step was to practice with the equipment and learn its uses, starting with the easiest operations and building up to the more intricate ones—all in the safe confines of the navy yard. Drill after drill we forced ourselves to perform alongside the dock, and before we took *Tirante* out for her first dive we were confident that every piece of gear operated as designed, and that every man knew his job.

Late in November the new ship stood out to sea. Her engines ran throatily, her stem breasted the waves daintily, her sleek length droned effortlessly on the cold, restless sea. Only the less-than-perfectly-ordered bustle of her crew belowdecks betrayed her newness as time drew near for her first dive.

"Stand by to dive." The uncustomary order pealed through the ship's announcing system. The crew stood to their stations, fingering the controls with which, in a moment, they would send her below. I was glad to see they were a little keyed up.

Ed Campbell, engineer and diving officer, looked inquiringly at me. As I nodded to him, he held up his hand, motioning as though opening a valve. High-pressure air whistled into the control room. A moment— he clenched his fist. The whistle cut off abruptly, as the auxiliaryman behind us whirled shut the stop valve. Ed and I inspected the barometer; it held steady, showing about half an inch more atmospheric pressure than before.

I climbed a few rungs of the ladder to the conning tower, far enough to speak to George Street at the periscope. He was already using it, though the ship was still on the surface. The conning tower hatch was shut tightly, I knew, because the ship had held air, and its "Christmas Tree" light was green. "Pressure in the boat. Green aboard. All set below, Captain."

George took his eyes from the 'scope and grinned at me. "Take her down, then," he said. "We can't learn any younger."

I reached over my head, grasped the conning tower diving alarm, and swung the arm twice through its short arc. Stiff with newness, it did not return to the Off position of its own accord, and I had to push it back each time. As the familiar reverberations died away—they, at least, sounded exactly as they had in *Trigger*—I seized the general announcing microphone. "Dive, dive," I called.

The vents popped as D. W. Remley, chief torpedoman and chief of the boat, pulled their hydraulic control handles toward him one after another. We could hear the rush of air escaping from the ballast tanks. The helmsman clicked his two annunciators over to Ahead Standard, and centered his rudder amidships. *Tirante*'s gently heaving deck seemed to change its motion; tilt ever so slightly down by the bow. Beneath me in the control room I could hear Ed quietly coaching his planesmen as they leaned into their big nickel-steel wheels. I could feel *Tirante* start to break surface and her down inclination become greater as I steadied myself against the side of the conning tower and made a note to have the diving alarm worked over.

George was going around and around with his periscope, alternately watching bow and stern. After a moment he spoke. "Bow's under." Then, in a few seconds, "Stern's gone." The sloshing sound of the water in the superstructure was replaced by the noise of the sea climbing swiftly around the bridge coaming and up the periscope supports. I thought I could feel the angle of inclination decrease imperceptibly.

"All ahead two-thirds." That was Ed's gentle voice calling up from the control room. The helmsman clicked the annunciators, got an answering click as the electricians in the maneuvering room responded. *Tirante*'s bow began to lift.

"Flood forward trim from sea." Ed again. She was coming up a bit too fast to suit him. "Secure flooding." The faintly heard rumbling of water flowing stopped. The deck continued to return to normal. "All ahead one-third." It is submarine custom for the diving officer to control the speed until he is satisfied with the submerged trim.

Ed was calling up the hatchway again: "Final trim, sir. Depth, six-oh feet, one-third speed." There was a barely perceptible tone in his voice. To hit the final compensation so closely on the very first dive of a new ship smacked of the miraculous. On *Trigger*'s first dive it had taken us an hour and a half of pumping and flooding before we were satisfied.

My new skipper was not one to pass by the moment, either; that was one of the first things I had begun to like about him. In a few well-chosen words shouted down the hatch, he let Ed know that he was without doubt the world's finest diving officer, and that we were extraordinarily fortunate to have him aboard.

Tirante's character developed rapidly, even before the training period was complete. Her radar was the most powerful I had ever encountered; her engines ran best when loaded to more than full rated power; she made 21 knots with ease whereas other subs of the same design struggled to reach 19. She carried four more fish than *Trigger*, and her torpedoes had been modified to eliminate the frustrations of the earlier war years. Many of *Tirante*'s crew were already veterans of the Pacific, some of them from *Trigger* herself. We built upon the virtues and mistakes of those from whom we had learned the business.

The prologue of *Tirante*'s first war patrol states laconically: "Ship completed on November 23, 1944, and commenced training in fog, storms, and freezing weather off Portsmouth. *Tirante*'s builders did a wonderful job." Somehow, starting with that first dive, everything seemed to work right the first time for us. After two and a half years fighting a ship which had gradually had more and more things wrong with her—whether the result of enemy action or just plain misadventure—despite which she had performed magnificently, it was an unprecedented delight to me to have everything go right.

During our two-week training period at New London prior to departure for the Pacific we worked out our fire control, our damage control, and all the other phases of submarine technique. Tirelessly, Ensign Bill Ledford, onetime chief torpedoman of *Trigger*, now assistant torpedo officer of *Tirante*, tinkered with his fish, and every torpedo we fired in practice hit the target. By the time we were ready to leave, *Tirante* had become a perfectionist, and we had no doubt of being able to pass any readiness inspection Admiral Lockwood cared to toss at us.

Then the day before setting out for Balboa and the Pacific our preparations were interrupted by an unexpected summons for the skipper. When he returned, he motioned Lieutenant Endicott (Chub) Peabody II and me into his stateroom.

"It was the force gunnery officer," he said without preamble. "He's got a hot potato on his hands and wants us to take it over."

"What is it, Captain?"

George chuckled. "It seems that the employees of the Westinghouse Corporation plant at Sharon, Pennsylvania, which makes electric torpedoes, got together and donated one special torpedo for the war effort. It's up in the torpedo shop now, tested and ready to go, and they want somebody to take it out with them."

"We've already loaded all our fish, sir," said Chub. "We'd have to take one back out . . ."

The skipper's grin widened. "Wait till I tell you the rest. This torpedo is painted up like a highway billboard sign so nobody can possibly mistake it. It's been photographed at least a dozen times, at least once at every stage of its construction and trials. Two admirals have publicly told Sharon that the fish will be delivered to the enemy with their compliments, and now—somebody has got to make good on all the bragging."

"You mean," I interjected, "they want us to take this particular fish out and plant it in the bottom of some Jap battleship? Don't they know battleships don't grow on trees and that even with a perfectly aimed salvo some of the fish are bound to miss?"

"Oh, they're not unreasonable. They'll settle for any decent-sized maru."

Chub said, "We'd sure look foolish if we took it out and then had to report we hadn't hit anything with it, wouldn't we?"

This didn't faze George. "You're right," he said, "and that's why taking it along is purely voluntary. A couple of ships have already declined the honor for that very reason. So the force gunnery officer is getting right anxious to get rid of it, and I told him we'd see that it reached the desired destination."

We might have known our skipper would never pass up this kind of challenge. There was a gleam in Chub's eyes, and I, too, felt a little pleased with the Old Man.

"It's on its way down right now," George added.

By the time it had arrived in a specially built torpedo carrier, accompanied by a bevy of high-ranking officers and half a dozen photographers, and we had tucked it aboard, we realized we had carried out the most thoroughly documented torpedo loading in history. And, as Ed Campbell commented after watching the performance, if we came back from patrol without having made good with it, we had better throw our hats in ahead of us wherever we entered.

On January 8, 1945, *Tirante* set forth from New London for Pearl Harbor. The passage took us thirty-three days, including eight days of exercises at Balboa, Canal Zone, and we drilled every day and part of every night. We had been out of the war zone for so long that there was a lot of catching up to do, and Street and I pored over our file of war patrol reports as we sped into warmer seas and through the Canal.

We were in a hurry, too, for it was already obvious that the war had not much longer to last. Our boats were crisscrossing the waters off the coast of Japan haunting the harbor entrances, or staying on the surface with impunity just offshore during daylight. One of our submarines had even entered Tokyo Bay on the surface during daylight to rescue an aviator who had ditched there during a carrier strike.

The Japanese merchant marine—what was left of it—lived in terror of the American submarines. In 1944 approximately half of the ships departing from the empire found their final destination at the bottom. Our executions at night had been the most horrendous of all. Once Admiral Lockwood had straightened out the torpedo fiasco, the heartbreaking failures and unexplained "misses" had been greatly reduced, and convoy after convoy had been wiped out in the hours between sunset and sunrise. The Japanese were now holing up at night, and running ships across the open sea only during daylight, when they figured our submarines would have to attack submerged, thus sacrificing mobility and giving them a better chance of getting their ships through.

So we worked our way through the training program at Balboa and Pearl Harbor with a vengeance and a will, finishing both of them in the minimum possible time, and then there remained only one thing before we could be on our way—the selection of our patrol area.

To us this meant a lot, for ComSubPac never gave a sign of how well or how poorly trained he considered any particular submarine. If she passed the stiff requirements he had set down, he sent her on patrol; if she did not, he held her up for more training; in extreme cases, he had been known to relieve the skipper and others of her crew. You could tell what Uncle Charlie thought of you only by where he sent you: the hottest ships went to the hottest spots, for obvious reasons. Finally our assignment came: the East China and Yellow Seas—just about as hot an area as he could hand out.

Once more the luck of the *Tirante* had proved good. We

carefully loaded our "Sharon Special" into number-six torpedo tube. Since we always fired in inverse order, with the first torpedo aimed at the MOT (Middle of Target), this location would give it the maximum chance of hitting with our first salvo from the bow tubes. And after that particular salvo had been fired, we would all feel much better.

Exchanging the play-acting of training for the reality of bombs, depth charges, warheads, and sinking ships is probably the most massive change which comes to an individual or a ship. At the same time, it is one of those things which cannot be approached by degrees. No matter how realistic the training, there is still the comforting knowledge that all participants will eventually find their way back to harbor. It is a common phenomenon to discover that the most expert, aggressive, farseeing person during training exercises somehow never quite finds the same opportunities open to him in battle. And an individual who never made much of an impression before might rise to astonishing heights of effectiveness under the stimulus of extreme danger. So is it with ships—especially submarines.

A psychologist could probably explain why it is that the first action on any patrol so often sets the tone for the whole cruise, and why the manner in which a new submarine handles her first contact with the enemy sets the character of the entire ship from then on. George Street and I did not know why, though we used to argue the reasons, but we knew it was so.

On the southern tip of Kyushu lies a huge bay, Kagoshima Kaiwan, protected by several small islands offshore. Our information indicated that many coastal freighters used the harbor. The chart of previous patrols off Kyushu showed few submarine tracks here, no doubt because of the restricted waters, but the water was deep all the way up to the shoreline. Not at all bad, if you didn't mind fairly close quarters.

Our object was twofold: to flood the ship as quickly as possible; and to get rid (honorably) of our VIT (Very Important Torpedo). So we resolved to venture into the precarious place, right off the harbor entrance, and patrol between the offshore islands and the mainland. I stayed up all night navigating, and shortly before dawn—on the morning of March 25—dived in the spot the captain had selected, five miles off the entrance. But this did not satisfy George; during the morning, while I caught up on my sleep, he closed the coast within less than two miles, and shortly after noon a ship was sighted coming out of the bay.

Our approach did not work out quite the way he had intended. We had stationed ourselves close to the beach, so that we would be on the shoreward side of any target coming out of the bay and heading up the coast. Thus we would be heading out to deeper water during the attack, and would be sure of firing our VIT from her bow tube. But the target, a small freighter, came by on our land side, apparently within inches of the rock-strewn shoreline. Submerged, our draft was so great that we could not turn toward him for a bow shot for fear of striking the bottom. So we fired a salvo from the stern tubes. The first torpedo blew the guts out of him less than one minute after we had let her go, and the other two exploded upon striking the shore. It took about a minute for our victim to sink.

The VIT still languished in the lower port forward torpedo tube, however, so we picked out a new spot well up the coast from Kagoshima Kaiwan—a precipitous cliff called Oniki Saki—and dived within a mile of it next morning. Three days we haunted the place, and right after lunch the third day our next victim came along.

The general alarm was still sounding as I reached the control room. I jumped up the ladder and crowded into the conning tower behind Chub Peabody where I could navigate if necessary, coordinate the fire control solution, and assist the skipper as might be required. Street was already at the periscope.

"Looks like a torpedo target," he said. "Take a look."

I could see an object resembling a small square building with a large black chimney slightly to the right of its middle. A cloud of smoke belched from the chimney and was carried flat to the right. Shimmering haze made the lines difficult to distinguish.

"Mark the bearing," I said, and snapped the handles as signal for the periscope to start down again. "Small, old-type freighter," I said to George. "Angle on the bow port ten. Seems to be making all the speed he can, probably ten knots."

George nodded. "That's my guess, too, Ned. We're using ten knots, and I put his angle on the bow as port fifteen." He glanced over Chub's shoulder to where the dials of the TDC reproduced a picture of the relative positions of the enemy ship and ourselves.

"Here's our chance to get rid of the VIT," I observed. Everybody in the conning tower nodded, and I checked the camera.

Several observations later George turned to me. "Make ready three fish, Ned, and spread them one to hit, one ahead, one astern."

We had already talked this over. Doctrine called for a spread of torpedoes equal to more than the length of the target, but this had been developed in the days of faulty torpedoes. Our first attack had proved that our torpedoes were all right. I ordered the spread, but aimed them so that all three ought to hit—one at the bow, one under the stack, and one at the stern. The VIT would go at the stack.

We had been twisting and turning, following the target's zigzag plan, maintaining ourselves in position while he approached. George, veteran of many patrols in the old *Gar* out of Australia, certainly knew how to handle a submarine. We never made a wasted motion, and his periscope technique was perfection. Now he put down the 'scope and gave several quiet orders. *Tirante* ceased maneuvering and slowed down.

"Stand by forward." George pointed to the telephone talker, who was already relaying the word.

"Range." He pointed to the sound operator.

"One two double oh," from the latter. Chub tapped his range dial and grinned tightly at the firing panel. Number six fish showed "Ready," and the switch was turned to On. The fire controlman stood with his hand on the firing key. I turned to Chub's setup. The TDC showed the enemy just coming into the optimum firing position. It was humming softly, and the Correct Solution lights were glowing for the forward tube nest. The Gyro Angle Order switch was in the right position.

"Gyros matched and ready!" announced Gene Richey, assistant TDC operator.

"Set!" I told the skipper. He rose with the periscope halfway—"Mark!"—and signaled for it to go down.

"Zero four three-a-half," sang out Karlesses, the periscope jockey. I saw that it checked exactly with the angle on the TDC.

"Fire!" I shouted. The fire controlman pushed the firing key, and we felt the recoil as a sudden jolt of air squirted out the first fish. Two more jolts followed.

"All torpedoes running normally," reported the sound man. Ensconced in a corner out of the way, a seaman was counting time. It seemed to take hours before he got to thirty seconds.

The periscope started up again. If all went well, the first torpedo would be hitting about the time it got up. Time stood frozen. I could feel the palms of my hands sweating, and wiped them along my trouser legs. They still felt damp.

WHRRRANG-G-G-! A tremendous explosion shook the heavy steel of *Tirante*'s frame. The periscope quivered in George's grasp, and he seemed to press his forehead even deeper into the rubber buffer. I was standing beside him, waiting for my chance, and in a moment he turned the 'scope over to me.

I could not see the center of our target, for it was obliterated in a column of water which had risen high above the tops of his masts. The bow and stern, as I watched, rose out of water and came toward each other. Then the water fell back, but the middle of the ship had disappeared.

As the skipper jostled me out of the way, I had a split-second picture of the hapless vessel cocked up, twisted away from us, and sliding under.

"Camera," George suddenly called out. Quickly I handed it to him; helped him fit it in the periscope. Just as he snapped the shutter, another, lesser, explosion in the target vibrated through our ship. Evidently a boiler.

When my next turn to look came a second or two later, there was just time to see the tip of the stern slide out of sight. Thirty seconds from the moment of the initial

explosion, the ship had ceased to exist. The two extra torpedoes, running a few seconds after the first one, were
robbed of their target and, neatly bracketing the stricken
hulk, sped on beyond into the empty sea.

The date was March 28, and we made a special note in
our log for that day that the torpedo which had wrought
such devastating effect was torpedo number 58009,
donated to the Navy as a contribution to the war effort by
the employees of the Westinghouse torpedo factory at
Sharon, Pennsylvania. It still bore its special paint job as it
streaked through the water on its final errand. Sharon
received pictorial proof of its special contribution about
four months after the Navy had accepted it.

That night, well offshore, I spread out the charts for
the captain as we debated where next to carry our hunt.
However, a message on the submarine Fox radio intercept
schedule brought a change to our plans. *Trigger*, which
had completed two unproductive patrols since I left her,
and was currently on her third, had been ordered to join
Tirante in coordinated patrol in the East China Sea. On her
present patrol—on which she had sunk two ships—she
had a new skipper, David Connole, whom I had known
slightly when he was a junior officer in the old *Pompano*
before she was lost.

Trigger was due to rendezvous with us that very night.
We should raise her by radio in a few hours. I became
rather excited at the prospect of seeing my old home
again. Since there would be some coordination to accom-
plish, someone would have to go aboard for a conference.
This was too good a chance to miss, and there were plenty
of volunteers from men who had once served in *Trigger* to
help man our tiny rubber boat.

Several times that night we called *Trigger* by radio, but

there was no answer. Silence. As morning drew near we dashed for the coast, submerged in a likely-looking spot, and waited impatiently for darkness again. Then we moved offshore once more to call my old ship. *Trigger from Tirante. Trigger from Tirante . . . S 237 from S 420 . . . S 237 from S 420 . . .*

All night long the call went out. Carefully we peaked our transmitter to the exact frequency; gently we turned our receivers up and down the band to pick up the answer in case *Trigger* was a bit off key. All during that long and sleepless night we heard nothing.

The third night was a repetition of the second, except that I spent nearly the whole time in the radio room. At irregular intervals Ed Secard tapped out the unrequited call. His face was inscrutable, his manner natural and precise. But Secard had made many patrols in *Trigger*, and when the time came for him to be relieved, he waved the man away. Fine beads of sweat broke out on his forehead, and a spot of color burned on his youthful cheekbones, but his right hand steadily and precisely pounded the coded call letters over and over again: *S 237 V S 420 . . . K . . . S 237 V S 420 . . . K . . . S 237 V S 420 . . . K . . . Trigger from Tirante . . . I have a message for you . . . Trigger from Tirante I have a message for you . . . Trigger from Tirante . . . Come in please . . .*

A spare set of earphones on my head, I watched the silent instruments as if by sheer concentration I might drag a response from them. Every time I glanced up to the open door of the radio room, there were intent faces staring at me—worried faces, belonging to men I knew well, who said nothing, and did not need to. Once someone handed in two cups of coffee.

There never was any answer, and deep in our hearts,

after three nights, that was answer enough. With your surface ships there are always survivors, messages, maybe a bit of wreckage. They always operate together, so there is always someone who can later tell what happened. With submarines there is just the deep, unfathomable silence.

We could visualize the sudden, unexpected catastrophe. Maybe a Kamikaze plane. Maybe a depth charge—a bull's-eye, after more than four hundred misses. Maybe a torpedo, or a mine, or even—inconceivably—an operational casualty.

In some compartment they may have had a split second to realize that *Trigger*'s stout size has been breached. The siren screech of the collision alarm. Instantly the angry water takes possession. The shock has startled everyone in other compartments, and the worst is instantly obvious.

Almost immediately she upends. The air pressure increases unbearably. Everything loose or not tightly secured cascades down to the bottom, against what used to be a vertical bulkhead. Some men have hung on where they were, but most are struggling around in indescribable confusion at the bottom of the compartment. Instinctively all eyes turn to the depth gauges and watch as the needles begin their crazy spin. Slowly at first, then faster and faster, they race around the dials. The shallow depth gauges soon travel past their limits; finally jam against their stops on the second go around. The deep-depth gauges and sea-pressure gauges soon afterward reach the limits of their travel. Nothing can be heard except the rush of water, the groaning and creaking of *Trigger*'s dying body, and the trapped, pounding pulses of the men.

Down, down, down she goes, to who knows what depth, until finally the brave ribs give way, the steel shell collapses, and *Trigger*'s gallant spirit ascends to the Valhalla of ships, bearing with her the souls of eighty-nine loyal sailors.

I could almost feel it happening, as the morning drew closer. We had decided to dive off Bono Misaki this morning, and finally I had to leave the radio room to plot our position. My heart felt like lead as I stalked out of the tiny hot compartment; a backward glance showed me Secard's head drooping into shaking hands.

That morning we sank a lugger by gunfire. It had refused to surrender when we fired a shot across his bow. We tried to pick up the survivors, but they dived into the water, and paddled away, clinging to bits of wreckage. It was only about six miles to the mainland of Kyushu, so we let them be and unceremoniously departed.

On the morning of April 6, *Tirante* dived off Shori To, on the south coast of Korea, and what followed is perhaps best told in the words of the patrol report itself:

APRIL 6

0540 Dived off SHORI TO. Saw numerous fishing schooners dragging nets astern. Kept busy staying clear all during the day. Decided to try to capture one and take the personnel back to base, since they ought to have information about the suspected anchorage at REISUE KAIWAN.

1918 Surfaced, going after one of the larger schooners.

1930 Having trouble coming alongside, and he

isn't cooperating. Fired a 40mm shell through his mainsail. The shell exploded, making a big hole in the sail; a 30 cal. machine gun cut his mainsail halyard so he lowered his sails in short order.

1940 Boat alongside. We look huge by comparison. Lt. Endicott PEABODY II (All American, Harvard 1942) and SPENCE, H.W. GM1c jumped aboard, both armed to the teeth in terrifying fashion. The dignity of the landing party was considerably shaken when Lt. PEABODY landed in a pile of fish and skidded across the deck in a tremendous "Prat" fall, but their efficiency was unimpaired. With many hoarse shouts and bursts of tommy gun fire, three thoroughly scared and whimpering fishermen were taken aboard. One KOREAN successfully hid by jumping over the side. Found out later he thought we were Japs, thus putting his days as a draft-dodger to an end.

SPENCE, having routed the last KOREAN out of a locker in the cabin where he had hidden, and having picked up a clock and pipe as souvenirs, reported to the Gunnery Officer that the search of the schooner below decks had been completed. The Gunnery Officer, not to be outdone, hurriedly looked about for a souvenir for himself before ordering "cast off." In the darkness he picked up something and sent it below. Nothing much was noticed topside but many curses immediately came from below decks and a burly seaman rushed to the bridge, holding his nose, and hurled "MR. PEABODY'S souvenir"—to wit, one very dead squid—over the side. One KOREAN was slightly wounded in the left arm when he had to be persuaded by a burst of tommy gun fire in the water to climb back aboard and join the party.

1958 Cast off schooner. Set course through the passages of the KOREAN ARCHIPELAGO at full speed, navigating by radar. Passed through fishing fleet of about 50 schooners. Hoped to rout out some of the shipping our planes have reported hugging the coast here.

The next night we received a message ordering us to proceed to a point off Tsingtao where ships running between China and Japan were reported to pass occasionally. It would take us a full-speed dash to reach the desired spot, but if we went more leisurely we might be out of action for a full extra day. And besides, orders were orders, to be carried out with dispatch. All night long we sped across the Yellow Sea.

The system we had evolved in *Tirante* was that I stayed up all night, more or less with the ready duty in case of a sudden emergency, and also to navigate. Just before diving, we called the skipper, and shortly afterward I would turn in until time for lunch. This day, however, I felt like a good breakfast, and left a call for 0800.

I ate leisurely and drank two cups of coffee before I began to sense that something was stirring. Then came a subdued clink of the annunciators, a faint whisper of hydraulic oil flow as the rudder went over. The gyro repeater in the wardroom overhead began to spin slowly. After a bit I heard someone in the control room tell someone else that there was pinging on the sound gear. One by one members of the ship's company began to drift by the wardroom—some one way, some another—but all, I noticed, in the direction of their battle stations. *Tirante* was girding her loins for battle, and it was time to go.

I gulp down the remains of the coffee, start for the conning tower. Pausing, I tell Roscoe Brown, one of our colored stewards, to call all the officers and tell them we'll be at battle stations soon.

Ed Campbell, I see, is already on the dive. As I swing onto the ladder leading to the conning tower, I hear the TDC start up. That means that Chub, or Gene Richey, is already there. George is looking through the periscope, and back by the TDC, Chub flashes me a huge, gap-toothed grin. The false tooth is out, which is Chub's way of getting ready for a fight.

Street is looking intently ahead. "That's them," he says, a bit ungrammatically. "Take a look."

There is a bad mirage effect on the horizon, but I can make out something which must be the mast of a ship, a shimmering something else which could be the tops of another.

"Better put it down again," says the skipper after a moment. "This mirage effect is tricky. It might look like a telephone pole to them."

That was something I hadn't thought of. He continued, "These are the most perfect sound conditions I've ever run into. We've heard them for nearly an hour before sighting them, and they shouldn't have any trouble bouncing an echo off us long before we're ready to shoot. We're going to have a tough approach and a rough time afterward."

"Shall I sound battle stations?" I ask him. It is obviously going to be quite a while before we fire torpedoes, but from what I've seen below it won't make much difference whether we sound the general alarm or not. George agrees with me, and the musical notes peal out. As we had expected, there is not a move belowdecks, but the "manned and ready" reports come through within seconds.

It isn't long before we can make out enough of the convoy to identify it. Two big ships and three escorts. The biggest looks like a passenger liner, with a long, square superstructure. The other is a freighter type. The three escorts are *Mikura*-class frigates—something like our destroyer escorts. All are zigzagging radically.

The approach is routine, except that we have to give unusual attention to the periscope to avoid being sighted. As the ships draw nearer we can see that both targets are crowded with soldiers, and that the three escorts have lookouts all over their decks. We identify the two big ships as *Nikko Maru*, an old passenger liner, and *Ramb II*, a brand-new, foreign-built freighter.

It is getting time to shoot. I check for the third time that all is ready, that the torpedoes need only pressure on the firing key to send them on their way. I watch George narrowly, to anticipate his every need, relay his orders, and receive reports for him. I also ceaselessly look over Chub's shoulder, and keep current on the tactical situation to have the latest dope for the skipper.

"Stand by forward, two fish!" says Street suddenly. This is unexpected, and can only mean one thing. We've been detected, and one of the escorts is after us.

"Down 'scope. Escort, passing close aboard," George explains briefly. "I don't think he's spotted us. He's passing now. No signs of having got us on sound?" The last is a question directed at me.

Sonar is on him, and the pings are coming in awfully loud. "How close?" I whisper to the skipper.

"Two hundred yards," he whispers back. Too close to

shoot now. The steady rhythm of his propellers comes strongly through the hull, grows steadily louder for several agonizing moments, then begins to recede. I heave a sigh of relief.

The escort is gone now, and from the setup on the TDC we can see it is time to shoot. George gets back on the periscope. I send to the forward torpedo room—we have no torpedoes left aft—to stand by with all six fish.

We wait two minutes. "Up 'scope! Final bearing and shoot!"

"Stand by forward," I order.

"*Nikko*—bearing—mark!" The 'scope slides down. George nods at me.

"Zero three two!" from Karlesses. Chub turns the target-bearing dial a fraction of a degree. The correct solution light seems to flicker momentarily, then burns bright and steady.

"FIRE!" I shout. *Tirante* lurches three times.

The periscope is up again. "*Ramb*," calls George. "Bearing—mark!"

"Three five seven-a-half." Chub's hand is a blur as he spins his bearing crank.

"Range—mark!"

"One six double oh." Chub doesn't have the bearing matched yet, so I grab the range crank and set the new range in myself.

"Angle on the bow, starboard 15," George calls out suddenly. This can't be right—it should be about forty. "Zig toward," the skipper adds—which explains that.

Feverishly we set in the new angle on the bow. It seems ages before the TDC catches up.

"Final bearing and shoot! Bearing—mark!"

"Zero zero two!"

"Fire!" Number four torpedo goes out with a jolt.

"Angle on the bow zero!" He hasn't finished zigzag-ging. I hold up my hand to stop the next fish. Chub franti-cally grinds his crank.

"FIRE!" as soon as it is matched.

"Angle on the bow port fifteen!" George is giving us all the dope he can. Furiously Chub spins the little crank.

"FIRE!" Our last torpedo tube is emptied. Street spins the periscope.

"They've seen us," he growls. "Flag hoist on both ships. Probably means 'sub sighted.' *Ramb* has reversed course. Not a chance of hitting him."

WHRANNG! A tremendous explosion shakes the con-ning tower. George spins the periscope again.

"*Nikko!*" he shouts. "Hit aft! Blew his stern off!"

WHRANGG! "Another one! Amidships!"

WHRRANGG! "Three hits! He's done for! Going down on an even keel! The first hit was in the after well and blew his stern off. The second hit under the stack. The third hit under the forward well and blew his bow off!"

"How about *Ramb?*" I ask.

"No luck there at all. She's got clean away."

"Escorts?"

"Here—they—come! Take her down. Take her down *fast!*"

Ed Campbell has been waiting for that one. The diving planes go immediately to full dive. Then the sudden increase in pressure telling us that he has flooded nega-tive and vented the tank. We ring up more speed to help him out, and *Tirante* claws for depth, hoping to get there before the ash cans arrive.

George crosses to the hatch, squats on the deck to speak more easily. "Keep her off the bottom, Ed. We've only got two hundred feet. Watch your angle carefully after we're down—it wouldn't take much of one to send one end of the ship into the mud."

At that moment the first depth charge goes off, and it's a good one. WHAM! our sturdy hull shudders and the piping twangs. WHAM! WHAM! A couple of men lose their footing. WHAM! Still closer. A cloud of cork dust rises into the air. WHAM WHAM! WHAM! WHAM! I have been holding more tightly than I realized to a piece of periscope drainage line in the conning tower overhead. Now I wish I hadn't—as I massage a tingling hand. George, standing with arms folded and feet spread apart, manages a grin. "That'll teach you," he says.

I'm not the only one who has relearned one of the tricks of the trade. The sonar operator is doubled up in agony: he had forgotten to take off his headphones, or at least to tone down his amplifier when the explosions came.

We have a slight respite, then another barrage bangs around us. After this one the skipper sends me through the ship to take stock of the situation and cheer up the lads. The latter part is a hard assignment. This is by no means the first time I've heard close depth charges, and *Tirante*, besides being brand-new, is a whole lot more rugged in design than *Trigger* was. But after all, it takes only one bull's-eye—and *Trigger*'s disappearance is fresh in my mind.

Throughout the ship, however, all hands are taking the beating stoically and with confidence. Despite the nerve-racking pounding, the tremendous noises of the separate explosions, the trip-hammer blows of the concussions themselves, they go quietly about their business. The experienced submarine sailors, by their example, leaven the reactions of those youngsters on their first patrol. In chief petty officers' quarters I come upon the ultimate in calmness. Remley, chief of the boat, on watch for many hours, had been sent by Ed Campbell to get some rest. He is carrying out orders, sound asleep on his bunk. The effect on the rest of the sailors is terrific.

As I look at him, another saintly series of close explosions shakes the ship, adding more dust and debris to that already strewn about the decks. Remley's eyelids flicker, then relax once more, and I walk gently away.

But it is in the forward torpedo room that I find the most remarkable reaction to a depth charging. Everyone is going about with a broad smile which somehow belies the strained look around the eyes. It seems that our Korean prisoners had been helping mule-haul the big torpedoes in and out of the tubes. Our men had told them, by sign language, that the torpedoes were meant for the Nips and this seemed to please them mightily, especially a few hours ago, when six fish had been hauled partway out, checked, and pushed back into their tubes. There had been many ribald gestures depicting what they hoped these fish would do to the Japs, and the Koreans had cheered for each one when it was fired.

When the hits came in, there had been more cheers which, so far as the Koreans were concerned, continued indiscriminately well into the first barrage of depth charges. The amusement was over the antics of the prisoners when they realized that there had been only six torpedoes but that there were many more than six explosions.

This much of the story I get between attacks, but the Koreans are nowhere to be seen, until a quivering canvas cot, rigged under an empty torpedo rack, is pointed out.

Moans come softly from a blanket draped over it. I lift up one end, and there is one of our Korean friends, hands clasped over his head, eyeballs rolling, moaning away.

Back in the conning tower I report everything normal, and receive the welcome news that we now have three ships working on us.

Street and I hold a small council of war. The time seems propitious to spring our surprise on the enemy. In the after torpedo room, covered with a tarpaulin, we have a little half-pint torpedo which, for want of a better name, goes by that of "Cutie." Cutie is an affectionate little fellow, always wanting to nuzzle up to fellows bigger than he is. His attentions are not very popular, however, as they are apt to terminate violently. Cutie is a homing torpedo.

"I've already told the after room to load it," says George. "Go on back with Chub and be sure they don't make any noise." I hurry away, for it's important to carry out this job quietly. Running silent as we are, the sound of chain hoists must not be permitted to get out into the water. Enemy tactics for a single ship attacking a submarine are usually to ping. With two ships they will alternately listen and echo-range, but with three there is always one listening.

Back in the conning tower once more, "We've got to wait till one of them makes another run on us," says the skipper. "Cutie hasn't much range and we've got to give the little fellow a chance to reach his target."

We do more than that. We take two runs in succession before there comes one to George's liking. Then, speaking softly over the phones, we give the order to let Cutie go.

Minutes pass. We had fired the little fish in the middle of a depth-charge run. Could it work its way through the roaring explosions? Would not its mechanism be damaged by the concussions which managed so to shake *Tirante*'s tough hide? We listen with growing impatience.

BANG! One tin can's screws stop abruptly. A subdued cheer rings out in *Tirante*'s conning tower—subdued, because there are still two others up there. And then, over the sound gear, comes the most eerie sound either George Street or I have ever heard. Distinctly audible in the receiver is the sound of voices in distress. We cannot make out what they are crying: they do not sound American, but they are obviously screaming in terror. The only explanation is that the Jap was nearly overhead when hit, and that the cries of his personnel were carried through the water. In sound tests conducted in training I had heard the human voice transmitted in this way, but this is the first time, so far as we know, of such an instance in combat.

In a few moments the other two escorts are back at us. Trembling and shuddering under the successive concussions, *Tirante* works her way toward deeper water, wishing that she had two more Cuties, that there were some way of striking back at her tormentors.

"Ned," says the skipper suddenly, "it looks as though this will be a busy night for you, keeping out of the way of these fellows. No doubt they'll expect us to surface after nightfall, and have some kind of search plan to find us. I can handle things right now. You go below and get some rest." So saying, he gives me a winning smile and a shove toward the hatch.

"I'm not tired, sir," I start to say, realizing all at once that I am.

"Goddammit, Ned, that's an order! I want you fresh tonight!"

While undergoing depth-charge attack it is customary

to secure unnecessary personnel, partly to make it easier on those who still must stay on duty, and partly to conserve oxygen by reducing the activity of the others. Besides, I had been up all night and most of the previous day, and as George said, would have a full night again. So rationalizing to myself, I climbed down from the conning tower and headed forward. When I reached the wardroom, an idea came to mind.

Seated there were all the officers who had already been secured—by coincidence the group included several who were on their first patrol. It was a tense bunch. There was not a thing any of them could do to help matters, which made things just that much worse. The game had degenerated into a contest between our skipper and the two tin can skippers, with an undetermined factor—how well the Portsmouth Navy Yard could build a submarine hull—in the balance.

Just as I arrived the screws of one of the enemy vessels became suddenly very audible, right through the thick steel hull. Someone said, "Here we come again."

Another voice, "We can't keep this up forever. Wonder how long our battery can hold out?"

I waited to hear no more. Stepping in, I announced that I had been up all night, and meant to get some sleep, and suggested that some of them do the same. The statement caught them by surprise—evidently they had not seen Remley.

The first of four close ones caught us as I climbed into my bunk, but resolutely I got in and lay there. With my head alongside the skin of the ship I could clearly hear the propeller beats, and knew when to expect the charges. I turned my face to the bulkhead so that no one would see my eyelids quiver, and forced myself to lie still.

I felt cold, The heat of my body was going right out into the Yellow Sea. It was warm within the ship, too warm, but the cold sea was sapping the heat right out of us. I realized that I was shivering, and then I realized it was mainly because I was afraid.

In the distance the swish-swish-swish-swish-swish of the propellers belonging to the chap who had dropped the last load took on a new note. At first it seemed that he was turning for a new run; but then another set increased in intensity, while those of the first remained steady.

Swish-swish-swish-swish-swish-swish-SWISH-SWISH-SWISH-SWISH-SWISHSWISHSWISH SWISH—*He must be right over us now—listen to that son of a bitch come*—SWISH-SWISHSWISHSWISH. *Drop, you bastard! Drop your . . . sonsabitching charges! Drop and be God damned to hell!* SWISHSWISHSWISHSWISHSWISHSWISHSWISH-SWISHSWISHclickclickclick *Here they come here they come here they come here they come!* WHAM! WHAM! WHAM!

My pillow is wet beneath my face, and I can feel my mind reach deep into slumber with the relaxation of tension. But it is wide awake again for the next run, and the next, and the next.

And then, somehow, the explosions seemed to lose some of their authority, seemed to draw away from us, and I slept.

APRIL 13

0612 Returning from SHANGHAI sweep at high speed. Sighted dawn plane and dived for the day.

Intend to make investigation of a reported anchor-

age on the north shore of QUELPART during darkness. Our six steam torpedoes left forward will be
ideal for this work.

The dearth of night traffic across the Yellow Sea was
almost sure proof that the enemy was anchoring somewhere. We had investigated all such anchorages within
reach. This one, though rather difficult to approach
because of the necessity first to negotiate a long, narrow
channel, looked as though it might be interesting for the
same reason.

We decided that going into the anchorage at night,
when the enemy, if present, would presumably have his
guard most relaxed and be least ready to retaliate, presented the most alluring proposition. There was a large
mine field off the general vicinity of the anchorage, but we
knew its approximate dimensions and location—shaped
roughly like the state of Nevada—between Quelpart and
the Korean coast. We planned to slip between it and the
shore of Quelpart, staying as close as possible to the land
so that Nip radars would find it difficult to distinguish our
pip from those of the beach.

Shortly after dusk on the night of April 13 the lean
gray form of *Tirante* swam to the surface and silently
headed toward the western tip of Quelpart. The plan of
action had been explained to the crew, and a special dinner prepared for the occasion, with sandwiches laid on for
later.

As soon as we had surfaced, of course, the crew's
entertainment radio was connected to an antenna, and
several of us were listening to it when mention was made
of "President Truman." An electric tremor ran through
the entire ship's company, and this was how we learned of

our country's loss. All during our long approach to battle we gleaned bits of information from broadcasters who assumed that the whole world already possessed all the facts. Even when the skipper said a few words about it on the ship's general announcing system, we listened avidly, as though from some occult source he had additional information to impart.

APRIL 14

0000 Approaching QUELPART ISLAND northwestern side.

0029 Radar contact. Patrol Boat. Went to tracking stations and worked around him. Sighted him at 4500 yards. No evidence of radar until we were nearly around. The patrol was suspicious for a short time; then went back to sleep. Continued working up to the anchorage.

It was something more than thirty miles up the channel between the coast of Quelpart and the mine field, and we had to make full speed all the way to carry out our schedule. Our radar continually swept to seaward to forewarn of the approach of enemy craft—in case the Japs had left a passage through the field for just this purpose—but concentrated ahead and astern. Most of the time I spent on the bridge, trying to compare our charts with what I could actually see, hoping to be able to spot hidden danger in time to avoid it. Chub stood at the TDC, assisting my navigation. George was ceaselessly climbing through the ship, talking to men in every compartment, explaining what we were up to, seeing for himself that every detail was in readiness.

For two hours we sped northeastward along the coast. The roar of our diesels came back to us from the dark hills. The night was pitch black. No moon. A thick overcast hung high over the silent land, stretching like a huge tent ahead, to port and astern, and the air had a musty tang with a suspicion of burning driftwood. There was a slight chop to the sea, but only an occasional wave broke high enough to dampen *Tirante*'s wood-slotted decks.

0223 Radar contact. Another patrol boat. Avoided by going close inshore. He was patrolling back and forth in front of the anchorage, had radar and was echo-ranging in the bargain. He also became suspicious, but our tactics of running inshore confused him, and he continued routine patrolling.

During the whole of the ensuing action, except when actually firing torpedoes, this patrol boat was kept on the TDC and both plots. He was always a mental hazard, and potentially a real one. The only chart of any use was the Jap "Zoomie" chart labelled "Japan Aviation Chart, SouthernMost Portion of CHOSEN (KOREA) No. V3-36." No soundings inside the ten fathom curve in the harbor and approaches were shown. Hoped the place wasn't mined and that none of the five shore-based radars reported on QUELPART were guarding the harbor.

George Street came to the bridge. "How about it, Ned? We think we have the harbor on the radar now. Too far to spot any ships, though. How well do you think you can see?"

I could see the shoreline off to starboard, lighter in color than the hills which rose behind it, or the sky and water in other directions. Beyond that I could see nothing.

"About six miles to go. We're all set below. How's the time?" the skipper asked.

"We're a bit ahead of schedule, but that's all to the good, Captain. What's this patrol boat doing?" I couldn't help wondering about him, although in our planned division of responsibilities this was entirely the skipper's worry, not mine.

"He's patrolling to seaward of us, fairly well out. I don't think he suspects anything. Chub has been following him ever since we picked him up."

"That makes two tin cans patrolling off this harbor," I mused. "Maybe there's somebody in this one."

"I'm beginning to think so too. These chaps don't look like ocean-going escorts. If they patrol offshore, there ought to be something there."

George leaned over the conning tower hatch and ordered the general alarm to be sounded.

0240 Battle Stations. Approached anchorage from the south along the ten fathom curve within 1200 yards of the shore line. Took fathometer soundings every 3 to 5 minutes. The smell of cattle from the beach was strong. Bridge could not see well enough to distinguish ships from the shore line in the harbor, though a couple of darker spots in the early morning mist looked promising—as did the presence of two patrolling escort vessels.

It was like poking your head into a cave on a dark night. Up ahead, where the harbor was, it seemed a little darker than elsewhere. The misty gray atmosphere of early morning seemed just a shade lighter than it had been. On our port bow I could see the bulky outline of the rocky island off the coast of Quelpart which formed the left side of the anchorage. Twice, dim on the port beam, I thought I could see a low-lying black shape. Dead ahead, where ships should be, if there were any, nothing could be seen. Radar could not be sure of ships, although there were certain outstanding possibilities among the confused jumble of the shore return. I could feel, rather than see, the presence of two or more dark spots in the atmosphere, with the suggestion of masts and stacks above them.

We pressed in more closely. The fathometer gave seven fathoms. Forty-two feet; not enough to cover the ship. Radar range to the islet was just over half a mile. Still no ships could be distinguished.

Doubts began to assail us. Maybe this whole thing was a wild-goose chase. Maybe this anchorage, like all the rest, was also empty. But if so, how explain two harbor patrols?

0310 Completed investigation this side of the anchorage from 1200 yards away. There may be ships here, but cannot see well enough to shoot. Started around the small island off the anchorage, staying as close as possible. The patrol vessel by this time was paralleling us 7000 yards offshore, still not overly suspicious, but annoying. Executive Officer on the bridge could see him now and then.

It was a relief to get into deeper water again. Non-divable water is murder, for it robs the submarine of her armor, her invisibility, and her haven all at once. We kept outside the ten-fathom curve going around the islet. We ran until we were due north of the harbor, then headed south.

0330 Having completed circuit of the small island, started in from northern side, cutting across ten fathom curve. At about

0340 Bridge made out the shapes of ships in the anchorage. Sound picked up a second "pinger"—this time in the harbor. Still too far—4500 yards and not sure of what we saw. Patrol heading this way. Sounding 11 fathoms. Current setting us on the beach. Decided to get in closer and have this over with. All ahead two thirds. Lieutenant Ted MARCUSE, radar officer, confirmed sharp pips of ships in the anchorage.

This is the first confirmation, other than my imagination, that there really are ships there. A load lightens. Whatever we manage to do about it, at least this has not been a wild-goose chase. *Tirante* glides into the harbor. Now we have the tall hills of Quelpart to port and the little island outside the anchorage to starboard. It is a bit lighter than before; the moon is now up. First light is still about an hour away.

Then, coming suddenly into view, I can see ships at last.

"Targets!" I bawl into the ship's announcing system. I can feel *Tirante* draw herself up. Dead quiet from belowdecks. I can sense the rumble of the hydraulic plant accumulator, the hiss of high-pressure air as the torpedomen check their impulse bottles. Water laps gently alongside, and the ship rocks slightly in the onshore current. Back aft, the four diesels purr softly, idling, and a small stream of water spatters out of their four muffler exhaust pipes.

0350 Bridge could definitely see ships. For the first time put targets on TDC, with zero speed and TBT bearings. Radar commenced ranging on largest ship—very difficult to distinguish from the mass of shore pips, and gave range of 2500 yards. Sounding 9 fathoms. Still getting set on. Land loomed close aboard and on both sides. Patrol still not overly alerted, passing outboard of us about 6000 yards away, pinging loudly. The land background is our saving grace. Secured the fathometer. If those ships can get in there, so can we. Both 40 MM guns are all loaded and ready with gun crews. Since it is too shallow to dive, we will have to shoot our way out if boxed in.

I clean off the TBT binoculars with a piece of lens paper. "Stand by for a TBT bearing," I shout into the announcing speaker.

"All back two-thirds!" I hear George order from the conning tower. "All stop!" a moment later. This, by prearrangement, is to be done just before firing. Having got this far, we want to get off our fish with the utmost deliberation.

Tirante lies dead in the water, every nerve keyed, every sense at its highest pitch. Six thumps in quick succession from up forward tell me that the outer doors of the torpedo tubes have been opened; that six deadly bronze warheads need only the word from George to be on their way.

"Bearing!" from the bridge speaker. My crosshair is bisecting the middle of the biggest target. I squeeze the right handle of the TBT, thus giving the "mark" to Chub on the TDC.

"Fire!" from the conning tower. A few seconds later a

streak of white bubbles comes to the surface, heading straight for the enemy ship.

Someone has joined me alongside the TBT. George. Both of us stare along the rapidly extending wake. Ed Campbell and the quartermaster add their binoculars to the watch. The streak of bubbles appears to curve slightly to the right. Current! The reverse of what we are experiencing from where we lie!

"Torpedo should be hitting now," says George.

But nothing happens. We wait longer. Can this have been a defective fish also? My God, I thought we were through with them! Admiral Lockwood personally assured the Force that they were now as perfect as they could be made.

Suddenly there is a flash of red-orange flame far up ahead. The location of the explosion proves that the torpedo functioned perfectly, and exploded when it hit the beach after missing to the right.

> 0359 Fired one torpedo aimed at the left edge of the largest target, to correct for current effect. Wake headed straight for the target.

> 0359-22 Fired another torpedo aimed same as the previous one—straight as a die. Exec's keen shooting eye looked right on tonight.

(It was nice of George to put that in the patrol report. Just like him, too.)

> 0401-05 A tremendous beautiful explosion. A great mushroom of white blinding flame shot 2000 feet into the air. Not a sound was heard for a

moment, but then a tremendous roar flattened our ears against our heads. The jackpot, and no mistake! In this shattering convulsion we had no idea how many hits we had made, but sincerely believe it was two. In the glare of the fire, TIRANTE stood out in her light camouflage, like a snowman in a coal pit. But, more important, silhouetted against the flame were two escort vessels, both instantly obvious as fine new frigates of the MIKURA class. Steadied up to pick off the two frigates.

0402 Fired one torpedo at the left hand frigate, using TBT bearings and radar range.

0402-16 Fired another torpedo at the same target.

0403 Fired last torpedo at the right hand frigate.

0404 Now let's *really* get out of here!

0404-20 One beautiful hit in the left hand frigate. The ship literally exploded, her bow and stern rising out of water and the center disappearing in a sheet of flame. Must have hit her magazines. Very satisfying to watch, though not the equal of the previous explosion, of course. Possibly two hits in him.

0404-40 A hit on the other PF also—right amidships! No flame this time, other than the explosion, but a great cloud of smoke immediately enveloped her and she disappeared. We jubilantly credit ourselves with three ships sunk with at least four, probably five hits for six fish. Not the slightest doubt about any of the three ships. Now only one torpedo left aboard. Immediately reloaded it . . .

On the bridge, the only persons who could not look at the fires we had left astern were Spence and the other three battle lookouts. Four of the most experienced sailors in the crew, selected for their steadiness, night vision, and marksmanship with the forty-millimeter guns, they made up a special lookout watch section who came on watch when action appeared imminent. As the harbor patrol increased speed and headed into the anchorage to see what had happened, and we raced away into the night, he was under the cold surveillance of Spence and his gang the whole time.

Once more we slipped along the shore, watching the patrol craft narrowly. A third frigate could be seen, but he did not come out after us. So we just ran down the coast of Quelpart, headed for the open sea, and transmitted results of attack to submarines in the area so they could avoid the antisubmarine measures certain to come.

0513 Radar and sight contact with the other patrol, which we avoided in the beginning. This time he was alert, as we got definite radar interference from him. Too light to evade surfaced, so dived and evaded submerged. He came over to the spot where we had dived and dropped a pattern. Many distant depth charges or bombs were heard and planes were sighted all day. This area will be hot tonight.

For several hours that day we labored over the message which we were to send to ComSubPac that night. There was much that had to be told, in addition to the results of the night's work. And besides, we now for the first time had the leisure to evaluate the passing of the man who had guided our country's destinies for twelve years. The message, when we finally sent it, read:

THREE FOR FRANKLIN XX SANK AMMUNITION SHIP TWO ESCORTS IN ANCHORAGE NORTHERN SHORE QUELPART ISLAND MORNING FOURTEENTH X NO COUNTERMEASURES X TIRANTE SENDS X ONE TORPEDO REMAINING . . .

APRIL 16

0537 Dived for a plane.

0854 Sighted dead Jap soldier. (Very dead.) Wearing kapok life jacket, helmet and leggings. Flooded down and hauled him alongside to examine pockets for notebooks, papers, etc. for our Intelligence Service, but corpse was decomposing, so secured.

1017 Sighted 2 PBM's headed for us. Fired one mortar recognition signal followed by another. PBM's still coming in. Suddenly heard one plane say, "Look at that ship down there! Wonder if it's friendly?" Promptly opened up on VHF and set him straight. Situation eased.

1043 Another dead Jap soldier similar to first. (Deader.)

1647 Sighted three Jap flyers roosting on the float of their overturned plane. Maneuvered to pick them up. Put our bow (well flooded down) against the float, but they defiantly straight-armed it and showed no desire to come aboard. Kept our boarding party on the cigarette deck behind armor plate. The pilot, identified by goggles and a flight cap, had something hidden in his right hand and suddenly threw a lighted aircraft flare aboard, in return for which Lt. Commander BEACH parted his hair with an accurately placed rifle shot. Our bridge .30 and .50 cal. machine gunners had to be firmly told not to shoot. At first it was thought that the flare might be some kind of a bomb or hand grenade. But this was obviously not so, and the flare was kicked over the side by the Gunnery Officer. The pilot kept haranguing his two crewmen. Things at an impasse. Brought one of our KOREANS topside to persuade them to come aboard.

The three flyers suddenly jumped overboard and swam away from their wrecked plane; so Lt. Commander BEACH, with a few rifle shots, gained the distinction of sinking a Jap plane single-handed. That left the three Japs with no refuge. The pilot went one way and the two enlisted men another. Brought one of the enlisted men alongside. At first he seemed willing to be rescued when yelled at by the KOREAN. Then evidently thought better of it, screamed "KILL, KILL, KILL" at us, ducked out of his life jacket, and swam away. He was observed to duck his head under water several times and swallow salt water, until finally he failed to reappear. One suicide for the Emperor.

We had actually gotten a boathook twisted inside this fellow's life jacket and were hauling him aboard when he broke free. Maneuvering a three-hundred-foot ship side-ways is rather a difficult operation, so we had to watch him drown before our eyes. Ensign Buck Dietzen's comment was perhaps the most appropriate epitaph: "The poor, stupid bastard!"

Brought the second enlisted man alongside. This was a nice looking lad, about nineteen. He was willing to be rescued after more cajoling by our KOREAN through a megaphone. Undressed him completely on deck searching for hidden knives and hand grenades. No lethal weapons found.

Brought the pilot alongside. He had shed his life-jacket, evidently thinking of suicide. He seemed conscious and in good control until close aboard, when he appeared to lose consciousness and became helpless. Lt. PEABODY and SPENCE, GMlc dived over the side with sheath knives and heaving lines tied around them, grabbed the inert Jap, and boosted him over the bow. He was still inert when undressed, and when examined below decks by the Chief Pharmacist's Mate, whose verdict was that the man was shamming. This was substantiated by the fact that, when startled by the general announcing equipment, he jerked upright, then relaxed into insensibility again. Evidently, having been brought aboard while unable to help it, his honor, or something, had been saved. He apparently had not the nerve to carry out his own suicide order.

We found nothing much of value in the pockets of either of the men we rescued except, perhaps, the notebooks which all Japs apparently carried. These were impounded for delivery upon arrival in port.

It took us nine days to reach Midway. During that time we let our Koreans repay a few old scores by making it obvious that they rated higher than the Japanese. The Korean with the wounded arm was placed in charge of the head-cleaning detail, a chore which our crew naturally hated, and the Jap pilot was placed under him. Since he had no rank insignia or identifying marks, and made no attempt to identify himself as an officer, we had no worries about the Geneva Convention as far as this fellow was concerned. Once the Korean realized what we wanted of him, the crew's head was kept nearly spotless. The Korean inspected it at least half a dozen times a day. Whenever it showed the least need of cleaning, his broad leathery face would light up, and he would hie himself off in search of his Jap working party.

Shortly before we reached Midway I presented each Korean with ten new one-dollar bills, which we hoped would alleviate to some extent their prison-camp existence. The Japs, of course, received nothing.

A huge crowd, including several movie cameramen, awaited *Tirante* when she moored alongside the dock at Midway. Several crates of fresh fruit were waiting on the dock for us, along with ten gallons of ice cream—which we didn't need because *Tirante* too had her own ice-cream-making equipment—and that most desired thing of all, mail from home. A band broke into "Anchors Aweigh" as the first line hit the dock—singularly inappropriately, I thought—and played the tune lustily as we warped our ship alongside. Then it let us have "There's a Long, Long Trail A-Winding," which seemed to suit the occasion better.

I dived into a packet of letters, immediately oblivious to everything else. Those from my wife I hurriedly shuffled until I found the latest one, which I immediately opened and read. All was well at home; I stuffed them into a pocket for more private and leisurely perusal. An official-looking missive next drew my attention: I was detached from *Tirante*, and from such other duties as might have been assigned to me, to report to Submarine Division 322 awaiting the arrival of USS *Piper*. Upon return of the *Piper* from patrol I was to report to her commanding officer as his relief.

The band was on "Dixie" as I realized that although my ambitions to have a command of my own were at last to come true, I would have to leave the magnificent fighting machine on whose decks I stood and the wonderful crew of submariners which I had had a hand in shaping.

"Swannee River" was playing as a natty marine captain saluted, then touched my arm to break the spell. I hastily returned the salute, the movement rusty from long disuse. "I've come for your prisoners," he stated. I pointed to the nearest hatch, just opening for the fifth time in as many minutes. Movie cameras perched all about it ground away solemnly as the Jap pilot, blind-folded, wearily climbed up for the fifth time and stood, swaying slightly, on its edge. Another salute, and the marine marched forward to claim his charge. Little did he know what he was in for, I thought, as the cameramen turned their machines on him with delight.

Ralph Pleatman, shocking black hair, smooth rosy complexion, hard as nails, approached with his hand held out. "Congratulations on your patrol," he said. "You and George have called out the biggest celebration I've seen yet on this damned island. Have you heard about your old ship?"

Hope flooded through me. "No. What is it?" Maybe, after all, there was some other explanation for her non-appearance a month ago—maybe she was all right after all . . .

"Awfully sorry, Ned. She's three weeks overdue. We've turned her in as overdue and presumed lost!" Ralph's sorrow was genuine, and I knew why he felt he had to bring *Trigger* up at this moment. He himself had survived *Pompano* in exactly the same circumstances, and Dave Connole, one of his shipmates then, had also.

"Oh," was all I could think of saying.

All this time George Street had been surrounded by a group of the biggest brass of Midway Island—not that anybody higher than a captain in the Navy ever managed to get shunted away in this spot—and now he broke away, beckoned to me.

"Ned," he said, "The commodore has invited me to his quarters for dinner tonight. He's got a big party on for us, and wants you to come too."

I knew where the commodore had got the idea of including me, but that didn't alter the anticipation of a big party with all the trimmings. "Swell," I said.

The band was playing, "There'll Be a Hot Time in the Old Town Tonight," which—even for Midway—could be true.

18

PIPER

PIPER WAS A STRONG and well-found ship, and I was happy to get her. She had preceded *Tirante* out of Portsmouth by only a few months, and was of almost identical design. The only flaw in her, so far as I was concerned, was that she had just begun her second patrol, and I had a long wait ahead of me.

In the meantime, *Tirante* completed refit at Midway and set forth on her second run. Ed Campbell had succeeded me as exec, and Jim Donnelly had been promoted into Ed's job. The rest of the crew was left essentially as before. When George took her out, I personally lifted her number-one line off the bollard, walked down the dock with the bitter end as Chub superintended hauling it in, and pitched it over so that the whole line landed on deck clean and dry. Then I stood on the end of the pier and watched the ship out of sight.

As she drew into the distance a light began to flash from the afterpart of the bridge. I made the Go Ahead sign with my arms. Slowly, so that I would not miss any of the letters, Karlesses—it must have been he—spelled out the message: GOOD LUCK NED K. I stood there a full minute with my arms outstretched in the R sign.

Piper, it seemed to me, was an unconscionably long time in getting back from patrol. She had drawn an unproductive area, and though she beat the bushes pretty thoroughly she remained at sea the full scheduled sixty days and brought back almost a complete load of torpedoes. All the while I stayed in Midway, assisting with the refits of other submarines as they came and went, and chewing my nails in exasperation. We could sense the war drawing to an end, and felt pride that the United States Navy had brought Japan to her knees almost single-handed. We argued whether Russia would enter the war in the Pacific. It was obvious that the war would shortly be over. I had to get to sea in *Piper* soon.

The messages I read daily were not calculated to make the wait any easier. *Tirante*, seemingly the only submarine able to find anything worth shooting these days, had entered another harbor—submerged this time—and had torpedoed a collier alongside a dock. To cap it, George had come out of the place with full motion-picture coverage! When I read his ensuing message, I would gladly have given up *Piper* to have been along.

Finally the long-awaited notice came, and I flew to Pearl Harbor to take command of my ship. But then came more delays. *Piper* was being fitted with special equipment to penetrate the Straits of Tsushima, between Japan and Korea.

Ever since *Wahoo* had failed to return from the Sea of Japan, back in October 1943, that area had not seen an American submarine. Mush Morton had entered via La Perouse Straits and had intended to exit through the same. We didn't know how the Japs had caught him, but suspected they had drawn a noose around *Wahoo* from which she could not escape. Tsushima was mined—

that we knew. Tartary was too shallow to pass through submerged, and was denied to us by the Russians; Tsugaru was shallow, and had swift currents, besides being heavily patrolled; La Perouse was deep, not too long, although also heavily patrolled. All in all, La Perouse seemed to be the best place for a submarine to make passage into the Sea of Japan, but once the enemy knew there was a submarine in it, trapping her there seemed a distinct possibility.

Then in June 1945, in Operation Barney, nine American submarines passed through the mined Straits of Tsushima into Morton's old patrol area in the Sea of Japan. They lay doggo for a few days, and then suddenly exploded into action. Twenty-eight ships they sank in twelve days, and Japan knew that her last lines of physical contact with the rest of the world were doomed.

Operation Barney was named after Commander W. B. (Barney) Sieglaff, who had been skipper of *Tautog* and *Tench* before going to Admiral Lockwood's staff. He did much of the work of readying and checking out the first nine boats. But the whole deal could have been just as appropriately called Operation Charlie, after the admiral himself, for the Boss had gone after that project with the same drive he had used in fixing up the torpedoes for us— and with equally effective results.

Worming our way through the mine fields would be tricky business, but nine boats had shown it could be done, and *Piper* was eager to be off about it. It was a big honor to have been selected, but we were the last of the second wave of seven boats scheduled to go through singly—and there was a strong possibility that we would be too late. When we were ready to leave Pearl, Admiral Lockwood came aboard to give us a final once-over. The special equipment which had just been installed didn't work well enough to suit him, so we had to lie over two days while the electronic experts adjusted it. Finally *Piper* got under way for Guam.

I had found, during the past few weeks, that being a skipper was far different from being an exec, no matter how much responsibility the Old Man had left you. Now I had *all* the responsibility, no matter to whom I delegated a specific problem. Now I had to be able to dispose of widely differing problems out of hand, sometimes without much consideration. Where before I had made suggestions and then loyally carried out the skipper's wishes, now it was up to me to make the decisions. Frequently they were hard to make, and harder to stick to. In all of them I held the sack if anything went wrong.

One decision I made, and clung to tenaciously: we were going to get *Piper* into action or break our necks trying.

At Guam two doses of bad news awaited us. Admiral Lockwood, who had preceded us by plane, decided that our new secret frequency modulated sonar was still not up to snuff, and held us over for more tinkering by a different crew of experts. Then, when number three main engine developed leaks in the fresh-water cooling system, inspection disclosed that seven of the ten cylinder liners were cracked and would have to be renewed. More delay.

There wasn't much time left, for it was already August. As soon as Admiral Lockwood was satisfied our equipment simply couldn't or wouldn't perform better, and that it was reasonably satisfactory as it was, I threw normal caution over the side and ordered *Piper* under way without the fourth engine. We would finish repairs at sea, and in the meantime could be gaining distance toward Jap-land. At 1700 on August 5, 1945, we backed away from our berth in Apra Harbor and set out for Japan at last, with all the speed our three good engines could give us.

We had not been long under way when a rather peculiar message came in describing some kind of bomb which had been dropped on Hiroshima and had done a lot of damage. I hardly gave it a second thought. Jerry Reeves, my exec, and I were busily planning the quickest way to get to Tsushima, and were considering the idea of running all the way on the surface. It could be done, we decided, even within sight of land during daylight—something no submariner would have considered a few months ago—but it seemed safe enough now until we got close to the Straits.

Repairs completed, number three engine was also put on the line, and *Piper* raced on four big diesels for the war zone. Somehow I felt it was slipping away from us—receding faster than we approached it. My emotions at this period I've never completely analyzed: rather than joy at the approaching end of the war, I felt an overwhelming impatience to be back in it before it ended. It was something like the feeling of the hunter who has been held out of the woods as the season draws to a close and finally is given a few fleeting hours to go out and find himself some big game. Certainly thoughts of pity for the Japs whose names were written on the twenty-six warheads we carried, and what would happen to them if I had my way, never entered my head. I think *Piper* and her skipper were as near to a remorseless engine of destruction as you could find. Now that the enemy was down, I wanted to stomp on him, kick him in the groin, destroy him completely if I could, just as he had *Trigger, Wahoo, Harder, Gudgeon,* and so many others.

At this juncture the blower lobes on number one main engine started to strike each other, and the engine had to be shut down. Once more our speed had to be reduced while it was dismantled and repairs effected. Furious, I put down the suggestion that we reduce speed further and take some of the load off the engines. We stayed on the surface and continued running, sighting neither planes nor ships belonging to the enemy, although we did see several of our submarines. After two days number-one engine was back in service, and our speed increased again.

Our plan was to transit Tsushima and enter the Sea of Japan on August 12. On the 11th a message from ComSubPac told us to patrol the Yellow Sea awaiting further orders. That night we vented our disappointment by destroying two fishing boats which had the misfortune to be caught in water deep enough for *Piper* to float. The surface firepower of a fleet submarine with everything shooting is frightening to watch. But we felt no pity for them, for they were the enemy. Sometimes these inoffensive-looking boats carried concealed radio transmitters and warned of the presence of submarines—this was our excuse for cutting up these two with our concentrated fire. I've since been somewhat ashamed of the episode, for obviously these particular fishermen were interested only in fish.

We disobeyed orders slightly, in that we did not enter the Yellow Sea, but instead remained in the vicinity of the Straits of Tsushima, in faint hope that Admiral Lockwood would relent. And he did, for during the night of the 12th orders arrived for us to go on through.

At 0500 on the 13th *Piper* submerged in the approaches to Tsushima. All during the day, with the crew at special mine-passage stations, we proceeded submerged, groping our way along, watching the special FM equipment for the first sign of detection of mines. Indication would be by visual presentation on a cathode-ray tube, accompanied by a gonglike ringing—which someone had named Hell's Bells—for each mine. Along about midday both indications came at once.

"There they are, Captain!" I was in the conning tower, but Arnold Christiansen, for the moment on the "mine watch," was the first man to spot them. The equipment began to ring continuously, and the cathode-ray tube showed a seemingly solid line of mines. There were no holes anywhere, but we had to find one somewhere and slip through it. The range of initial detection was such that there was no hope of turning around for another go at them. Holding my breath, I watched the tube. The mines could not be planted that solidly—there simply *had* to be holes between them! There was dead silence in the conning tower, broken only by the bell-like chimes of the mine-detection gear as we slowly approached. I concentrated on the tube, watched the phalanx of mines coming closer and closer, Hell's Bells ringing louder all the time. It was up to me to find a hole and maneuver the ship through it. Watertight doors and bulkhead flappers were shut tightly throughout the ship, and there was no communication except by telephone. I could sense, however, that everyone in the ship's company had got the word.

There! A hole at last! Slightly to the right. "Right full rudder!" I ordered, speaking as calmly as I could and deliberately pitching my voice low.

Ever so slowly the opening drifted to the left, until centered directly in front of our bow. I ordered the rudder amidships. Seconds passed. We commenced to pass directly between two mines, equidistant from each. The mines disappeared from the indicator, but we could still hear the chimes. They were abeam now—now abreast the after torpedo room. "We're clear!" somebody said. But I continued to watch the FM equipment indicator, for just before the mines passed clear, a veritable nest of them had shown up, dead ahead, accompanied by an incessant cacophony of jangling chimes.

No hole at all this time! Cold sweat on my forehead. Too late to change course—it had already been too late when we picked up this latest group. Nothing to do but remain at slowest creeping speed and hope to see a hole as we get closer. A trapped, panicky feeling rises just beneath consciousness, but I manage to keep it there. It's up to me, only me! A small hole develops, to the right again—and cockeyed—but it's the best there is.

"Starboard back emergency! Port ahead emergency! Right full rudder!" That's all we can do. I haven't taken my eyes from the screen, and so I see us swing into the hole. We just seem to get into it. The mines draw up alongside, pass aft, ringing incessantly, along the hull. I open my mouth to give the order to put the rudder amidships again and equalize the screws, when the telephone talker interrupts rapidly:

"Mine cable scraping port side after battery!"

Disturbing the cable might set off the mine floating on the end of it. Or even if it doesn't actually snag as the ship moves ahead, the cable might readily drag the mine down on us. Either way means disaster.

Instantly I tell the helmsman, "Shift everything!" He's heard the report, too, and responds with amazing celerity. We had drilled for just this situation. Without further ado, the helmsman switches the starboard annunciator from back emergency to ahead emergency; the port one from ahead emergency to back emergency and nearly rips the steering wheel from the bulkhead as he swings it to left full.

As I watch him go industriously through the routine, an incongruous thought intrudes: "Bet even old Wilson wouldn't have got it all done any quicker!"

Back aft, the electrician's mates are also on the phone circuit, and the order to shift everything has been relayed to them via the talker. The shift in direction of the twist is nothing short of remarkable, and the cable stops scraping outside.

At 2000 we surfaced, safe and sound, in the Sea of Japan, and began running at full speed for our assigned patrol area.

AUGUST 14

1640 Sighted swamped lifeboat with man and woman clinging to it. They both appeared young; the woman quite pretty with her many-colored scarf around her head. The wolves could be heard howling throughout the boat. Decided to take them aboard. Came alongside three times, flooded down, bow planes rigged out, trying first to coax them aboard, and that failing, to frighten them aboard by a few shots well overhead. Both methods failed; each time we maneuvered close aboard they paddled away on a floating thwart; it was believed that girl had seen wolves before.

During the procedure the entire boarding party, both first and second waves, were on deck with guns and equipment. After the third attempt, it was decided that enough was enough, and the Gunnery Officer, Lt. W. A. BOWMAN and LECLAIR, R.J. Slc (225 pounds of very solid gun-striker), stripped to skivvies and with long knives clenched in their teeth (like John Silver) went over the side after them.

This ended all argument. The young lady was towed alongside with her hands clasped in front of her face, praying in Japanese; the man followed suit, struggling somewhat.

It was decided to strip and search both prisoners on deck, and in deference to maidenly modesty a shapely mattress cover with arm and leg holes was provided. This was quite unnecessary, as without a scarf and a pair of pants, the beautiful she turned out to be a young he. The other prisoner was suffering from a deep scalp wound closely resembling an old bullet crease. Both men were bathed, given medical attention and dry clothing.

Before this could be completed, sighted a raft ahead with four more customers. These were more willing to come aboard under their own power, with the exception of a serious young man who first tried to swim away, then deciding this was no good, floated on his back and gazed up at the riflemen as he waited to be shot. LECLAIR went over the side and brought him aboard in a manner that left little doubt in his mind that we wanted him alive.

We had been running at full power ever since breaking out of the Tsushima area, and remaining on the surface all day in order to increase distance. Picking these characters out of the drink within a half hour's flight from land delayed us, and was a risky operation as well. A submarine has no business being on the surface during wartime, unless it is ready for instant submergence. When Bowman and LeClair went over the side, they must have realized that we might have been forced to leave them up there, although of course we'd have stuck around and picked them up later. Nevertheless, I breathed much easier when everyone was once more safely below and we had resumed running at full speed for the Jap coast.

Nary a ship had we seen, except an old waterlogged and abandoned wooden landing craft. The radio, which we kept tuned in, continuously reported the progress of the peace feelers going on. It was obvious that this was to be the last patrol, the only question being—would it last long enough for *Piper* to get a few licks in at the enemy?

Rescuing our six prisoners had cost us several hours, and though we raced through the night, we were not able to get close enough to the coast by daylight next morning to patrol for any coastal shipping. We tried to run in on the surface, but twice planes forced us to dive, and the second time we stayed down. However, we kept our radar antenna mast out, since it could be used as a rather poor radio antenna, and thus it was that at seven minutes after one that afternoon we heard that Japan had surrendered, and the war was over.

A wild cheer rang through the boat. We had known it was coming, and had been following the signs, but now it had come. The fighting was over. We had made it. I could well understand and appreciate the joy felt by everybody on the ship.

My own feelings I could not understand so well. Instead of wild exultation, a fit of the deepest despondency descended upon me. I tried to join in the happiness of my officers and crew, but after a while I left them. I went to my stateroom and drew the curtain. I didn't bother to turn on the light—just sat there on the bunk, not stirring. During the next several hours I was aware that the curtains fluttered once or twice, as though someone had started to call me and then had thought better of it, or had been stopped by someone else.

Eventually it was time to surface. After we had brought *Piper* up, I told the officer of the deck that I was going out on the main deck for a while. This, of course, was never permitted without good reason, and never without the captain's express permission. But I was the captain, and I kept my reasons to myself.

The night was clear and cloudless, with just a hint of the moon soon to rise. The air was warm, seemingly devoid of the oppressive mustiness I had so often noticed. The sea was nearly calm. It was a night of peace. I wearily paced the deck, around and around from bow to stern, and back to the bow again. The same old thoughts were still running through my mind. After this, what? Why *Trigger*, and not *Piper*, or *Tirante?* Why Penrod Schneider, Johnnie Shepherd, Stinky, and Willy Kornahrens? What about Johnnie Moore, the man who had ordered me to submarine school against my will, back in September of 1941? He had gone down as skipper of *Grayback*, after a series of outstanding patrols.

What about Penrod's wife, Sammy, who had christened *Dorado* as she was launched? And Al Bontier, who had had the bad luck to run his new *Razorback* aground off New London, as a result of which he was transferred off the ship and to Pearl, where they gave him the recently overhauled *Seawolf?* And what about the skipper of that destroyer escort who to his dying day must reproach himself for not having tried harder to identify the submarine which desperately signaled him as he ordered the fatal hedgehogs thrown?

What was the difference between Dave Connole, cut short after bringing *Trigger* back into the payoff column once more, and Jack Lewis, who caught pneumonia on our first run up in the Aleutians three years ago—what indeed was the difference, except that one of them was dead?

As I turned about the deck, always it came back to the same thing. We had won the war. It was over—finished—and somehow I had had the incredible luck to be spared. But what little divided those of us who were alive to see this day from those who were not? Just a few feet over the side, the long, cool, clean, silent water was the answer. It could claim many secrets—had claimed them for thousands and tens of thousands of years—one of them might as well have been me—could still be me . . .

I shrank from the abyss of lunacy yawning in front of me. The revulsion from four years of tension, and ultimate rejection of the subconscious idea that I might not make it after all, had plumbed its depth. Stinky and Johnnie Shepherd had not taken my place in the *Trigger*; it had simply been their bad luck, and my good.

A call from the bridge, with a sort of wild, half chuckle to it: "Captain, Captain. Here's a message for you!" I walked swiftly forward.

Jerry Reeves was standing there, holding a piece of

paper in his hand. "You old bastard, sir!" he said. "Why didn't you tell anybody?"

The message said: FOR PIPER X MESSAGE TO COMMANDING OFFICER FROM MRS. BEACH SAYS DAUGHTER BORN AUGUST TENTH X BOTH WELL X CONGRATULATIONS X COMSUBPAC SENDS

The war had come to an end, and life, for some of us, was beginning.